Housing in the Metropolitan Area of Barcelona

IMPSOL

2015—2024

Housing in the Metropolitan Area of Barcelona

IMPSOL 2015—2024

AMB IMPSOL

Foreword

We present *Housing in the Metropolitan Area of Barcelona. IMPSOL 2015—2024,* a publication that brings together the housing developments promoted by the Institut Metropolità de Promoció de Sòl i Gestió Patrimonial (Metropolitan Institute of Land Development and Property Management, IMPSOL) over the last decade. It is designed as a reference guide that takes a new look at metropolitan public housing, a paradigm shift that transforms the conception of the traditional form of dwelling.

This publication suggests new ways of understanding and experiencing domestic space, highlighting its evolution towards innovation, inclusion and sustainability. Metropolitan housing policies, from the architecture project to the construction of the building, explore a narrative that aspires to go further and give shape to new housing types that reflect emerging needs and diversity. They are also the means to provide affordable housing to all citizens who are excluded from the market.

Gender perspective is also a fundamental element of these policies. The push for a major redefinition of traditional gender roles and dynamics in the field of housing calls for inclusive measures and practices that are fundamental to creating home environments that are welcoming, inclusive and safe.

This book aims to acknowledge the work and efforts of a large group of agents: councils, project drafting and construction management teams, competition entrants, construction companies and IMPSOL staff. Aimed at public administrations, the general public and architecture professionals alike, it is an invitation to explore the paradigm shift taking place in metropolitan municipalities to create cities that are more liveable, sustainable, egalitarian and fair, and ways of addressing the challenge of facilitating access to housing.

Antoni Balmón Arévalo
President of IMPSOL
Executive Vice President of AMB

Prologue Ramon M. Torra i Xicoy – Amadeu Iglesias Unzué

Access to quality affordable housing is one of the priorities of the Barcelona Metropolitan Area (AMB) and a vital element in promoting social cohesion. The need to adapt future developments to the requirements of our time, as regards both type and construction, in environmental and social terms, raises a new scenario in housing policies in the metropolitan area. Architecture competitions play a key role, and simplifying and minimizing administrative procedures makes it easier for the collective of young architects to take part.

In this framework, AMB exercises competences in land and housing policies, among others, through the Metropolitan Institute of Land Development and Property Management (IMPSOL), which promotes quality social housing that is affordable, sustainable and innovative, and responds to gender requirements, with the aim of meeting both the local needs of municipalities and the development strategies of the metropolitan territory to knit it together and bring quality and continuity to the urban fabric.

Public institutions must work to avoid compromising the well-being of future generations. For this reason, taking into account the climate and housing emergency situation, and the risk of exclusion due to energy poverty, our basic principles prioritize the quality architecture and energy efficiency of projects. Sustainability has to be one of the priorities of new development, since in addition to meeting residential needs, buildings have to aim for nearly zero consumption (NZEB), which means reducing their ecological footprint and CO_2 emissions, the waste generated during construction and their subsequent energy consumption. The benefits and construction systems of the developments' buildings must be improved accordingly, and complex installations avoided. At the same time, radical commitment to intermediate spaces, both private and communal, improves heating and cooling, thereby minimizing energy demand as well as socially strengthening communities.

Another criterion of IMPSOL developments is typological and technological innovation, which takes into account the inclusiveness of new homes and gender perspective. New forms of dwelling have to give rise to a new housing model, designed both for traditional family models and new shared households, where corridors are eliminated to increase the size of the rooms so that they all have similar dimensions, offering flexibility of use and allowing adaptation to future changes. The kitchen spaces, with the same level of quality, are generally more open to encourage more than one person to work there at the same time.

The COVID-19 pandemic highlighted the need for a change in perspective in citizens' dwelling habits and requirements, making it necessary to strengthen all the qualitative strategies that were already incorporated in the competition model and the developments previously designed by IMPSOL.

Committing to typological and technological innovation with tight budgets and schedules involves significant risks, which we assume by generating an environment of trust among everyone involved in the development process. The same philosophy is applied in the after-sales phase, when the various agents involved in the construction process approach the users to explain the building's target values, provide them with information and accompany them throughout so that they can use the building as it was designed and take advantage of its full potential. Disseminating new housing paradigms beyond the circles of those who design and construct them enables their evolution and good functioning.

IMPSOL's activity in the development of affordable housing with these characteristics calls for special attention in the definition of quality processes to implement technical improvements, monitor them and analyse the results together with everyone involved: technicians, construction companies and residents. Energy saving, the industrialization of construction, the creation of multifunctional communal spaces and other proposals that are considered necessary have to be understood and accepted both by those who develop housing and those who live there to achieve the goal of constant improvement.

The period illustrated by the developments built between 2015 and 2024 has been recognized by multiple prizes and awards that reinforce the process that has been begun and encourage all the professionals involved to continue working towards these goals.

Ramon M. Torra i Xicoy
Architect. Managing Director of AMB and Chief Executive Office of IMPSOL

Amadeu Iglesias Unzué
Architect. Managing Director of IMPSOL

Index

Works and projects. 2015—2024

Competitions. 2016—2021

Locations

Castellbisbal
Sant Andreu
de la Barca
Corbera
de Llobregat
92
La Palma
de Cervelló
Pallejà
El Papiol
Sant Cugat
del Vallès
Cervelló
Molins de Rei
Begues
Sant Vicenç
dels Horts
86
154
224
Torrelles
de Llobregat
Santa Coloma
de Cervelló
72
Sant Feliu
de Llobregat
120
Sant Climent
de Llobregat
54
Sant Just
Desvern
Sant Joan
Despí
Castelldefels
252
238
232
148
198
Esplugues
de Llobregat
160
190
42
Sant Boi
de Llobregat
210
Gavà
Viladecans
L'Hospitalet
El Prat
de Llobregat
Cornellà
de Llobregat
0
2000
5000
10000

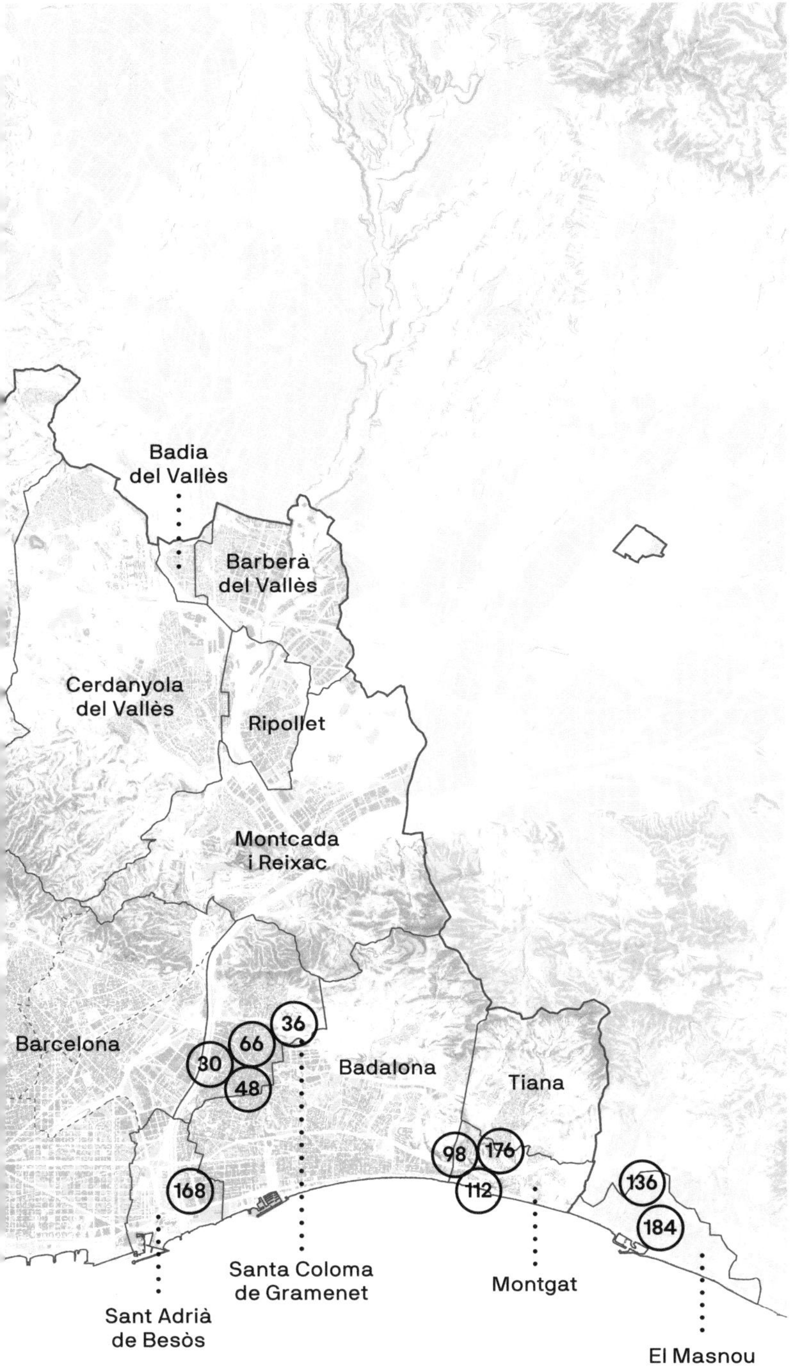
Badia
del Vallès
Barberà
del Vallès
Cerdanyola
del Vallès
Ripollet
Montcada
i Reixac
Barcelona
Badalona
Tiana
36
66
30
48
168
98
176
112
136
184
Santa Coloma
de Gramenet
Sant Adrià
de Besòs
Montgat
El Masnou

Housing unit type

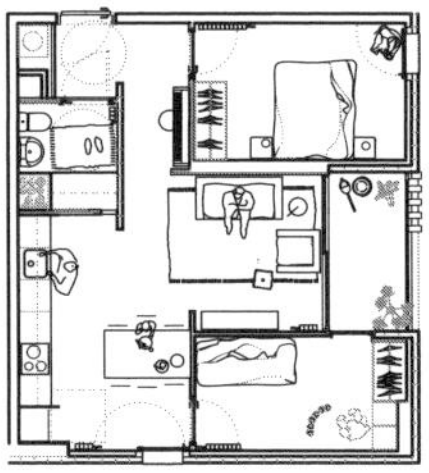

(136) El Masnou
52.62 m^2

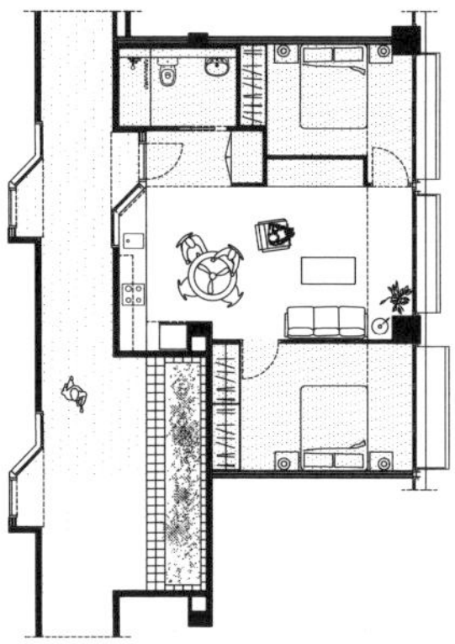

(72) Sant Feliu de Llobregat
52.65 m^2

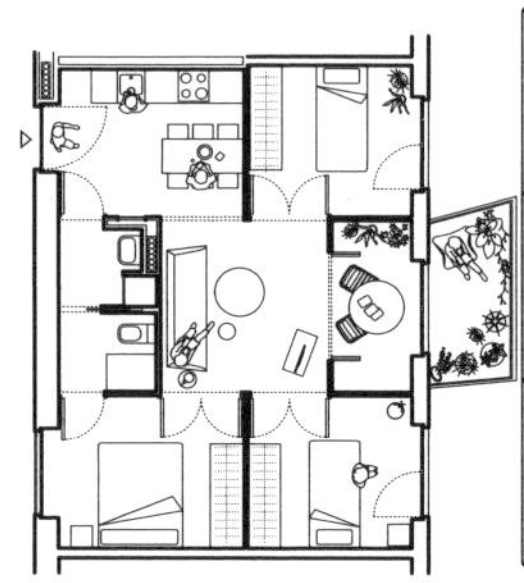

(120) Sant Feliu de Llobregat
61.74 m^2

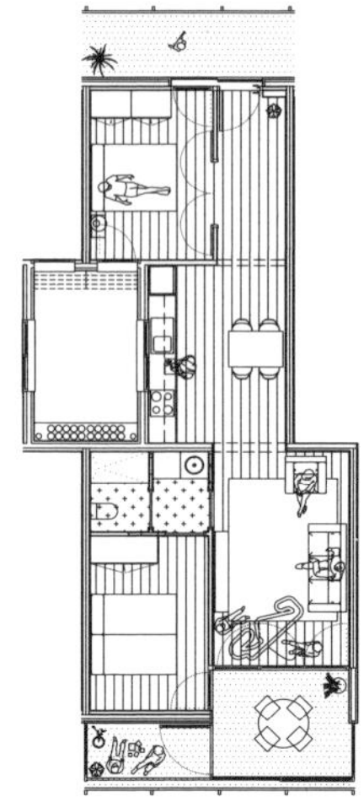

(154) Molins de Rei
63.40 m^2

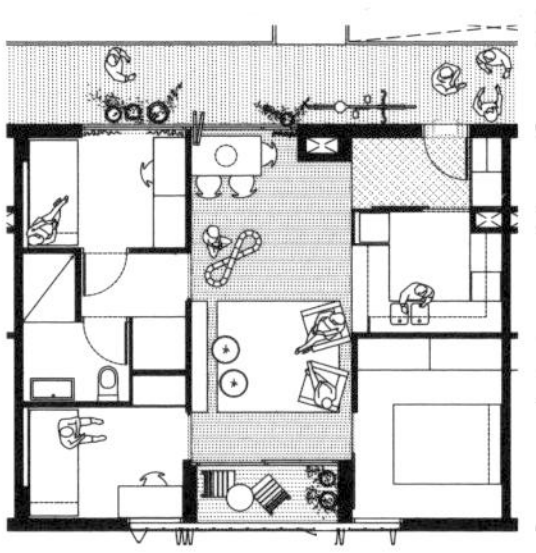

(66) Santa Coloma de Gramenet
58.60 m^2

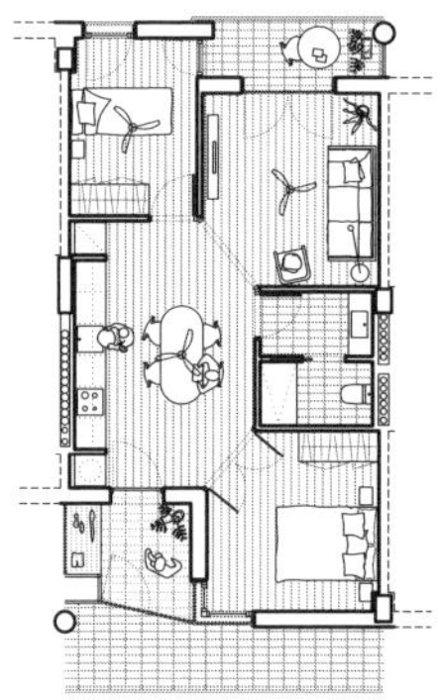

(184) El Masnou
58.56 m^2

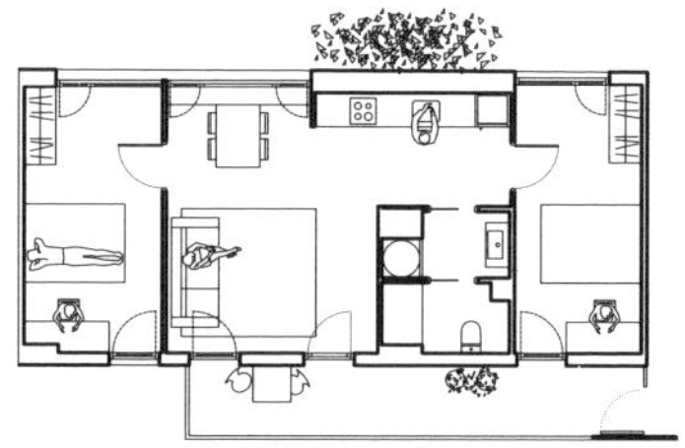

(232) Viladecans
63.25 m^2

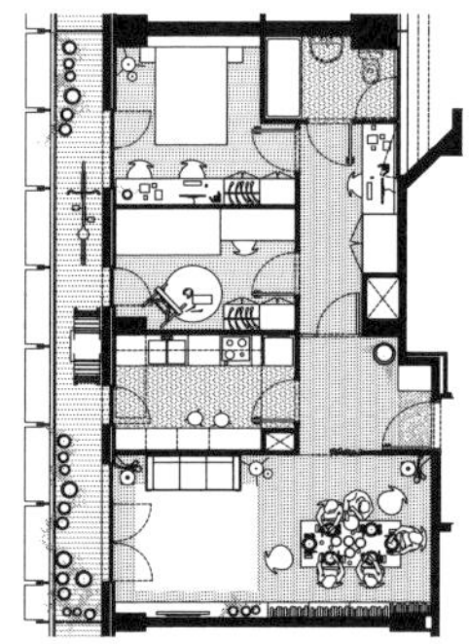

(252) Gavà
66.25 m^2

(160) Cornellà de Llobregat
59.34 m^2

(92) Sant Andreu de la Barca
65.00 m^2

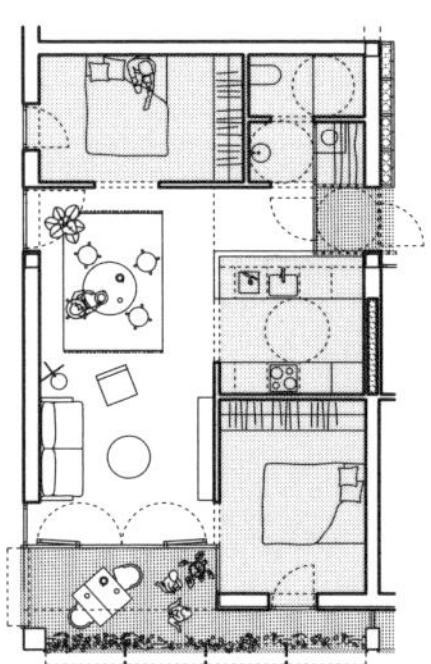

(148) Sant Boi de Llobregat
59.74 m^2

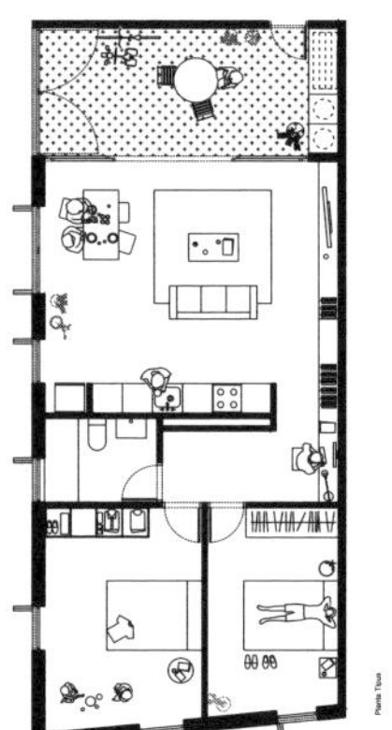

(48) Santa Coloma de Gramenet
60.48 m^2

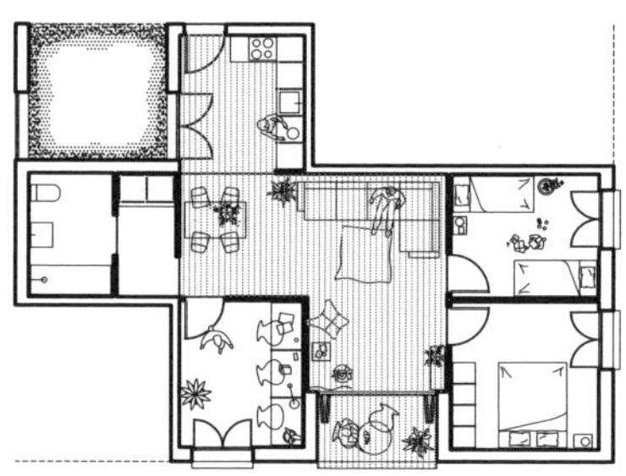

(190) Castelldefels
68.42 m^2

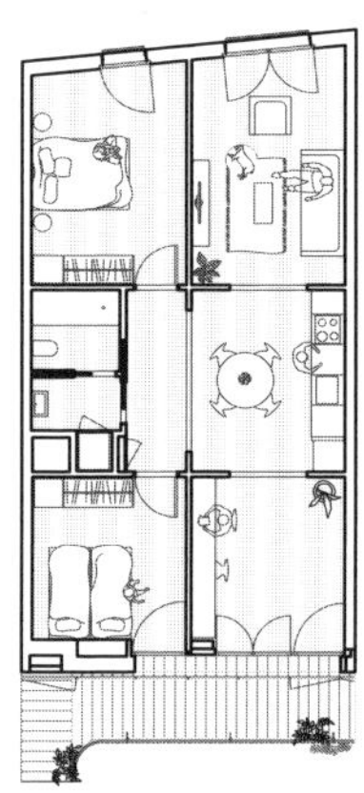

(42) Viladecans
68.60 m^2

0 1 5 10 20

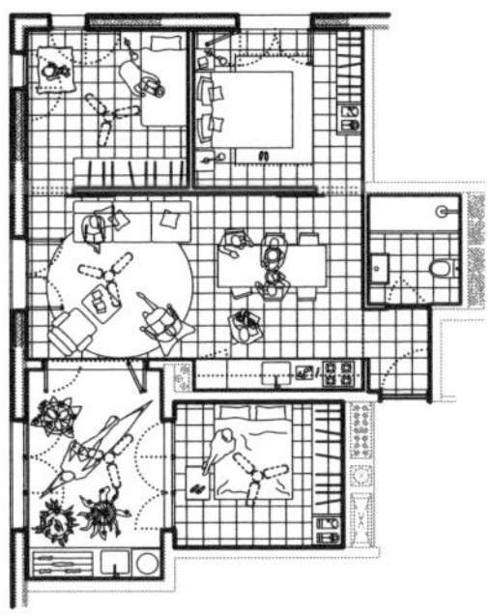

(86) Molins de Rei
70.07 m^2

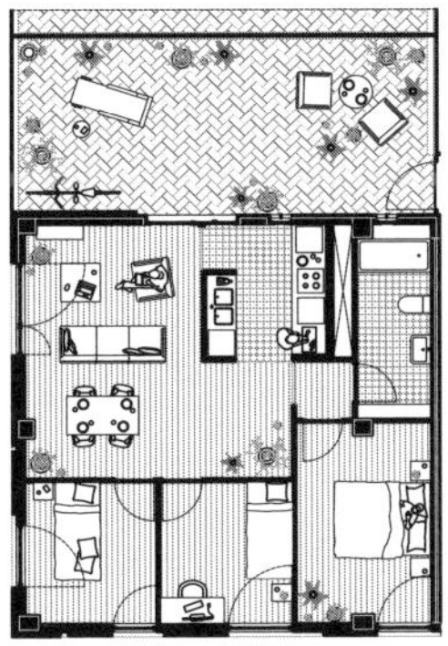

(198) Sant Boi de Llobregat
70.92 m^2

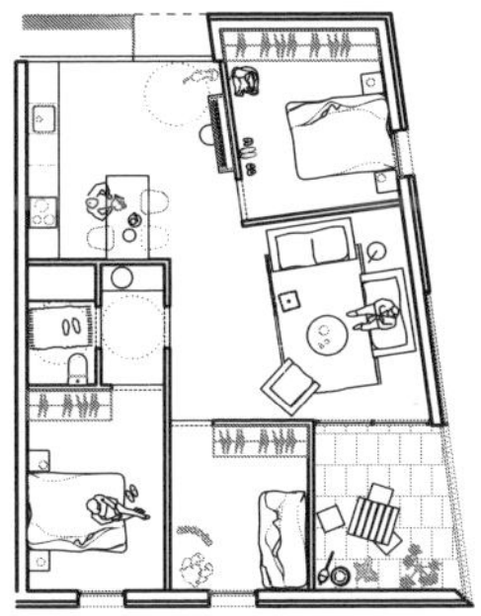

(30) Santa Coloma de Gramenet
74.96 m^2

(54) Sant Just Desvern
78.58 m^2

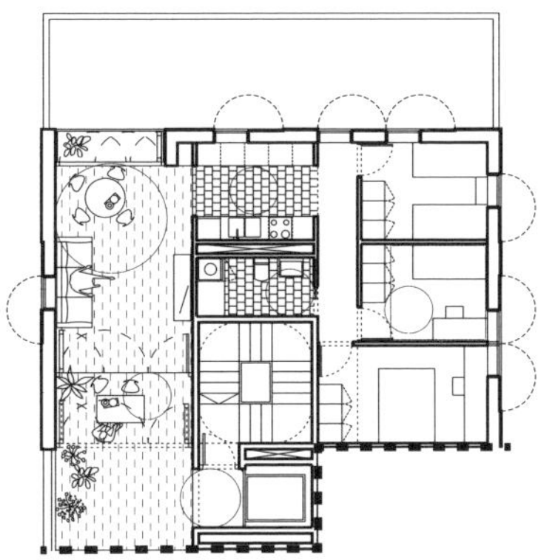

(36) Santa Coloma de Gramenet
70.80 m^2

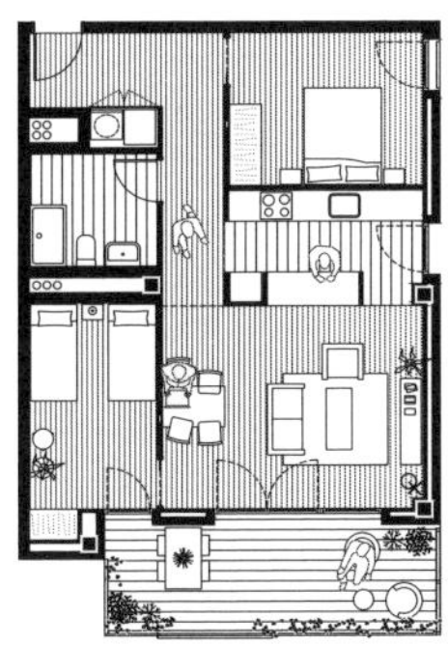

(224) Molins de Rei
72.05 m^2

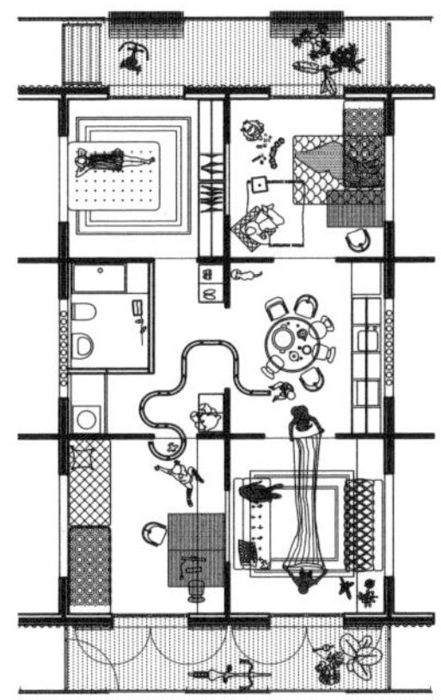

(210) Cornellà de Llobregat
82.64 m^2

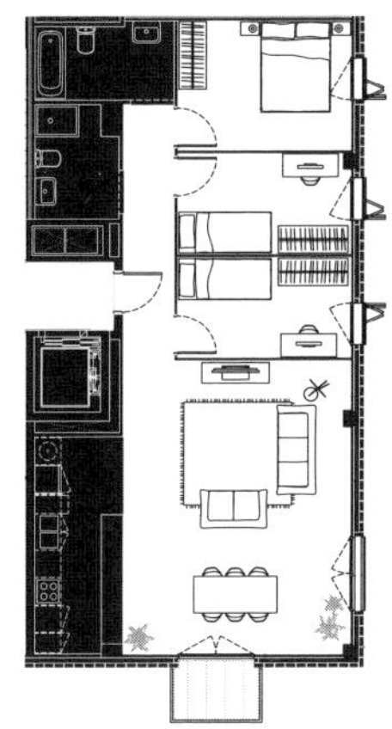

(176) Montgat
85.80 m^2

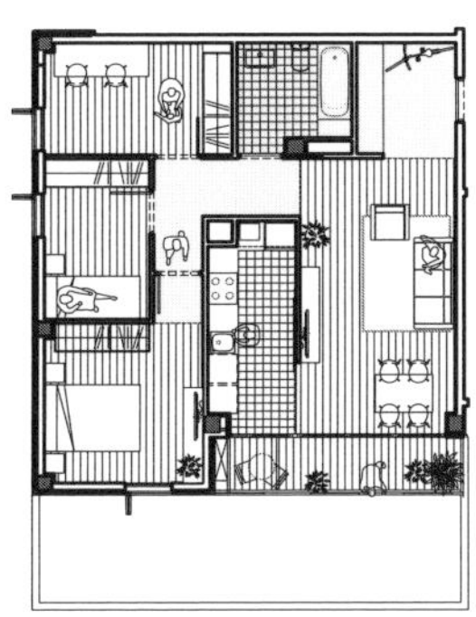

(112) Montgat
71.60 m^2

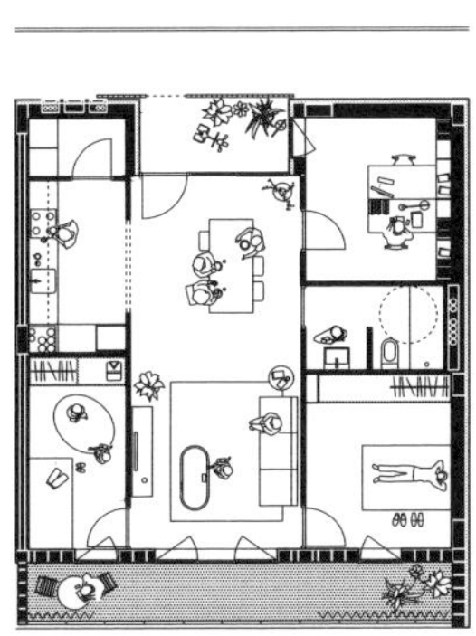

(98) Montgat
77.97 m^2

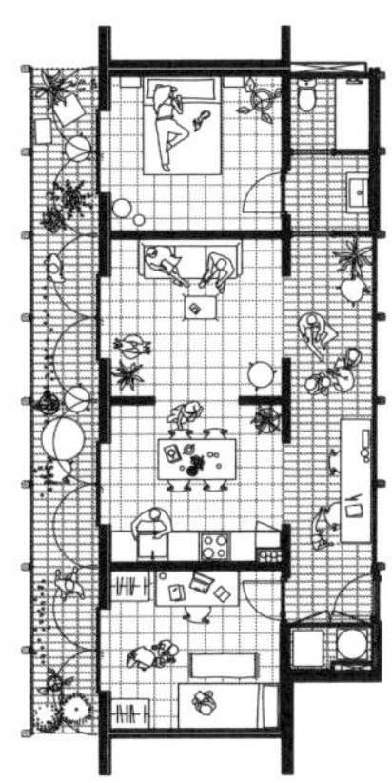

(238) Gavà
86.96 m^2

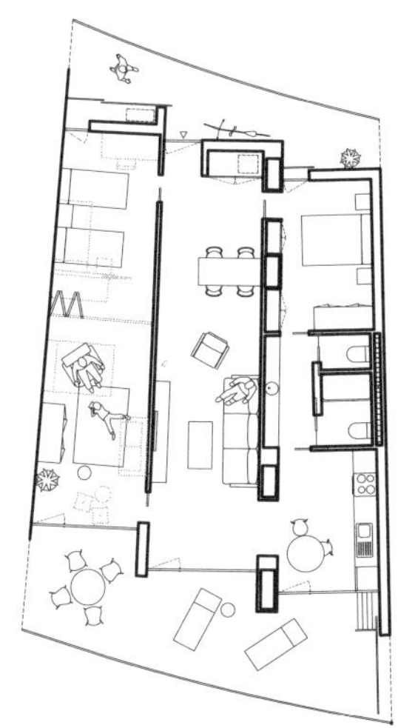

(168) Sant Adrià de Besòs
90.00 m^2

Housing: key issues for dealing with change

Josep Maria Borrell Bru, architect, technical coordinator of IMPSOL.

Buildings speak. As a whole, they are a reflection of our cultural values, our identity, our singularities and our society. Architecture is the material heritage of the intangible value that we are as a collective. This is why governments must work to set an example; in our case, of the highest quality of both what we develop, and our subsequent promotion and management of it.

This publication brings together the projects and construction work developed by IMPSOL since 2015, when we were immersed in economic crisis and, consequently, in throughgoing reflection on what the direction of future developments (possible at that time) should be. It was the moment to ask the big questions to which all the participants have offered answers in the years since then. It is not difficult to see that there has been a notable evolution in typology, technology and environmental response in most of the proposals explained here compared to previous stages, and changes in architecture are a sign that collective thinking and behaviour are evolving. This collection of developments aims to give a broad, real vision of IMPSOL's production, with works built in various stages, works under construction, projects at the design stage and even a section on competitions to highlight the importance of this moment and the many proposals that, for their quality, also deserve to be built.

The first key issue in this evolution in developments is the idea that housing is a permanent social infrastructure, so each building we develop has to be seen as a new facility that will become the heritage of society as a whole and, accordingly, an opportunity for improvement for the city and citizens alike. The users are circumstantial, but the environmental, social and even pedagogical values benefit all of society. When viewed in this way, the approach and the resulting decision-making process change completely; individual sacrifices may be made for the common good. This is the perspective that the public service must adopt: any decision has to be explained in terms of the general good. From this viewpoint, it is also reasonable that the response to the increasing diversification of people requesting housing and the permanence that we require of buildings must be resilience and versatility of all their spaces: communal areas, homes and rooms. We know how we live today in the metropolitan area of Barcelona, but we do not know how our regular practices will change in the space of a few years, and this has led us to the ambiguity and optimization of spaces that make up a building so that it can be easily adapted.

The second issue is the architecture competition model as a vital moment in the development process, with a very clear objective: to achieve the highest architectural quality of the proposals by recruiting the best possible professional talent. This involves democratizing the procedure and promoting the universal participation of the collective of architects; rigorous conditions of entry aim to clearly convey the ambitious environmental, social and economic objectives, and encourage innovation and flexibility at all levels; the diversity and the professionalism of the jury, with the inclusion of the town councils, help to detect opportunities and facilitate the symbiosis between the buildings we develop and the environments in which they are implanted; and, finally, appropriate financial compensation for both the finalists and the winning teams is also key.

The response from the collective of architects has been extraordinary, with tireless involvement, commitment and dedication. We not only asked them to lead the multidisciplinary teams in charge of developing the projects, but they also accompanied us in the subsequent processes of disseminating the values and after-sales management with the residents in a mutually enriching process of shared visions and experiences.

The third of the key aspects was simply that, as a public developer, we had to be equal to the task and, having attracted the best talent and obtained the best proposals, be able to carry them out and make the most of them by facilitating the process, on the basis of trust. It seems obvious, but this means changing the role of the public developer, breaking with many preconceived ideas and encouraging proactive leadership within the public administration, in addition to managing the risks. With the general interest at the centre, it was necessary to create flexible attitudes, seek consensus, and work—political and management posts, and technical and administrative staff alike—in the same direction, synchronizing internal attitudes to work with councils and external teams on the same footing, with no taboos or hierarchies, instead understanding the role of each, with determination, exigency, breadth of views and generosity.

These values, along with expertise, characterize the IMPSOL team, without which it would certainly not have been possible to take on the challenges posed.

The fourth issue is the need to disseminate the architecture we develop and explain what it entails. Residents must be aware of the management processes and understand the reasons for decisions that affect their way of living as well as the values, virtues and needs of the new developments—in short, their rights and responsibilities. The architectural discourse must be made accessible to citizens, and citizens and the collective of architects have to come together to gain understanding on both sides and to continue innovating at the service of greater quality of life for people, which must be everyone's main goal. This required a concerted effort in three areas. The commercial teams and managers of existing properties receive training to explain at first hand the developments' characteristics to the inhabitants. IMPSOL mediates to bring about direct interaction between the teams that created the projects and the people who live in the homes, in the form of visits and information sessions, and meetings when the buildings are lived in, producing very productive debates. And, finally, expositions, talks and visits to the buildings and homes with very diverse groups are organized, which also helps to spread this valuable knowledge.

For us, the developments are a collective product, the sustainable sum of the thinking, experiences and accumulated effort of all those involved, including the users who bring the proposals to life. We wanted to explain the projects in the opposite way to what is usual, from the inside out, from type to location, in order to underscore typological innovation as a response to changes in ways of living, which is also what distinguishes IMPSOL. We also wanted to explain the projects as seen both by the architects, who imagined specific situations and explain them by means of the final photographs of their works, and in everyday life, incorporating the visions of day-to-day activity and the passage of time, in which the residents can share these logics or interpret the spaces differently.

We are proud to say that it has been a worthwhile process with many acknowledgments both from residents and official bodies, which encourage us to continue working for the highest quality and the decarbonization of what we build. With humility and undiminished enthusiasm, we embark on a new phase in which we will incorporate the experience and try to correct any mistakes; we aim to focus more and more on rehabilitation, valuing existing construction, and on social innovation, considering people's new needs and habits, because public policies can no longer take into account just a general, homogeneous public that is no longer a majority.

Ambiguous spaces

Versatile, flexible, undefined spaces: towards a sustainable and resilient domestic architecture

Rafael Gómez-Moriana is an architect, educator and critic. He studied architecture at the University of Waterloo (Canada) and the Berlage Institute in Amsterdam. He directs the Barcelona programme of the School of Architecture, Planning and Landscape of the University of Calgary, and is a contributor to periodicals such as *The Architectural Review*, *Bauwelt* and *Detail*.

Over the last decade, a significant shift has taken place in the architecture of IMPSOL social housing, a wave of innovation that has not occurred in half a century. These latest projects break radically with models that were unquestioned for decades, especially when it comes to the design of dwelling unit types, the most private realm.

In the eighties and nineties, Barcelona excelled in the design of its *public* spaces: new democratic institutions, infrastructures, public squares and parks. This public architecture captured the world's attention, and so in the first decade of the 2000s, the time of the 2004 Universal Forum of Cultures, the city's "Olympic model" became transformed toward spectacle and tourism. The early 2010s, however, saw a deepening economic crisis that led to an unprecedented interest in social housing, a field that had hitherto occupied the background. It was then that a new generation of architects emerged with an interest in affordable housing offering greater flexibility and energy efficiency, and less gender discrimination; homes in tune with the times. Many of these innovative projects have now been completed and are inhabited, making it possible to appreciate, analyse and evaluate work that will probably mark a before and after in the development of social housing in Barcelona.

This growing architectural interest in social housing comes at a time of important cultural, social, economic and political changes that have great effects on this discipline. Issues such as access to housing or the well-being of our planet are being addressed like never before. Faced with an increase in inequality and political polarization that coincides with a climate emergency, architects are questioning our extractive economic model and the excessive use we make of natural resources, both in the construction and during the lifetime of buildings. Primordial questions are resurfacing, and the home—the shelter—is the most primordial architecture of all.

Housing is a subject of great architectural and planning complexity, even more so when it comes to social housing. Most of the built floor area of our cities is residential, and the home is also where we spend most of our time (even when there is no pandemic). Housing is, by its very ubiquity, the architecture that most defines us as a society.

The new housing is above all characterized by residential unit types that radically reconfigure domestic space. Housing is being rethought accordingly, starting with the most private and primordial space, that of the home. The dwelling unit is the basic module of any collective housing project, and its transformation can affect the configuration of our cities. In the past, social housing innovation in Barcelona was mainly focused on urban massing and the architecture of communal spaces, which is consistent with an interest in public space. The architecture of residential units was mostly taken for granted and left unquestioned. The projects included in this publication, however, break with custom in order to respond to more diverse ways of living.

Although no clear unifying trend can be identified in the varied projects that follow, all share a concern with creating domestic spaces that are more generic and adaptable to different styles and ways of life. Compared to the social housing of former decades (as can be seen in previous IMPSOL publications, for example), more experimentation with dwelling unit types can be perceived. If there is a guiding thread among the many innovative projects presented in this book, it is perhaps the introduction of more *ambiguous space* into the dwelling unit. Domestic space is now less defined with respect to use or to limits; it can be interior, exterior or both; public, communal or private… Indeterminacy is precisely what enables greater versatility and freedom. Ambiguous spaces are more versatile since they do not have to conform to exact—and therefore limiting—designations.

Ambiguity is a characteristic of our uncertain and unstable times. The Anthropocene, our present geological era, is conditioned more by human activity than by natural phenomena, specifically by carbon dioxide emissions due to our intensive use of fossil fuels. Architecture must respond in two different ways to climate change: on the one hand, buildings must consume less energy in their construction and during their use to minimize contributing to climate change, and on the other hand they must also be designed to be more resistant to the new climatic conditions. In these less predictable times, we need an architecture that is more resilient and more adaptable to change.

Architectural ambiguity—spaces that are less strictly defined and more versatile—is one way to achieve buildings that are more adaptable in the long term and therefore more durable, sustainable and resilient.

In the case of social housing, which is highly regulated and must be compact and efficient, architectural ambiguity also entails designing spaces that are perceptively larger in addition to being more versatile. Architecture has to be flexible and adaptable to all sorts of possible scenarios when the eventual inhabitants and their needs are unknown, as is the case with social housing. A space intended strictly for a specific purpose is no longer useful when that purpose becomes obsolete, which is why many functionalist-era buildings are no longer very functional today. "Form follows function" is unsustainable by definition, as sustainable architecture is, above all, one that is useful over a long duration; one that does not need to be demolished and replaced every time a technological or cultural change occurs in society.

Architecture's new interest in residential unit types is a characteristic of the present moment. In the five decades prior to 2010, the dwellings of affordable housing projects varied relatively little. This can be seen by the way the rooms of a typical late-twentieth century Spanish flat are clearly separated from each other, connected only by means of a long, often narrow corridor. Each function has its specific space, and each space its function. This produced the flat that we all know, which is accessed from a stairwell via an entry vestibule that quickly becomes a long corridor from which rooms are accessed. The first door usually leads to the living-dining room, the largest space in the home and the one that is most representative and public. The next door typically leads into a narrow, enclosed kitchen that is so cramped that only one person can work there at a time. Then come the doors to the bathrooms and bedrooms that vary in size according to traditional family hierarchies. On the exterior façade of the flat, in front of the living room, there is often a balcony barely a metre wide—a bit of outdoor space for plants, storage, or the air-conditioning unit. Almost all post-war Spanish flats follow this basic layout, the only difference being geometry and the exact number of bedrooms and bathrooms. The enclosed kitchen, narrow balcony and long corridor separating hierarchically organized bedrooms formed part of an unquestioned architecture for over half a century.

This standard model of the past no longer serves most of today's population. The first thing we see in almost all the projects published here is the new placement of the kitchen, now more typically an integral part of a dining room located in or near the centre of the home. Now, rooms open directly onto this central kitchen-dining room via large double or sliding doors that allow spaces to be joined and avoid the need for a corridor. The living room, meanwhile, is now only an optional use of one of the generic rooms, which are now larger thanks to the elimination of the corridor. The balcony has in some cases become an intermediate social space between an external communal walkway and the front door, a place where residents can also greet their neighbours while enjoying some fresh air. Rather than exclusive uses, these spaces can fulfil multiple functions, an ambiguity that allows inhabitants to adapt apartments to their needs rather than the other way around.

Today's society is more diverse than ever, and architects who design social housing never know in advance who will occupy their building once complete. Years ago, social housing was designed for the most *typical* occupant, and the rest had to adapt; today, it is designed for *most* occupants through built-in flexibility. It is true that in the past there was much more social uniformity, the typical occupant being the traditional family. Now that this kind of family is increasingly a minority, there is no typical occupant of a home today.

The way social housing projects are displayed in this publication is a sign that the dwelling unit type has become relevant and decisive. Projects are explained in terms of the way they can be inhabited, showing their *interiors*. Before, social housing publications only showed photographs of the outside of a building, or of communal areas such as lobbies, stairs, walkways or courtyards. This new approach reveals that the social housing unit is now considered a field of architectural research.

It is true, as Gustau Gili Galfetti argues in his book *Model Apartments: Experimental Domestic Cells* (1997), that many avantgarde architects took an interest in the dwelling unit throughout the twentieth century, often experimenting with prototypes. But as the author also demonstrates, these experiments were in many cases carried out for exhibitions, fairs, private clients, or inside the architects' own homes. In this case, however, experimentation in the design of dwelling unit types occurs in real developments commissioned by the public sector through architecture competitions. New ways of dwelling are actually made available to citizens in the numerous developments carried out by IMPSOL. The private housing market, by contrast, lacks experimentation because it is risk averse, highly dependent on financing and obsessed with resale value. Social housing, because it cannot be financially speculated with, is the only kind where experimentation in architecture seeks to genuinely promote the well-being of its occupants. Indeed, social housing is the field of experimentation for housing in general.

The *ambiguous spaces* of recent IMPSOL housing unit types can be roughly classified as follows:

1 Open-plan kitchens
2 Generic rooms
3 Interconnecting rooms
4 Intermediate climatic spaces
5 Intermediate social spaces

Open-plan kitchens

The kitchens of most of the dwelling units published here are no longer conceived as separate, enclosed spaces to be used exclusively for cooking. The kitchen is now the main social space of the home. Also known in Spain as an *American kitchen*, probably because of the popularity of 1970s TV sitcoms imported from the USA, the kitchens in these projects form part of larger, more central daytime spaces which, in many cases, are the nexus of movement in the home. Some of the projects situate the kitchen as part of the *entrance* to an apartment (see pages 30, 120, 136, 184, 190, 198, 232), doing away with the entrance vestibule, or else in a *daytime* space such as a dining room or living-dining room (see pages 42, 48, 54, 72, 86, 92, 154, 160, 176, 198, 210, 224, 238). There is also an example of a closed kitchen through which bedrooms are reached (see page 36). Only a minority of the projects feature an enclosed kitchen, and in these few cases the separation is partial rather than complete.

The open-plan kitchen, doing away with the enclosed kitchen as a workspace intended mainly for women, is an important example of the integration of gender mainstreaming in architecture. The open-plan kitchen encourages a more collaborative approach to housework, is less formal, and is also a space of leisure and sociability. Combining a kitchen with a dining room reduces the compartmentalization of the home moreover, creating rooms that are more equal in size and importance to each other.

In many cases, the open-plan kitchen consists of a room with a single piece of kitchen furniture built in along one wall, leaving space for dining furniture in the centre. When cooking, the dining table can be made to serve as an extension of the kitchen (for food preparation, for example), and when dining the kitchen furniture can serve as a dining table accessory.

By combining the kitchen with the dining room, the living room is now relegated to one of the other rooms, offering the possibility of living without one if a kitchen-dining room suffices as a home's social space, as may be the case with a shared flat. In fact, in the past, working-class homes and rural farm houses did not have a living room, only a dining room; a well-known example being Casa Bloc, a social housing project designed by members of the GATCPAC, Spain's first avantgarde architects. A living room should be an option, not an obligation, especially during an affordable housing emergency such as the one we are currently experiencing.
By combining kitchen with dining and relegating the living room elsewhere (if anywhere), the rooms of a flat acquire dimensions that are more similar and less hierarchical.

p. 54

p. 72

Generic rooms

Another novelty in many of the projects published here is the similarity of the rooms, in terms of both size and proportion (see pages 36, 42, 48, 54, 86, 92, 120, 148, 154, 160, 168, 190, 210, 232, 238). The default is no longer one double bedroom (for the parents) and then single rooms (for the children). This model works very well for traditional families, but today there is greater diversity: there are more single-parent families, more childless couples and more shared flats than ever before as living alone becomes less and less affordable, forcing many to live in shared flats not unlike university students. More and more people are working from home, which can generate the need for an office. To accommodate this growing plurality of domestic situations, it is best for rooms to be generic—that is, similar in size and proportion. A generic room can be converted into a double bedroom, a single bedroom, a guest bedroom, a living room, an office, a home cinema room or a room for yoga, dance, gymnastics, video games... or whatever. It is also notable that all the rooms in the projects included here face either the exterior or a generously-sized courtyard. None receive their daylight and ventilation exclusively through a light-well or stairwell, as is common in nineteenth- and twentieth-century housing. Furthermore, the rooms in all the projects allow cross ventilation, which is essential in the context of an energy and climate emergency.

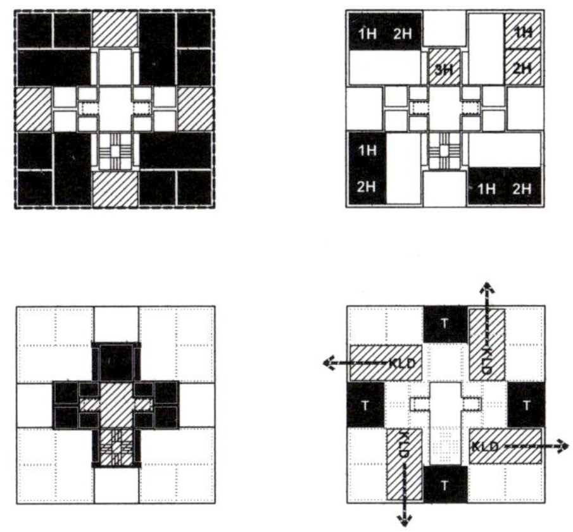

p. 86

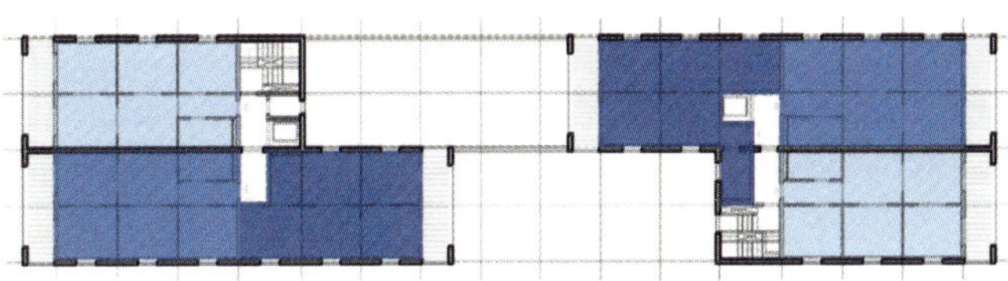

p. 92

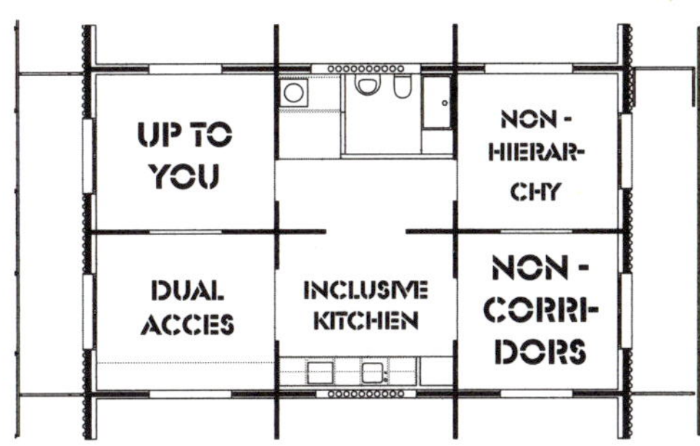

p. 210

Interconnecting rooms

Another characteristic of many dwellings in this publication are enfilades of rooms that interconnect instead of being reached through a corridor (see pages 30, 42, 54, 66, 72, 86, 92, 98, 120, 136, 148, 168, 184, 190, 210, 232, 238). This leads not only to gains in useful square metres and greater efficiency of movement, it also increases the perception of light and spaciousness. The elimination of corridors enables larger generic rooms to be created, which makes them more versatile. The doors between interconnecting rooms are usually floor-to-ceiling double or sliding doors, which means that rooms can be joined together temporarily. Spaces can therefore be combined spontaneously as need arises, such as during a celebration with guests.

In some cases, the interconnecting rooms form part of a larger geometric pattern that extends throughout the building floor plan, usually a grid (see pages 42, 86, 92, 120, 190, 210, 238). This contemporary architectural trend creates a more abstract floor plan in which the walls dividing flats become less prominent. Rooms do not need to be square to be interconnected, but it is obvious that when they are, an image of greater architectural rigour emerges. Although generic rooms of equal size and shape are less hierarchical, this does not mean that they can be used perfectly equally or that there is a total absence of hierarchy: a room at the end of an enfilade is not the same as one in the middle that necessarily acts as a distributor to other rooms. There is still a certain hierarchy in a grid. But interconnecting rooms can nevertheless be joined together—an impossibility for rooms separated by corridors—and this gives the home much greater architectural and spatial quality.

p. 72

p. 120

p. 238

Intermediate climatic spaces

Intermediate climatic spaces are those situated between two climates: an indoor and an outdoor one, forming a kind of buffer between the two. They can be private, like a greenhouse or a balcony, or semi-public, like a lightwell or a communal courtyard (see pages 30, 36, 48, 54, 72, 86, 92, 98, 120, 136, 148, 154, 160, 190, 198, 210, 232, 238). In some projects, the courtyards have operable glass roofs that open when it is hot and close when their sensors detect low temperatures or rain, thereby becoming greenhouses or solar chimneys. This kind of control serves to preheat air for domestic ventilation in winter, providing significant energy savings. The idea is to harness the renewable energy of the sun to heat the home and that of the wind to cool it by means of cross ventilation, and to capture and store this thermal energy in materials with high thermal inertia (such as ceramics, concrete, earth or stone). Incorporating these traditional climatic principles into modern homes can lead to considerable energy savings. Faced with growing energy poverty, social housing must set an example of sustainability.

p. 54

p. 98

p. 238

Intermediate social spaces

Intermediate social spaces are those that are located between the private home and public or communal realms, forming a buffer between them. The concept has always existed, so it is not new, but it is now being reinterpreted and enhanced to promote new kinds of relations between neighbours (see pages 30, 36, 42, 54, 72, 98, 120, 148, 154, 168, 184, 198, 210, 232). Intermediate social spaces are often located in communal spaces in front of the entrances to homes, where residents can put a doormat, plants or even a chair, personalizing a stretch of communal space that would otherwise be empty and sterile. They are small but very important spaces, the perfect place for neighbourly relations in an apartment building. In some of the projects (see pages 36, 42, 54, 98, 148, 154, 184, 210, 238) *private* intermediate social spaces have been created, with operable enclosures that can be opened to offer a space of interaction. These are actually balconies along an exterior access walkway from which flats are entered, making them ideal places to store bicycles. In others, the strategy used is determined by the arrangement of volumes or access to the various stairways, modifying the plan to generate communal transition spaces between public and private space, such as squares and gardens (see pages 136, 190, 210, 224, 238, 252). Finally, there are projects that generate spaces for the community to appropriate, such as courtyards, premises and terraces (see pages 36, 66, 72, 86, 92, 120, 148, 154, 232). In seven cases, the intermediate spaces are both social and climatic (see pages 36, 42, 54, 98, 120, 148, 184, 198), bringing even more ambiguity to the housing typology.

p. 72

p. 98

p. 210

The projects presented in this book display many more architectural qualities than those discussed here, such as urban integration, new materials and construction systems, and innovative community spaces. This text concentrates solely on the architecture of the dwelling unit type, the most revolutionary element in these projects after decades of little change.

The five types of ambiguous spaces discussed here are the factors that mark the greatest departure from (or reinterpretation of) outmoded dwelling types. These spaces will probably require a period of adaptation on the part of occupants, who will not be used to them. Buildings create habits and customs, as Walter Benjamin reminds us in his essay *The Work of Art in the Age of Mechanical Reproduction* (1936), and habits and customs do not change easily. But there are many habits that we must change for the good of humanity in this period of climate change.

It would be interesting to study, in a few years' time, how the occupants of these flats are making the most—or not—of the options and possibilities that architects have provided them with. There are sure to be some surprises. It will also be interesting to see how many years it takes for the *private* housing sector to adopt the ideas and the ambiguous spaces presented here. The fact is that change is urgent if we are to advance in the decarbonization of our environment. Let's hope that the private housing sector joins up with the changes proposed by public administrations, and that many more innovative homes continue to be built, perhaps with new types of ambiguous spaces that are still unimagined.

Bibliographic references

BENJAMIN, Walter. "The Work of Art in the Age of Mechanical Reproduction." *Illuminations* (ed. Hannah Arendt), translated by Harry Zohn, from the 1935 essay. New York: Schocken Books, 1969.

GILI GALFETTI, Gustau. *Model Apartments: Experimental Domestic Cells*. Barcelona: GG, 1997.

Works and projects

2015—2024

Santa Coloma de Gramenet 12 homes

Housing unit type

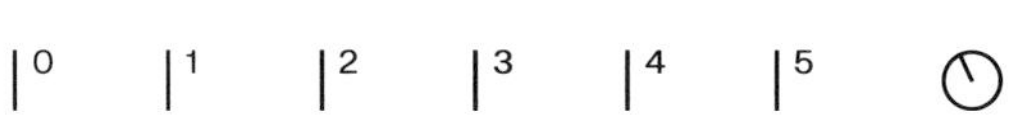

Open-plan kitchen

Interconnecting rooms

Intermediate climatic spaces

Intermediate social spaces

Housing unit type – Aggregation
The organization of the floor consists of grouping the bathroom, kitchen and installation ducts along the party wall in order to free up the rest of the space.
The rooms are thereby located at the extreme of the apartment, eliminating corridors and generating a living-dining room area that absorbs and organizes circulation. The terrace grows as a result of optimizing circulation, creating a wintergarden with a large enough surface area to be used as an outdoor room. The living-dining room is separated into two distinct but visually connected spaces.
It is a mixed aggregation type that combines three homes per landing, a total of 12, which are accessed via an outside walkway.

Urban context – Urban response
The aim is to integrate the proposal into the existing urban fabric (a deep, narrow, small-grained parcellation), adapting its geometry to the irregular topography by means of two elements that cover the neighbouring party walls and sew together the existing cornices. Instead of following the street layout of the chamfered corner, the project breaks off the corner to create the entrance court to the building and allow connection with the space at the centre of the street block.

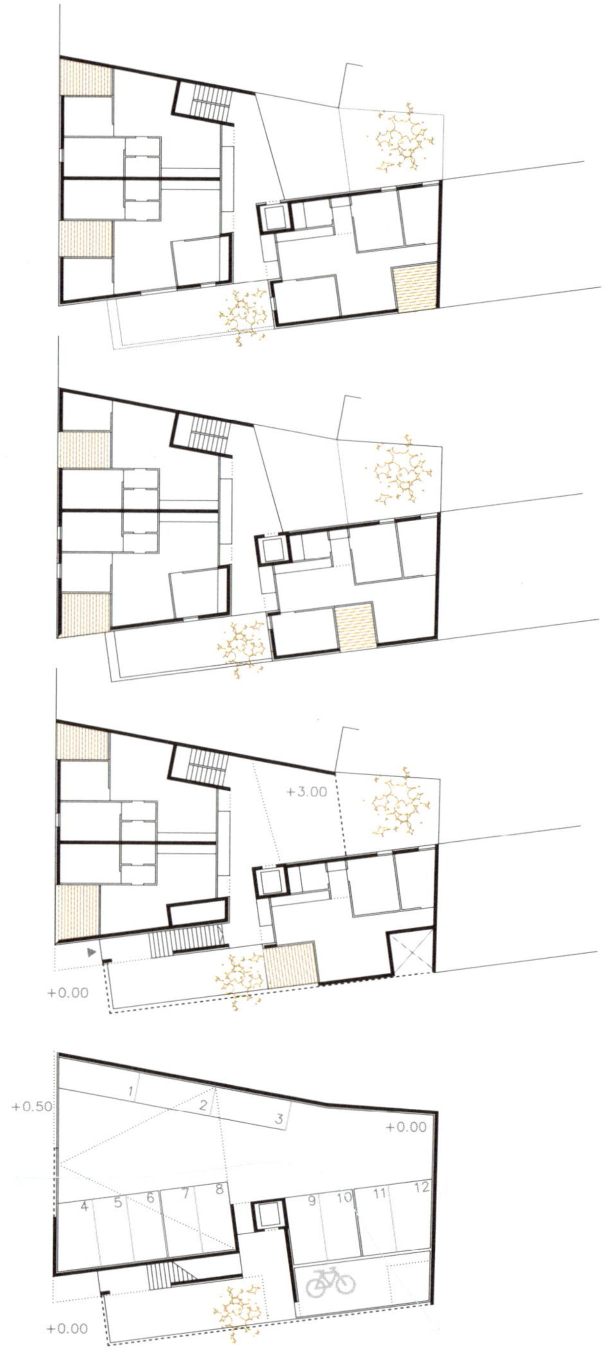

Plans

Communal space
The walkway leading to the homes is designed as an open space that allows daylighting and ventilation of the walkway itself and the apartments, guaranteeing cross ventilation throughout. The arrangement of the aggregation units produces two courts, interconnected on the ground floor, that cool the building and the centre of the street block.

Energy strategy
- Cross ventilation in all the homes.
- Intermediate spaces: terrace with glass curtains, a space that captures heat in the winter and dissipates it in summer.

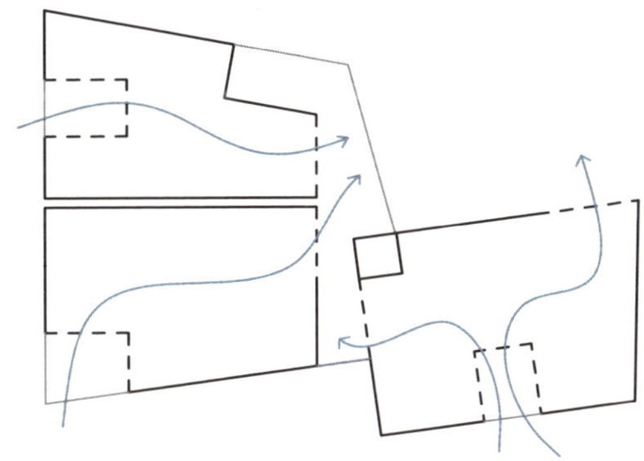

Ventilation diagram

Section

0 1 2 5 10

12 homes

Typical floor plan

No. rooms	3	2
Total surface area (m^2)	74.96	61.11
Kitchen-living-dining room (m^2)	31.81	29.99
Outdoor room (m^2)	8.64	7.92
No. homes	**8**	**4**

Architects: Marta Peris, José Manuel Toral. Team: Ana Espinosa, Izaskun González, Guillem Pascual, Maria Megías, Cristina Porta, Miguel Bernat. Collaborators: Bernuz-Fernández Arquitectes (structures), ELETRESJOTA (installations), Societat Orgànica (environmental consultancy). Location: Carrer Pirineus, 114. Floor area: 1,496 m^2.

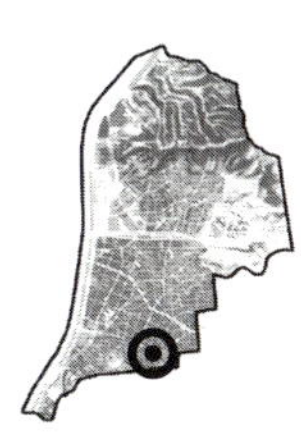

Site

Location

Santa Coloma de Gramenet   16 homes

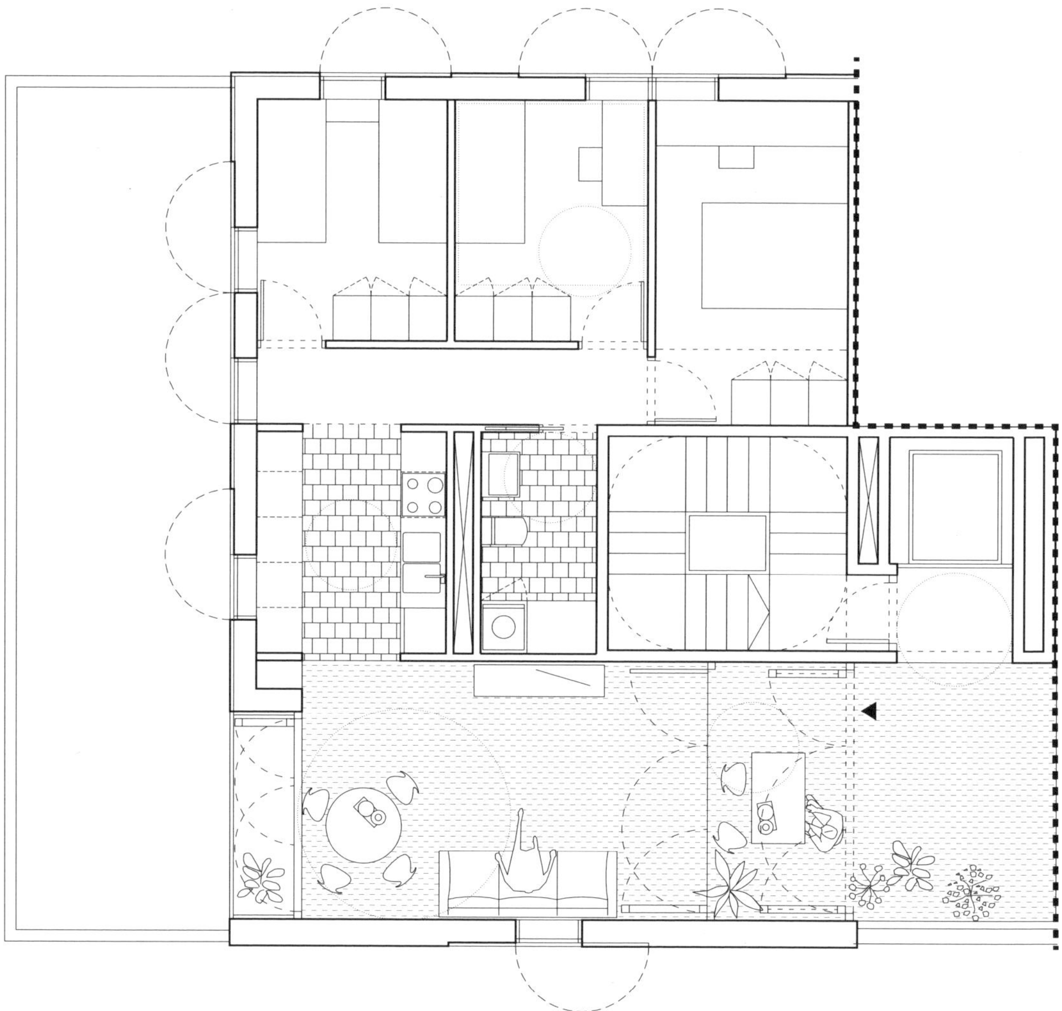

Housing unit type

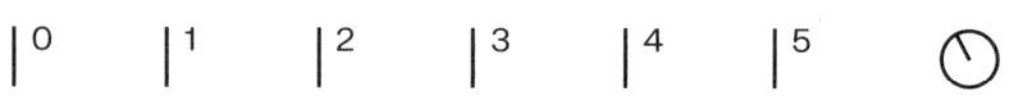

Open-plan kitchen

Generic rooms

Intermediate climatic spaces

Intermediate social spaces

Housing unit type – Aggregation

The homes are laid out around a central through space (living room) that opens onto two façades. To either side, a filter space creates different levels of privacy from the shared area and provides thermal and acoustic control. The wet areas are located in the central space of the block, and the rest of the rooms are located on either side. The rooms are all the same size, giving the home great flexibility.

The apartments are arranged in threes on each floor around a communal space, a south-facing glazed porch that filters sunlight, offering views of Santa Coloma.

The floor plan contains nine rooms of the same size, with no hierarchy. This design serves to formalize different housing typologies for different user profiles, allowing for two-, three- and four-bedroom homes.

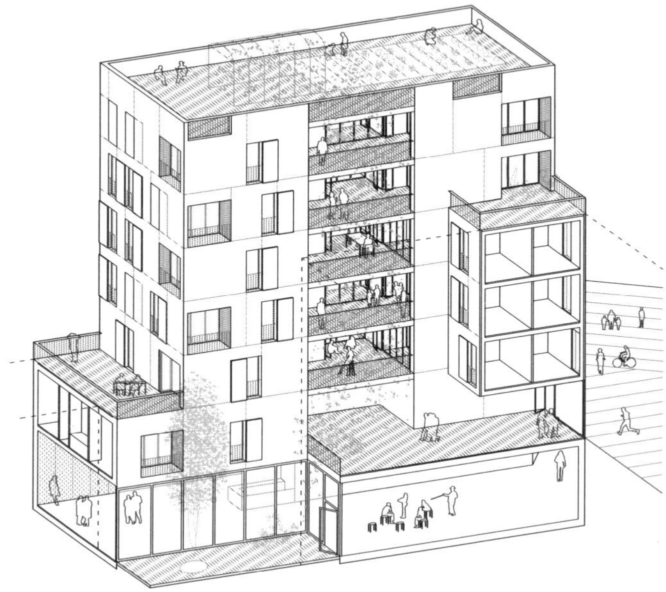

Homes and community

Flexibility

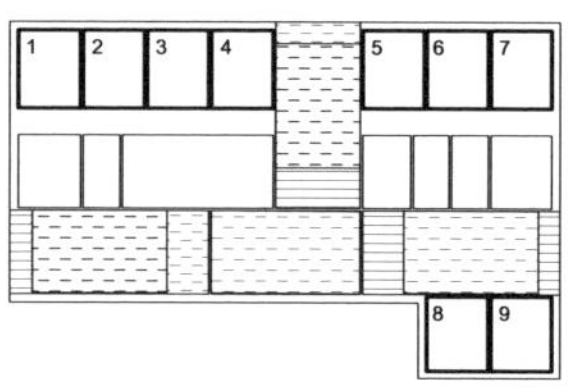

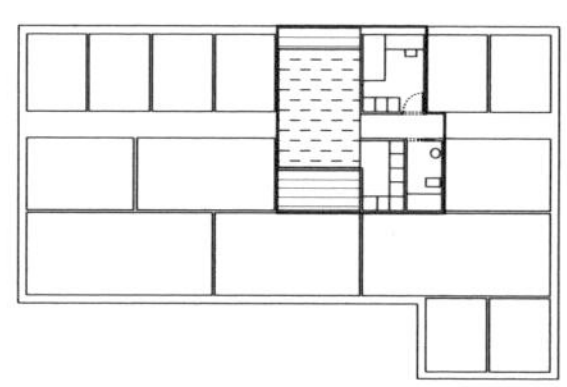

Entrepreneur
Single person

GFA: 50 m²

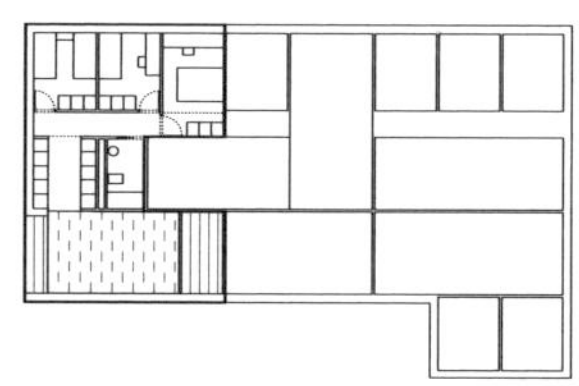

Young family

GFA: 83 m²

Climatic and filter spaces of appropriation

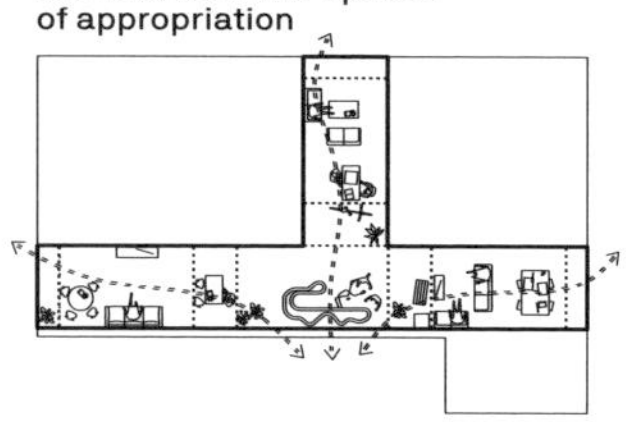

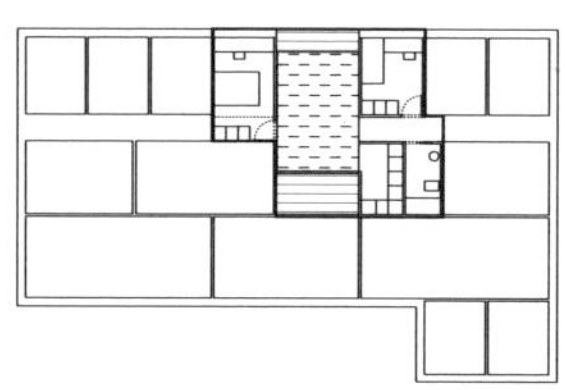

Couple

GFA: 63 m²

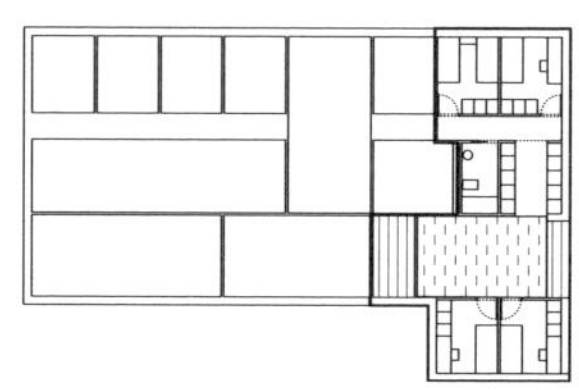

Single-parent family

GFA: 90 m²

Structure and service strip

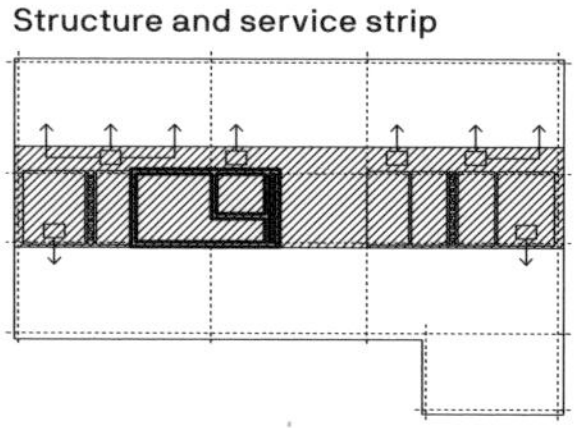

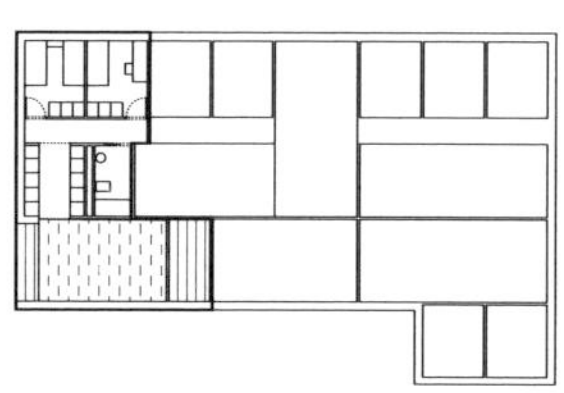

Retired persons

GFA: 71 m²

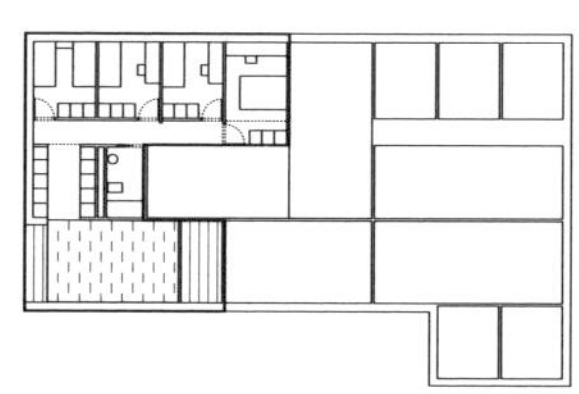

Large family

GFA: 95 m²

Urban context – Urban response
The ground floor of the building organizes the two levels of public space.

Communal space
On the ground floor, linked to the entrance halls, there is the main communal area, a porch that connects to public space.
On all the floors, access to the apartments is via a generously proportioned outdoor porched space, onto which all the living rooms give.
The building has a walk-on roof terrace, with community vegetable plots.

Energy strategy

- The apartments are all cross ventilated, turned to face south-west and north-east.
- Maximum solar capture, with sun protection in the form of shutters.
- Ventilated façade in the most exposed orientations and non-ventilated in the opposite ones.

16 homes

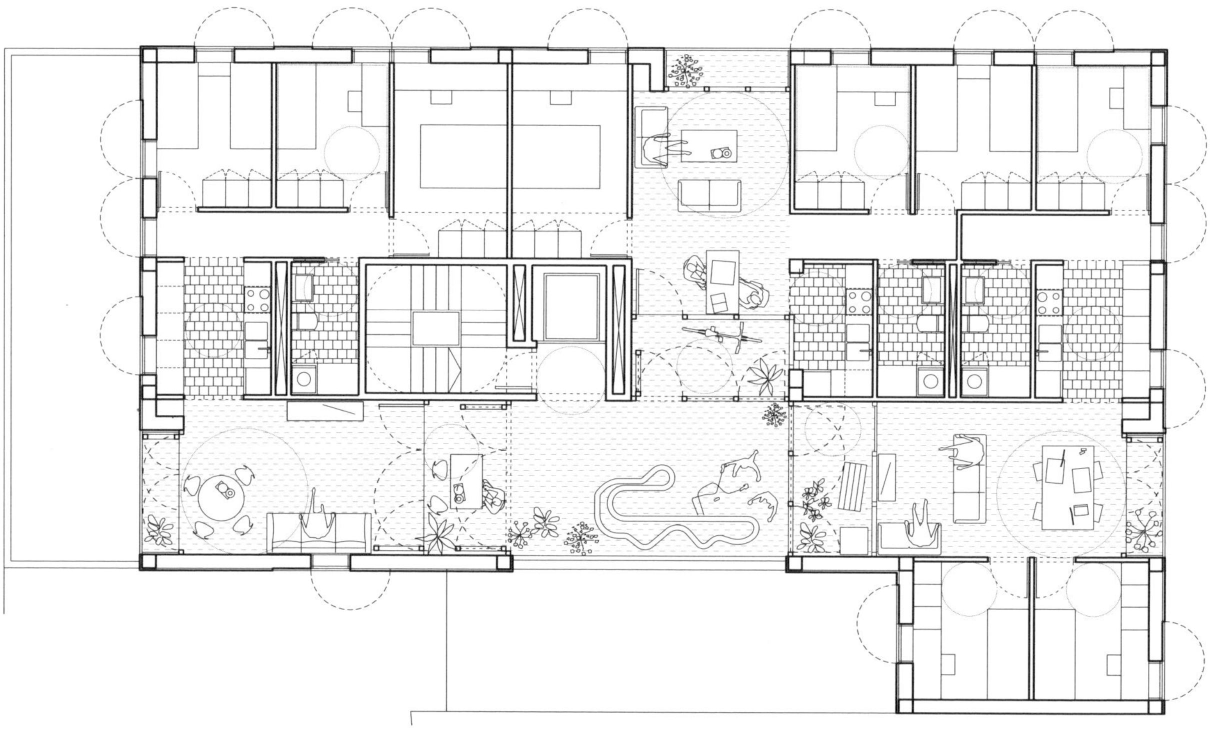

Typical floor plan

No. rooms	3	2
Total surface area (average) (m²)	67.73	55.00
Intermediate space (m²)	5.80	5.80
Living room-Dinner (m²)	21.15	21.15
Room (m²)	10.00	10.00
Balcony (m²)	2.20	2.20
No. homes	**11**	**5**

Architects: Pere Buil, Toni Riba, Ivan Pérez, Adrià Calvo. Team: Zoí Casimiro, Alex Etxeberria, Pol Bosch, Gonzalo Pérez, Santi Pérez, Eduard Resina, Jaume Garcia, Cristina Acosta. Collaborators: ikokora (renders). Location: Carrer Sant Pasqual. Floor area: 1,667 m².

Site

Location

Viladecans

22 homes

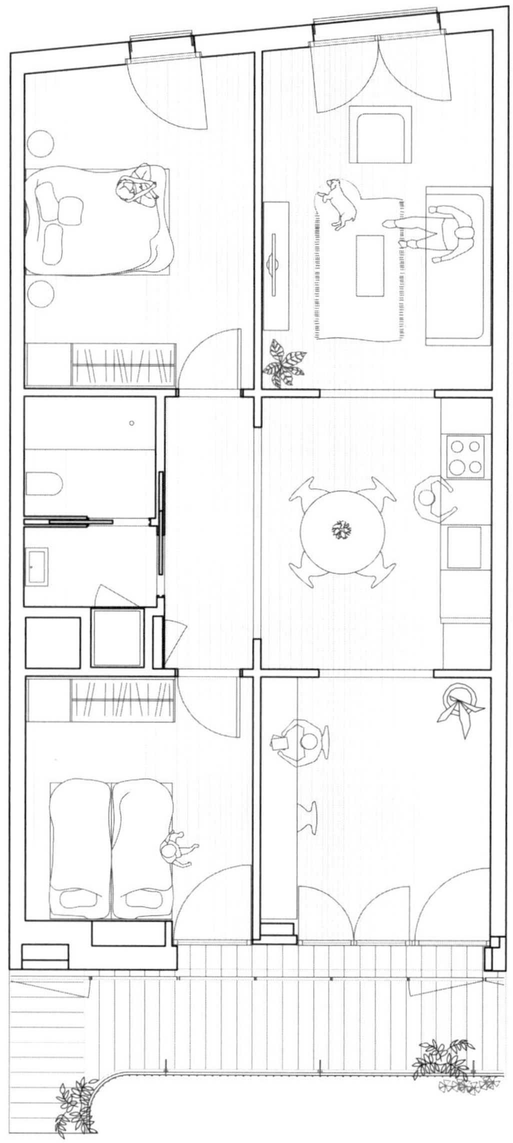

Housing unit type

Open-plan kitchen

Generic rooms

Interconnecting rooms

Intermediate social spaces

Housing unit type – Aggregation

The project proposes a prefabricated structure of large spans that produces an open floor plan with a flexible layout to allow changes in configuration and use over time. The proposed typology responds to the central service shaft scheme, freeing up the inner and outer façades for the rest of the rooms.

The aggregation applies an isotropic matrix to the particularity of the L-shape of buildable space and to the urban morphology. The two volumes, GF+2 and GF+4 respectively, form one building with a walkway leading to the homes. A single communication shaft and an open walkway on the inner façade produce a compact, optimized system that frees up the ground floor for commercial use.

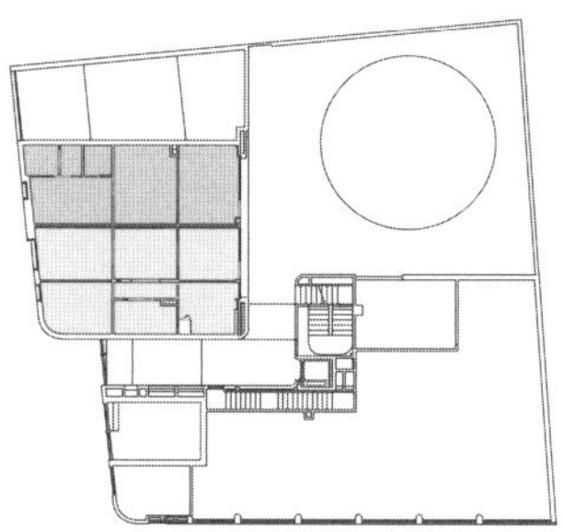

Ground floor plan

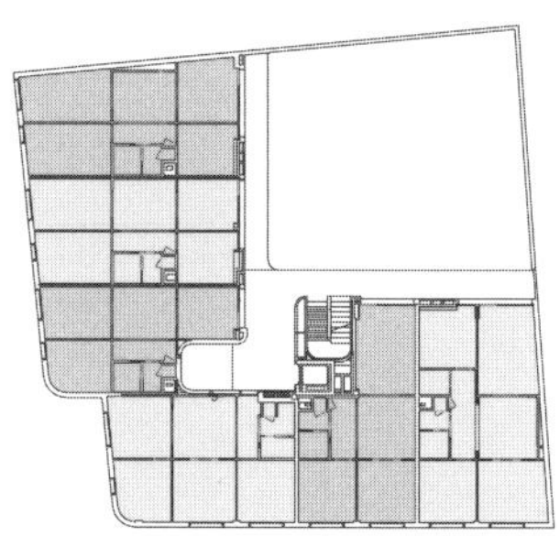

Second floor plan

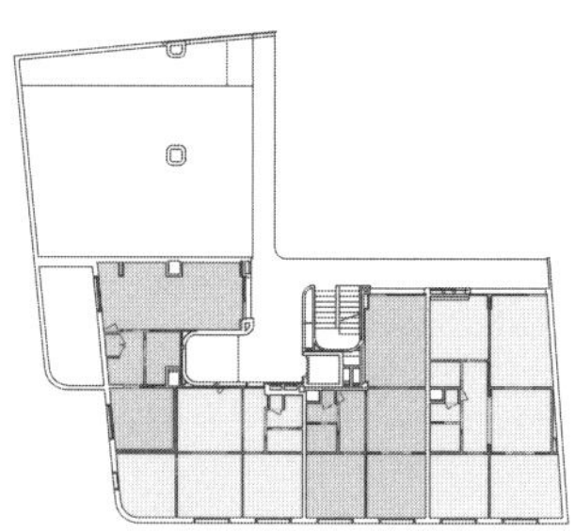

Third floor plan

Aggregation schemes

Urban context – Urban response

The project responds to the particularity of the plot, located between two different neighbourhoods, while reaffirming at urban and residential level the transition in volume proposed by planning. In order to generate the transition in scale between Passeig de la Marina and Carrer Balmes, two façades with different characters are created: the one at the centre of the street block is more domestic and communal, opening up to the inner garden, and the outer façade is more urban with occasional openings. The ground floor is perceived as a plinth that transitions to Carrer Balmes, and a semicircular geometry of the vertex of the volume in this street is proposed to promote the fluidity of urban space and generate an area that leads to the building.

Communal space

On the ground floor there is access to an open inner space that functions as a green community courtyard/garden. This space is directly connected to the system of walkways leading to the different homes via an outdoor stairway that is the building's communication shaft. The system of walkways is an intermediate communal space that becomes a private outdoor space for the homes situated at the ends of the volumes.

Energy strategy

- All the homes are cross ventilated and face two directions.
- A prefabricated modular system with a low ecological footprint is used, guaranteeing fast construction, and reducing emissions and energy and water consumption.

Energy certification: A.
- Non-renewable primary energy consumption: A (25 kWh/m^2 year).
- Carbon dioxide emissions: A (4 kg CO_2/m^2 year).

Section

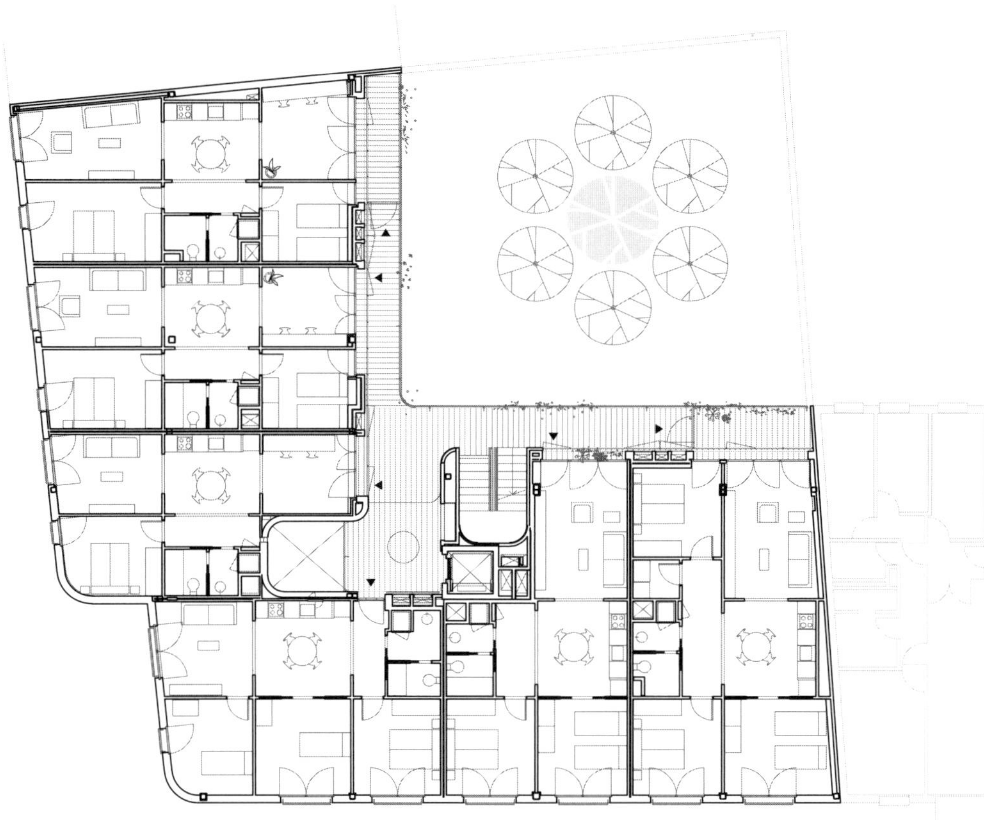

Typical floor plan

No. rooms	3	2	1
Total surface area (m^2)	80.50	64.65	54.39
Central shaft (m^2)	19.92	19.92	19.92
No. homes	**6**	**10**	**6**

Architects: Toño Foraster, Pilar Calderón, Marc Folch. Team: Paolo Calarco, Ivo Azevedo, Nieves Gómez. Works management: Núria Petit, Marc Solà (SBS). Collaborators: ELASTIC POTENTIAL (structures), TDI (installations), Ecopenta (sustainability).
Location: Carrer Balmes, 2. Floor area: 2,928 m^2.
Construction budget: €2,878,071.37

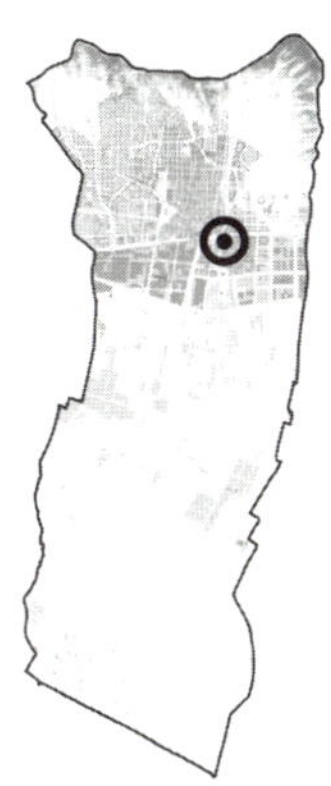

Site

Location

Santa Coloma de Gramenet 26 homes

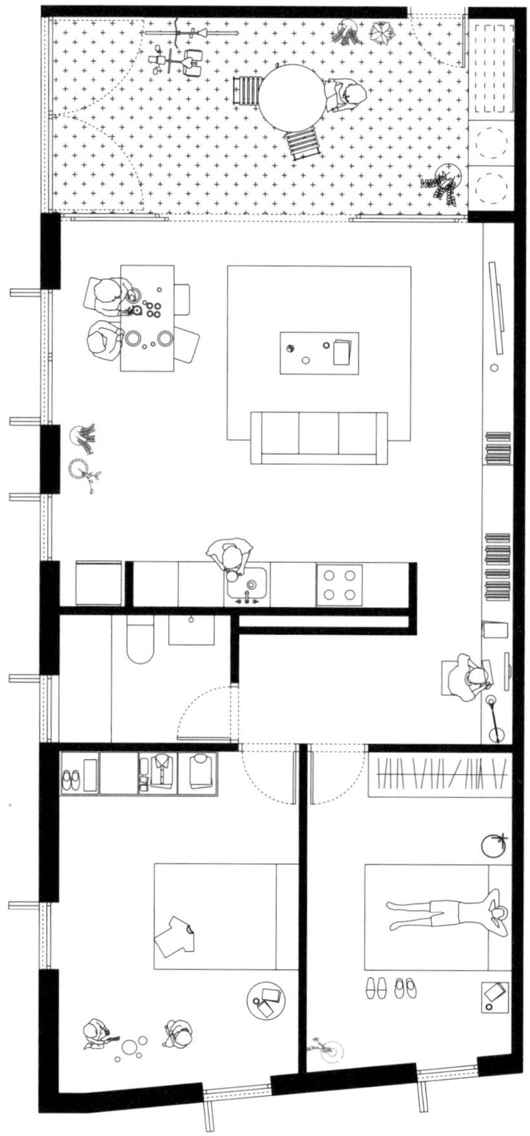

Housing unit type

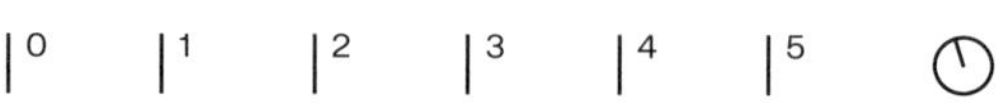

Open-plan kitchen

Generic rooms

Intermediate climatic spaces

Housing unit type – Aggregation

The proposal incorporates the courtyard house typology. Entrance to the apartments leads through an intermediate terrace-glazed balcony space that functions as a greenhouse for passive thermal collection and a filter between private and communal space. It is an extension of the home itself. The layout of the kitchen is inclusive, open to the living-dining room-terrace. The rooms are similar sizes to promote multi-functionality.

Due to the complexity of the site, the homes are grouped in a mixed, staggered layout: four, three and two homes per floor according to planning requirements, around a single communication shaft for the 26 homes.

Urban context – Urban response

Situated on a plot on a chamfered corner, the project addresses a big difference in levels and the confluence of two very different building typologies: the local district and an intensive high-rise fabric.

Energy strategy

- All the homes have natural cross ventilation.
- The wintergarden terrace functions as a passive thermal collector and a buffer space.

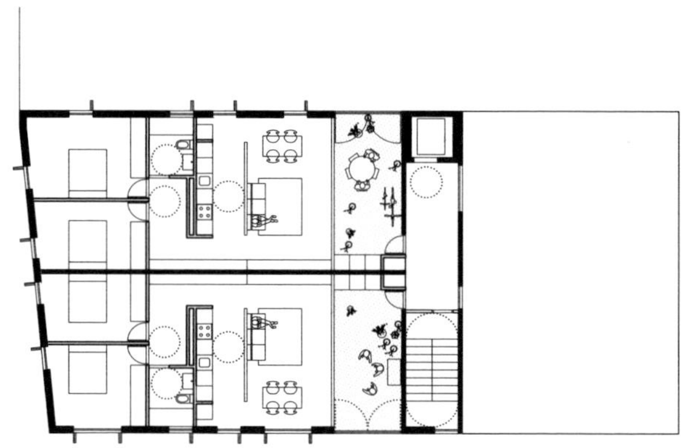

Sixth and seventh floors plan

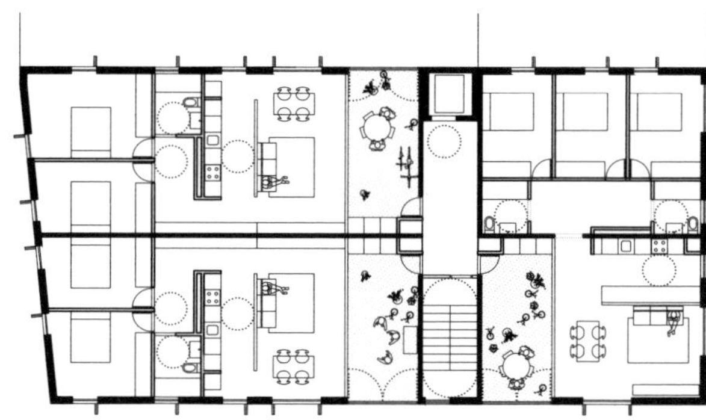

Second, third, fourth and fifth floors plan

Ground floor and first floor plan

Climatic section

0 1 2 5 10 20

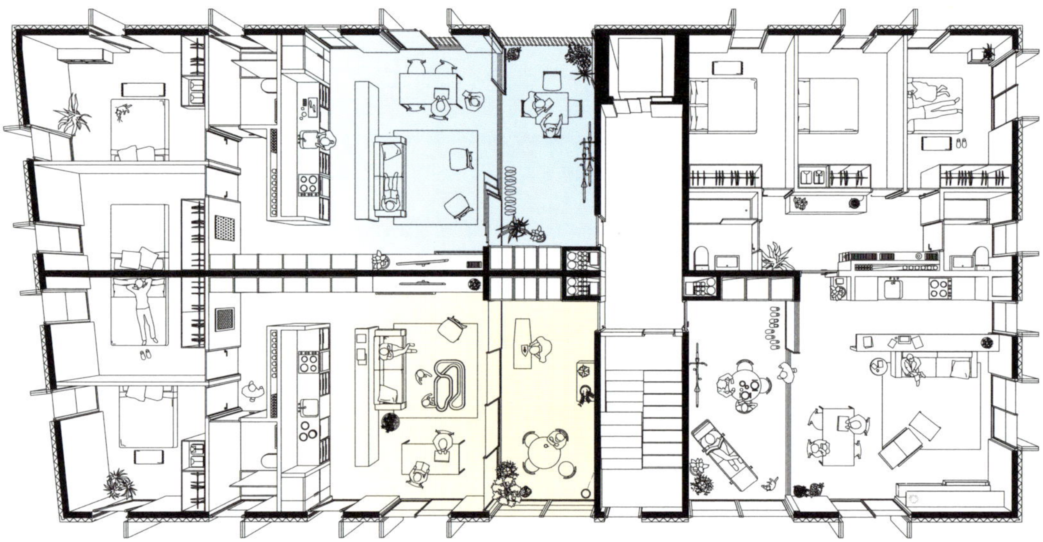

Typical floor plan

No. rooms	3	2
Total surface area (m²)	75.61	60.48
Kitchen-living-dining room (m²)	21.40	21.77
Entrance courtyard (m²)	15.31	15.31
No. homes	**4**	**22**

Architect: Joan Ramon Pascuets.
Location: Passatge dels Pirineus and Carrer de la Circumval·lació.
Floor area: 2,721 m².

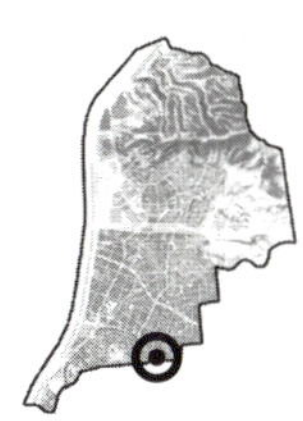

Site

Location

Sant Just Desvern

30 homes

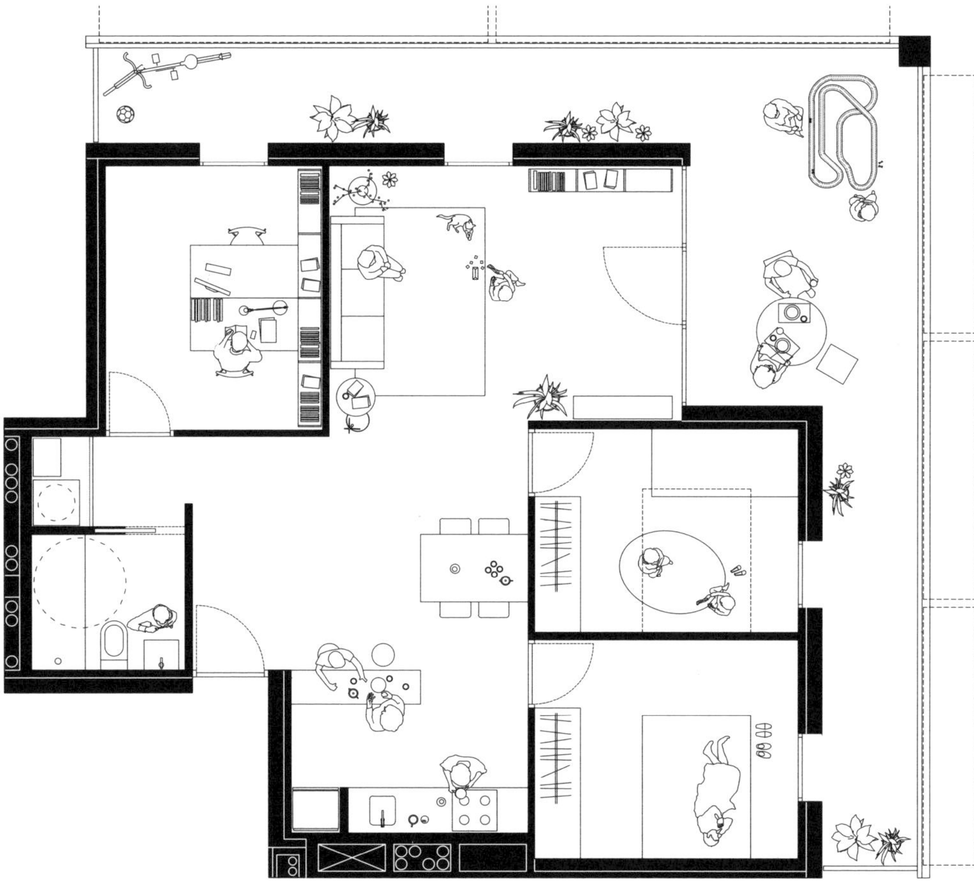

Housing unit type

Open-plan kitchen

Generic rooms

Interconnecting rooms

Intermediate climatic spaces

Intermediate social spaces

Housing unit type – Aggregation
The typology is organized according to a system of cross views and diagonal flows that guarantee lighting in all the spaces and visual connection between the terrace, living room, dining room and entrance. The central space distributes all the rooms in the apartment nonhierarchically along the outer edge of the house, in contact with the balcony. The kitchens and the sanitary and distribution spaces are located on the inside edge of the home. The balcony forms the outer ring that regulates contact between the various spaces and the outside, widening at the corners to create terrace spaces in direct relation with the living areas. The 30 homes are organized in a square floor plan around a central atrium with a communication shaft located in the northeast façade. In this way the homes enjoy the best views and orientation, freeing up the corners for terraces. There are five apartments per landing, four with three bedrooms and one with two, in the GF+5 building.

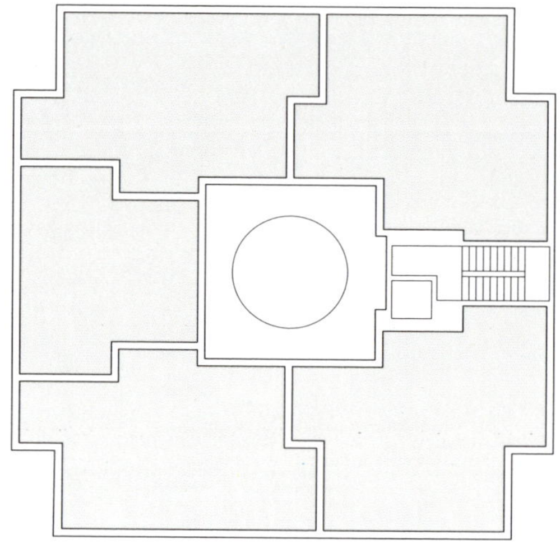

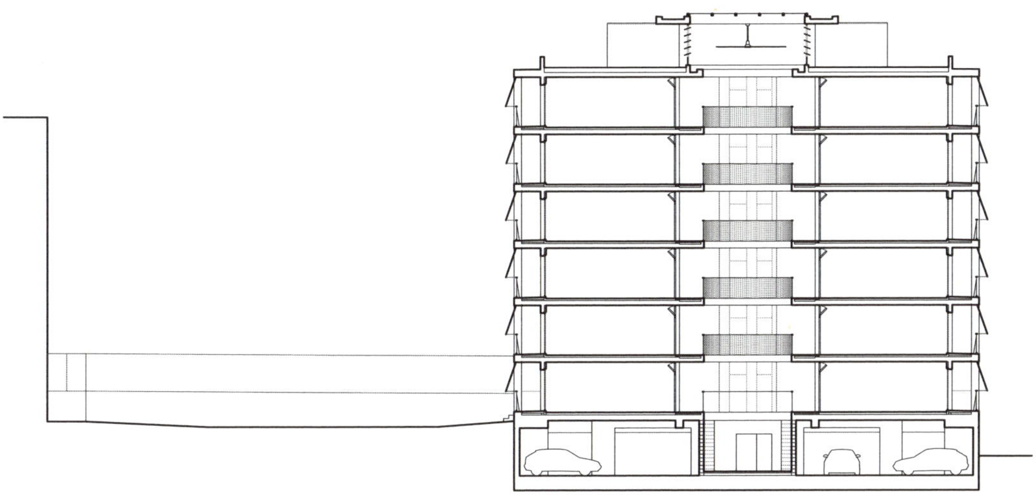

Section

0 2 5 10 20

Urban context – Urban response
The building presents an open, extroverted image with continuous terraces in all the façades that prioritizes the relationship with the landscape in a suburban setting in direct contact with nature and the community garden.

Communal space
The project proposes two intermediate spaces: the central atrium and the perimeter terraces. The central atrium is a bioclimatic collective space that closes in winter and opens in summer; the building is characterized by having a dynamic form factor, compact in winter, and open and dissipative in summer. The perimeter terraces of the homes are also intermediate spaces for private outdoor use that regulate sunlighting.

Materiality
The building is a masonry construction with a reinforced-concrete structure and façades that provides an economical solution to thermal bridges and leaves the entire structure of walls and ceilings visible. It is a robust construction that reduces maintenance and improves the durability of the building. The floors are also made of concrete: polished concrete pavements outside, precast concrete terrazzo indoors. The decision not to apply finishes or claddings serves to allow low maintenance and good ageing.

16

Energy strategy

- High thermal inertia of the building.
- Good orientation, with ventilation through the central atrium.
- Sun shading in the form of awnings.
- Cross ventilation.

Energy certification: A.
- Non-renewable primary energy consumption: A (25 kWh/m² year).
- Carbon dioxide emissions: A (5 kg CO_2/m² year).

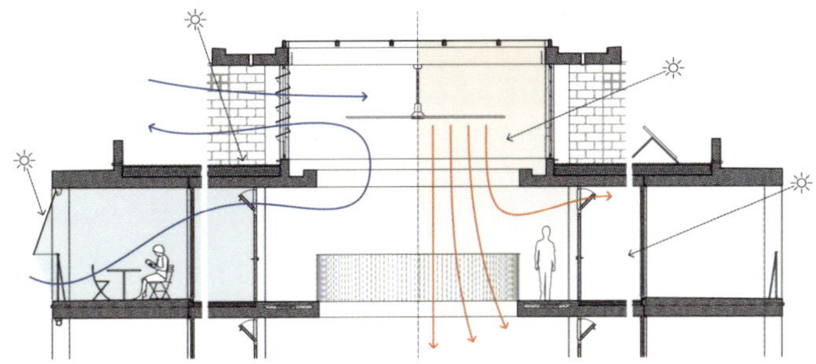

Building section

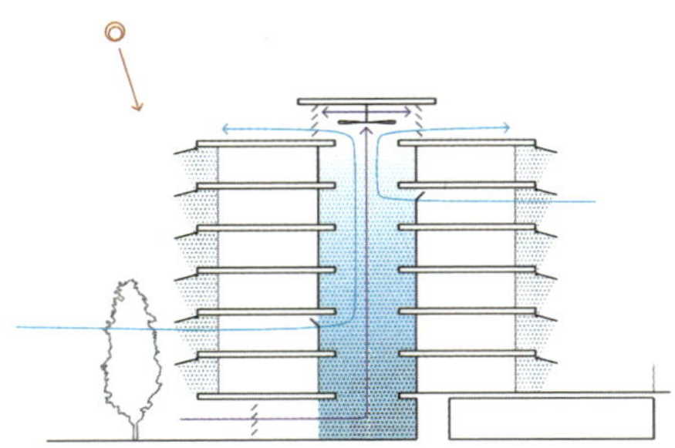

Atrium section, summer

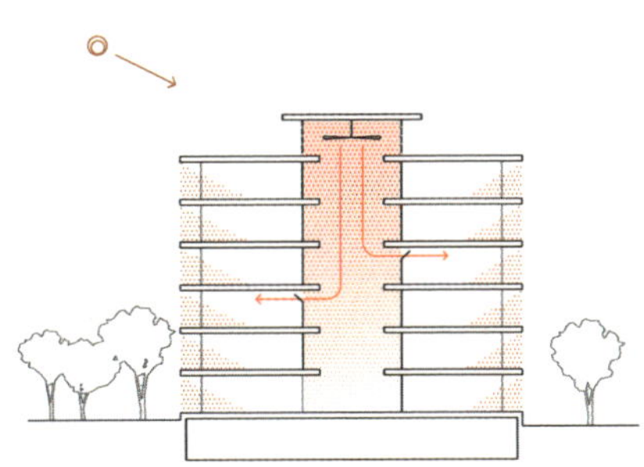

Atrium section, winter

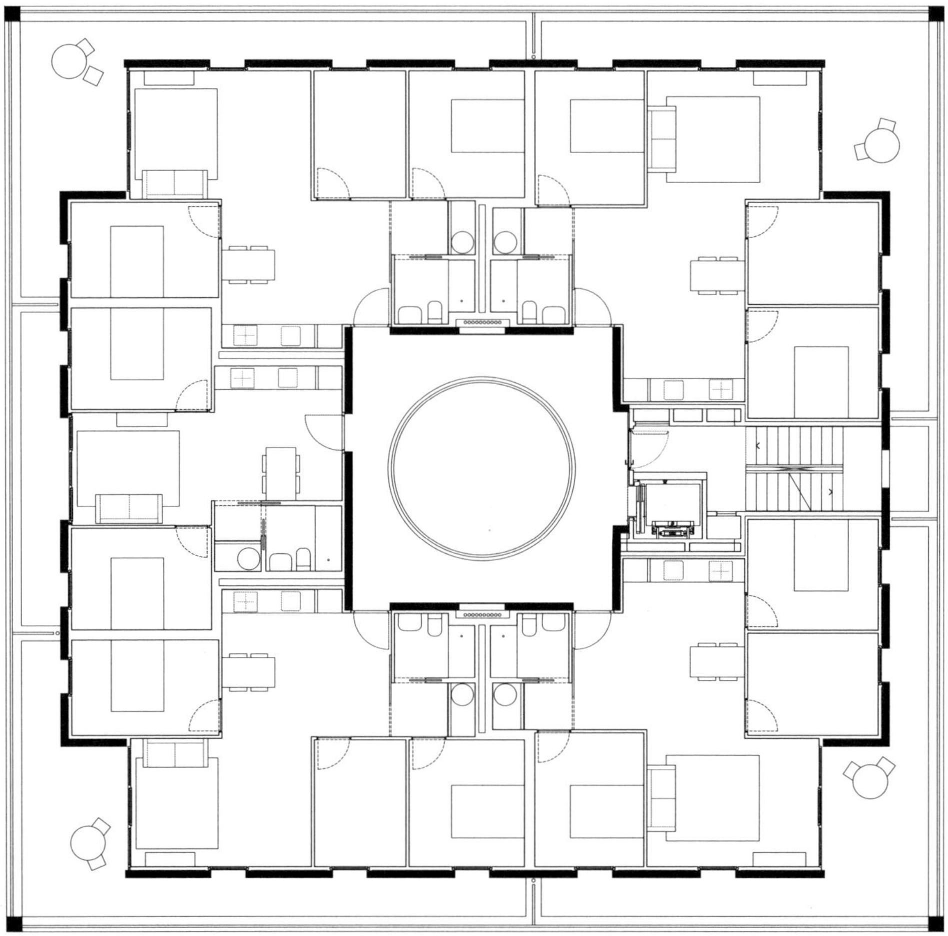

Typical floor plan

No. rooms	3	2
Total surface area (m²)	76.07	61.90
Kitchen-living-dining room (m²)	34.23	28.29
Terrace (m²)	31.87	20.50
No. homes	**23**	**7**

Architects: Claudi Aguiló, Albert Domingo, Xavier Vendrell.
Team: Javier Gavín. Works management: Brufau Cusó estudi d'arquitectura. Collaborators: Bernuz-Fernández Arquitectes (structures), ELETRESJOTA (installations), Àurea Acústica (acoustics), Societat Orgànica (environmental consultancy).
Location: Carrer de Carolina Catasús, 7. Floor area: 3,828.09 m^2.
Construction budget: €2,997,118.28

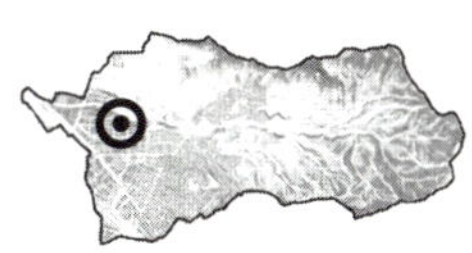

Site

Location

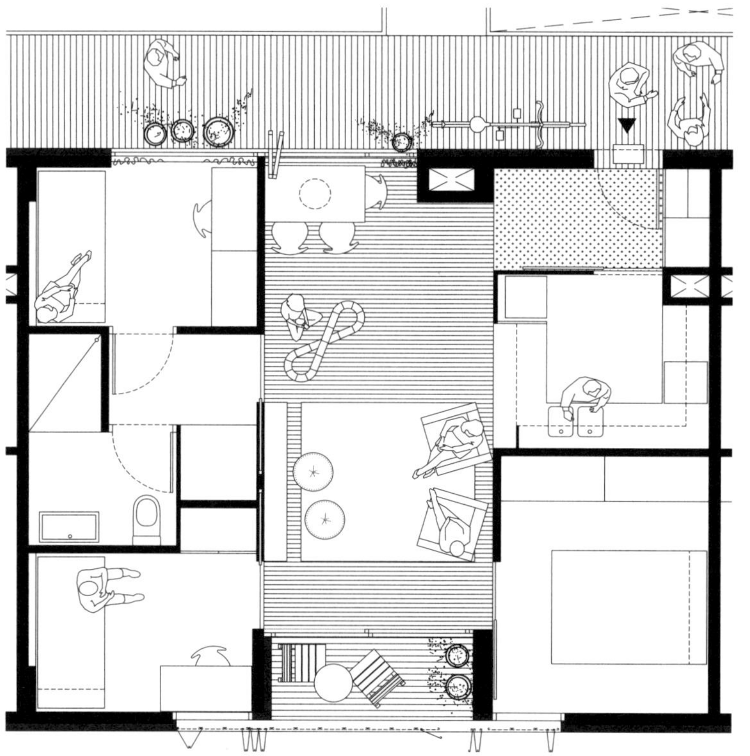

Housing unit type

Brullet de Luna

2017—design phase

Interconnecting rooms

Intermediate social spaces

Housing unit type - Aggregation
The chosen housing typology minimizes corridor space. The homes are made up of three strips of approximately three metres, perpendicular to the façade: a central one, with the living-dining room and a glazed terrace, and one to either side, containing two rooms in the façade. The entrance, kitchen, bathrooms and a third room are laid out along the walkway leading to the homes.
The aggregation pivots on a central axis that is partially open to the court at the centre of the street block, with a communication shaft located at each end. The typological units on the two stairways of the building respond to the same model. This takes the form of four homes per floor in the sections that coincide with the existing GF+2 building, with the same building depth, and three homes per landing on the upper floors.

Urban context – Urban response
The building makes up the large difference in level between the two streets, Carrer de la Circumval·lació and Carrer Sant Pascual, and makes the transition between the height of the existing buildings and the new proposed height, so that no party walls are visible and the new buildings become an integral part of the existing blocks.

Communal space
The communal stairways become intermediate spaces that act as thermal buffers. The idea is that the two roofs will be community spaces. They are designed as large outdoor living rooms, sheltered by the façade that surrounds them and with the incorporation of awnings to provide shade.

Energy strategy
- The aim is to reduce the demand for air-conditioning to below 15 kWh/m^2 a year, and for primary energy to below 120 kWh/m^2 a year.
- In the winter, the private glazed balcony serves as a wintergarden, and the communal glazed balcony as a buffer space. In summer, the adjustable solar protection turns the gallery into a shaded space.

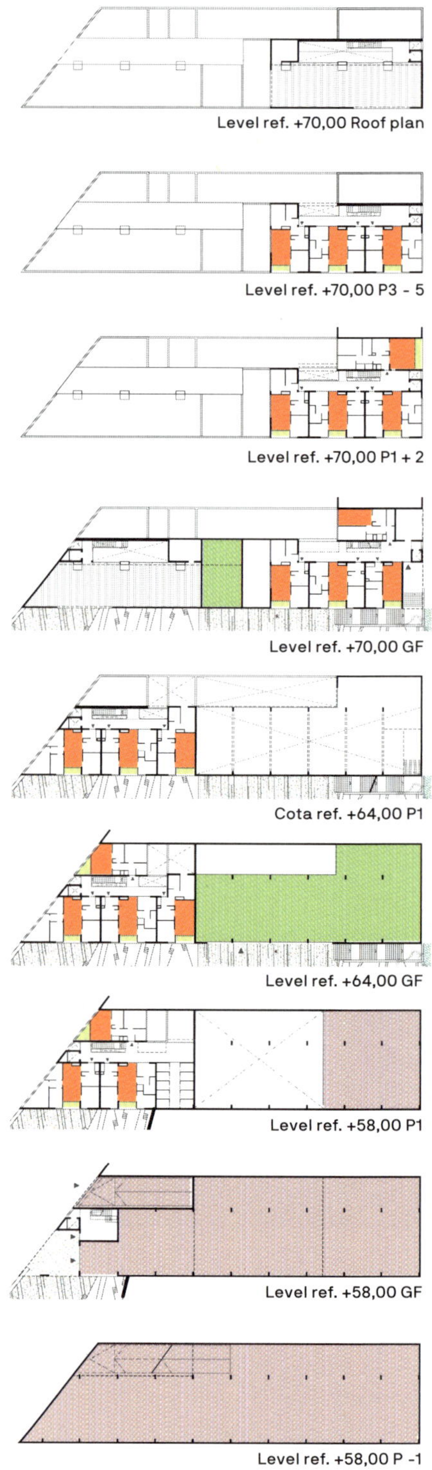

Floor plan diagrams

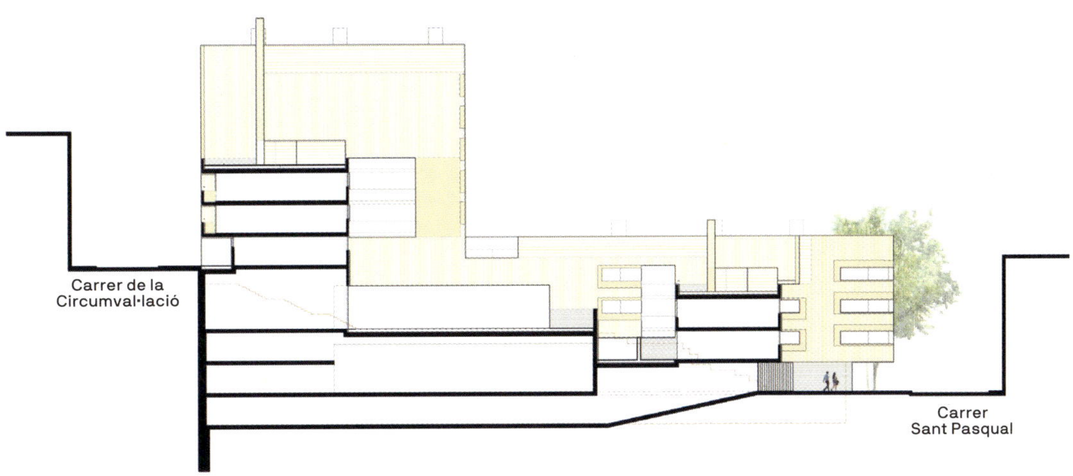

Longitudinal section

|0 |5 |10 |20 |50

Typical floor plan

No. rooms	3	2	2
Total surface area (m²)	58.60	53.80	63.30
Living room-diner (m²)	17.70	17.50	19.60
Terrace-glazed balcony (m²)	2.50	2.60	4.90
No. homes	**18**	**11**	**2**

Architects: Manuel Brullet, Alfonso de Luna. Team: Jaume Piñol, Mitra Modarressi, David Casadevall, Mateusz Obolonczyk. Collaborators: Manuel Arguijo y Asociados (structures), Maria Morillo (sustainability). Location: Carrer Sant Pasqual. Floor area: 5,546.12 m^2.

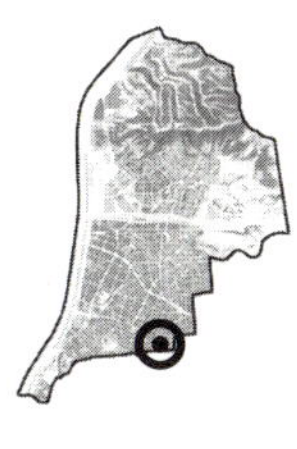

Site

Location

Sant Feliu de Llobregat

34 homes

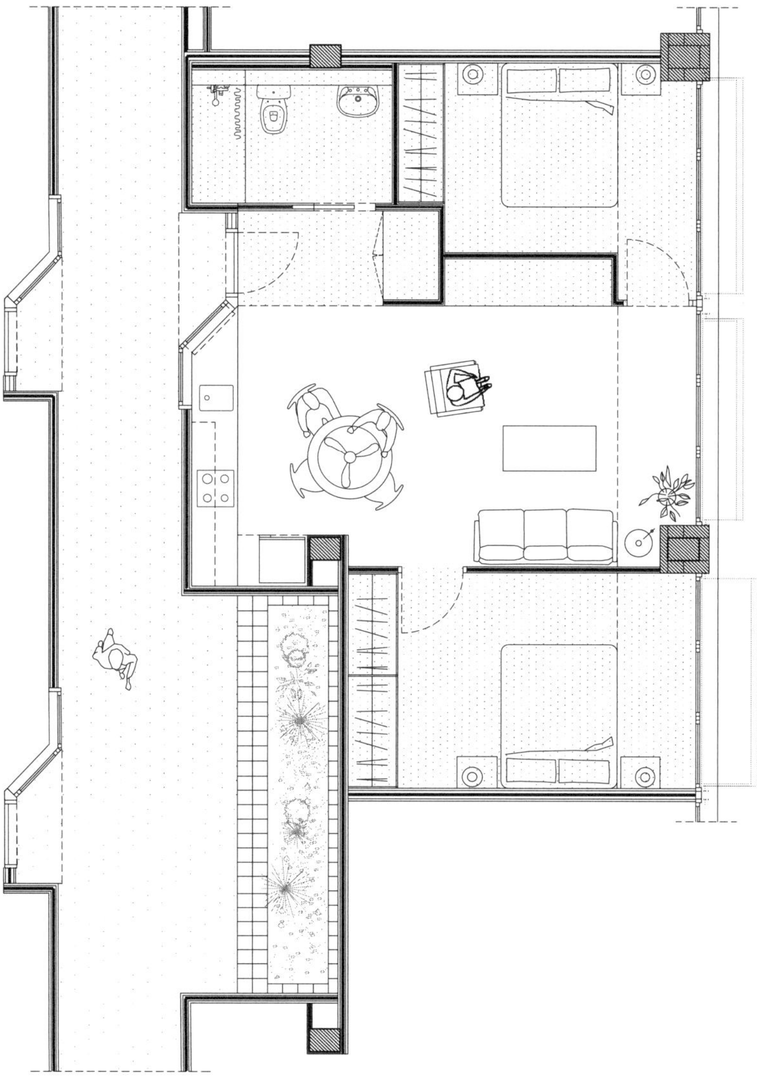

Housing unit type

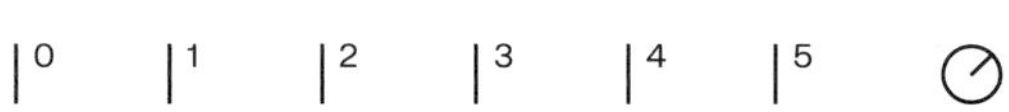

Open-plan kitchen

Interconnecting rooms

Intermediate climatic spaces

Intermediate social spaces

Housing unit type – Aggregation
The homes are arranged in two halves perpendicular to the façade: one open plan, occupying the living room, kitchen and dining room, and aiming to enhance cross ventilation and the relationship with the common space; and a second half, closed and compartmentalized, housing the entrance space, cupboards, bathroom and bedroom, seeking privacy and order. The completely open-plan kitchen is arranged parallel to the corridor, concentrating the fittings, freeing up the maximum space for the dining room and eliminating gender roles.

Due to the dimensions of the space, orientation and views, the project arranges the 34 homes to either side of central corridors. The aggregation is simple and the position of the one- and two-bedroom homes and communal spaces sets out to ensure that the entrances of light to the central corridor are uniform and equidistant. In front of each of the entrances to the homes, spaces are created that widen the corridor with windows to connect it with the homes and the exteriors.

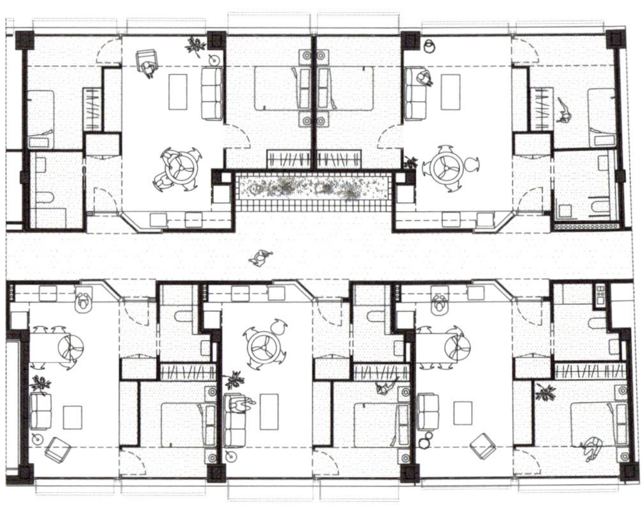

Aggregation floor plan

0 1 2 5 10

Communal spaces
The project positions the common spaces strategically and alternately to expand the central corridors. At the exit from the lift, it includes a communal parking space for bicycles to encourage their use in the town or on the many paths along the riverside park. Further inside, in front of one of the planters, there is a laundry with ventilated drying racks for the community's clothes since the existing façade makes it impossible to create outdoor spaces. Finally, at one end there is a multipurpose room for games, meetings, celebrations, study, work, or whatever activities the inhabitants choose.

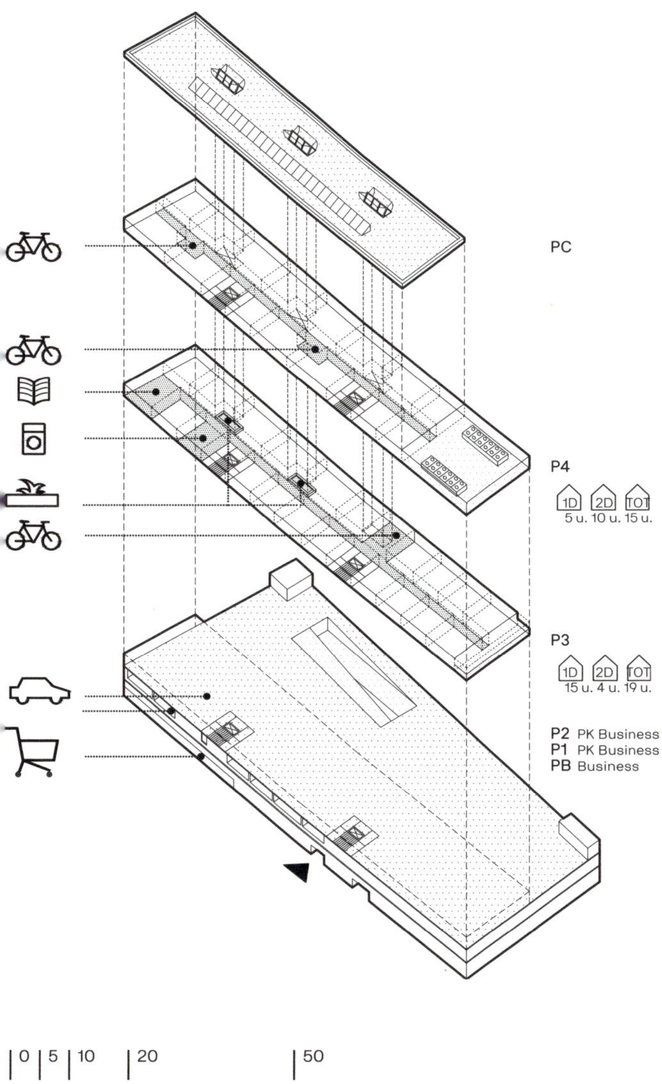

34 homes

Urban context – Urban response

This is an urban recycling operation. The project is introduced into the two top floors of an existing mixed-use building (shops/car park/offices) that had fallen into disuse and are being reactivated to address the housing emergency. The floors that had to be repurposed were characterized by measuring approximately 86 × 15 metres, with two circulation shafts, long windows, 1.10 m from the ground, and a structure of reinforced concrete pillars supporting a reticular slab.

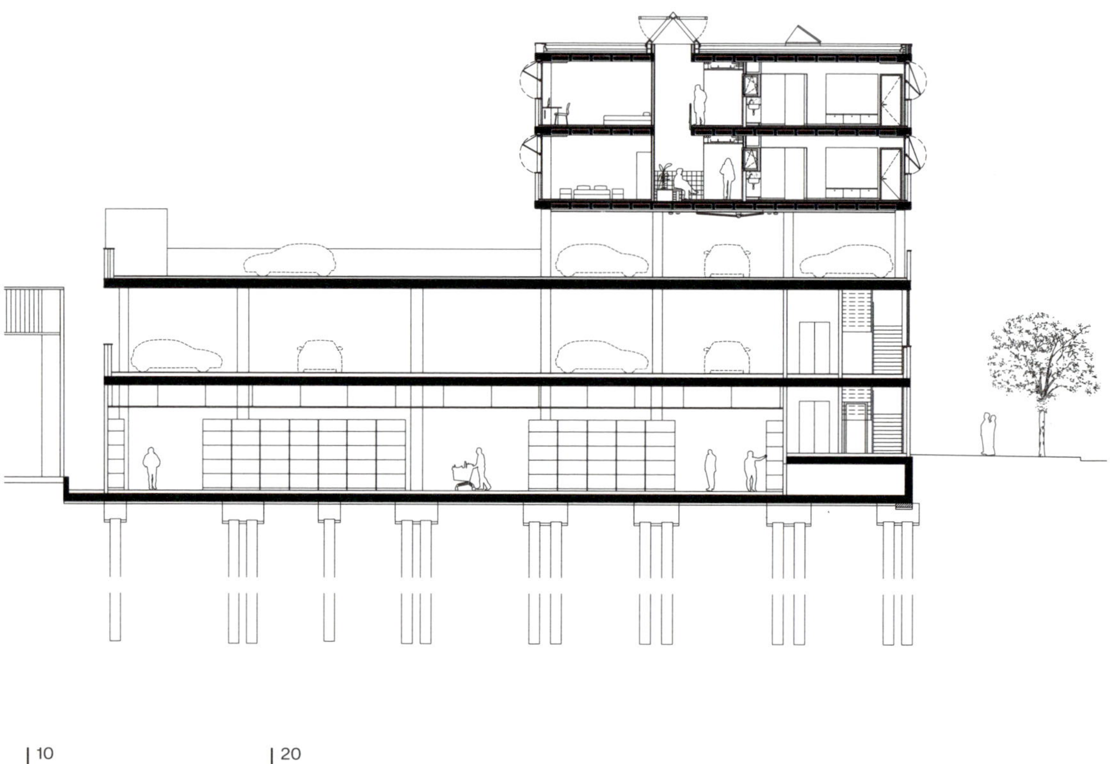

Cross section

The project proposes a series of strategies to ensure the best environmental qualities for movements between the street and private space, creating areas to spend time and interact with neighbours: three spaces are carved out up to the roof to let in daylight, interrelate the two floors spatially and give all the homes cross ventilation. These empty spaces become benches/ planters on the lower floor, a balcony on the upper floor and a skylight in the roof.

Materiality
The starting conditions are the existing structure and façade. The façade will be insulated from the extrados, with improved waterproofing and new tilt-and-turn windows with upgraded aluminium frames. Dry-construction compartmentalization is proposed for the structure to minimize the added weight, and points around the new courts are reinforced with carbon fibre. The common spaces are clad with warm materials: glazed ceramics in the communal areas and wood for the corridors and front doors. Wood continues inside the homes in the living room furniture.

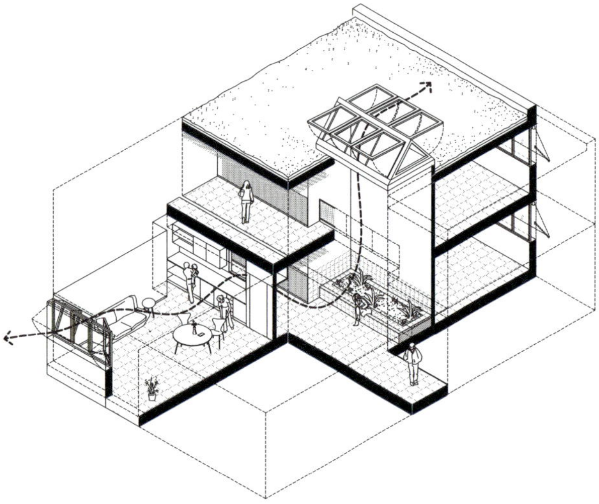

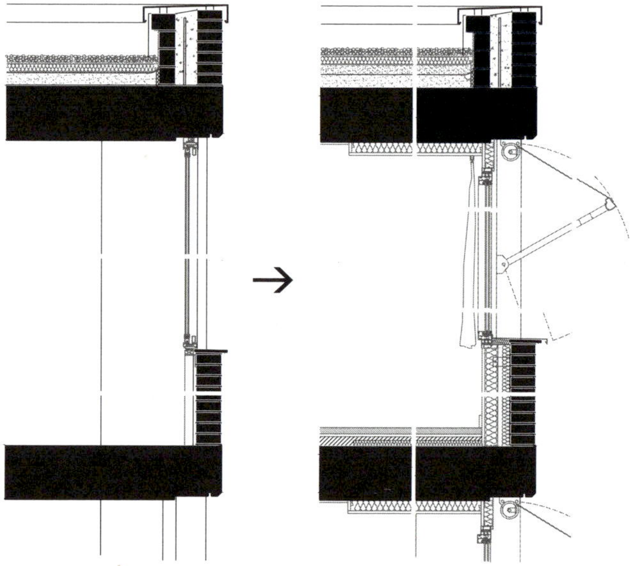

Details of window frames

| 0 | 0.5 | 1

Energy strategy

- Insulation of façades, roof and floor slab on level three.
- Solar protection for the interior in the form of curtains and for the outside with adjustable awnings.
- Natural cross ventilation encouraged by adjustable skylights and windows at the end of the corridors.
- Cross ventilation of the homes thanks to the installation of tilt-and-turn windows in the kitchens.

<u>Energy certification:</u> A.
3rd floor:
- Non-renewable primary energy consumption: A (22 kWh/m^2 year)
- Carbon dioxide emissions: A (3 kg CO_2/m^2 year).

4th floor:
- Non-renewable primary energy consumption: A (11 kWh/m^2 year)
- Carbon dioxide emissions: A (2 kg CO_2/m^2 year).

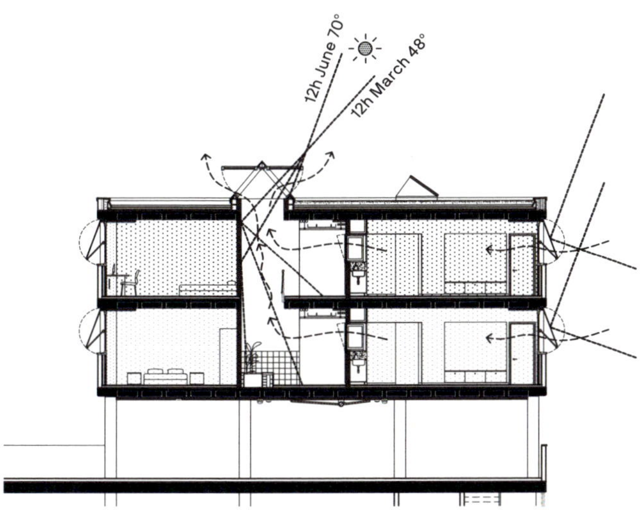

Summer section

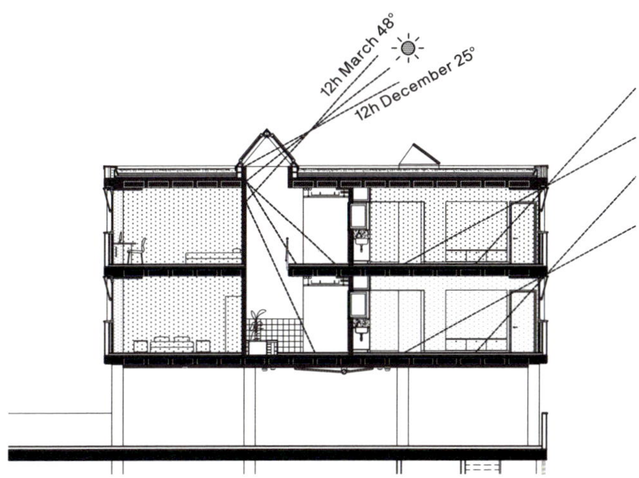

Winter section

0 1 2 5 10

34 homes

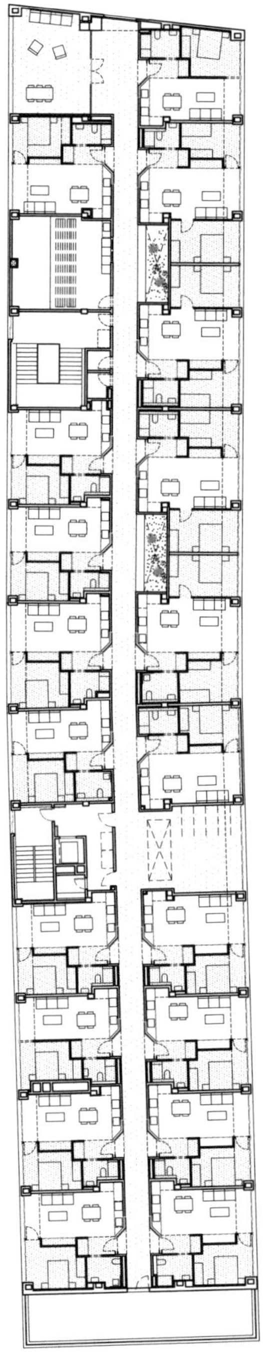

Typical floor plan

No. rooms	2	1
Total surface area (m²)	55.00	39.00
Kitchen-living-dining room (m²)	27.00	25.00
No. homes	**14**	**20**

Architects: Mariona Benedito, Martí Sanz. Team: Xavier Isart, Clara Vidal. Works management: Xavier Badia (VINCLAMENT), Alba Subirada (Gruart). Collaborators: Manuel Arguijo y Asociados (structures), AIA (installations). Location: Carrer del Pla, 2F. Floor area: 2,474.05 m^2. Construction budget: €1,708,616.97

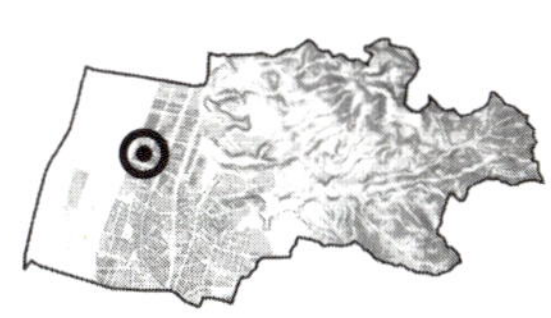

Site

Location

Collective housing responses to the socioeconomic context

In recent decades, our country has undergone major socioeconomic changes, but our housing developments have not. Economic practices and everyday lives have been profoundly transformed, but the market continues to develop the same type of housing. Fortunately, these past few years the government has fostered research in new forms of public housing that can better adapt to contemporary society, and which are now yielding the first built results. With the COVID-19 pandemic, it became even more evident that researching new housing arrangements was an urgent task. The shortcomings of our homes became apparent across social strata, traditional housing typologies were increasingly brought into question, and the attendant confinement furthered the multidisciplinary debate on multifamily housing and domestic spaces. This gave designers and policymakers the final push to step out of their comfort zones and seek better answers to new problems.

One of the key social shifts that designers need to grapple with today is the profound change in our forms of living together. The traditional family consisting of a father, a mother and their children is no longer the norm. Groups of people who live together are increasingly more diverse and transitory. And it is not possible to anticipate who the users might be, their genders, their ages or their ties. Nor is it easy to estimate how long their domestic living relationship will last. Housing has the responsibility to respond and adapt to these changing realities. This is why the blank canvas approach is gaining popularity—a neutral, non-hierarchical arrangement in which each family can adapt organically according to its changing needs. In this approach, the rooms are similar in terms of dimensions, daylight, relation with the outside, and relation with the kitchen and the bathroom. No space is favoured over others; there are no distinctions between “noble” and “service” spaces that still echo historically unequal social relations within the home. All the rooms can be used for everything and by everyone, and they are interchangeable over time. This approach is not new—it was already widespread in the twentieth century across Barcelona’s Eixample and in different types of Spanish popular architecture, with flexible layouts that allowed for multiple changing uses. But this flexibility was replaced, in the mid-twentieth century, by more hierarchized housing arrangements that mirrored the traditional family model and its entwined political project.

Since the pandemic, it has become evident that such multipurpose housing typologies can better adapt to the growing range of activities that now take place inside the home. In addition to cooking, eating and resting, people now play sports, play and listen to music, make phone and video calls, and work remotely. These activities require spaces of certain sizes and proportions for different types of furniture. And they also require spaces that can be cut off from one another at any given time. Indeed, during lockdown we all realized how important it was to be able to close a door for both privacy and comfort. But we also saw that it was necessary to be able to open that door and escape the growing isolation that the digitization of work, leisure, education and communication had brought about.

Social isolation is without a doubt one of dangers of the digitization of our everyday lives that the pandemic exacerbated, and one that architects can help address. It is increasingly possible to do everything from home—a safe, comfortable territory that is now also digitally hyperconnected. It is now possible to work and earn a living without having to go to the office. You can get an education—even a university education—from the comfort of your bedroom. You can buy anything from home. Accordingly,

Maria Amat, an architect and founding partner of METRONOM, combines her professional activity with teaching at ETSAB-UPC and in various workshops.

leaving the home is increasingly less of a pressing need, but not doing so can affect our mental health and our ability to socialize.

In the design of new public housing typologies, then, the tendency is to include spaces for social interactions to alleviate the dangers of isolation. Such spaces can offer residents a reason to leave their homes and meet with neighbours, fostering a sense of community and a much-needed support network. The functional common spaces (foyers, lifts, stairways, bicycle parking) where chance encounters occur is therefore becoming a primary design concern. It is also increasingly common to include spaces for community use: laundries, multipurpose rooms, communal kitchens, shared teleworking spaces, formal and informal meeting rooms, spaces for care or for guests, etc. Outdoor spaces can also fulfil this function: green roofs and gardens where residents can sunbathe, play sports, study, meet and celebrate. In short, housing blocks are being reconceived as generators of chance encounters and deliberate gatherings of residents who are increasingly exposed to the risks of social isolation.

These types of community spaces also offer an opportunity to share material goods outside the home, such as washing machines, clothes lines, maintenance tools and screens. In this respect, cooperative housing models are one step ahead and are often an inspiration for public housing. One would hope that, as a consumer society, we learn to see this sharing ethos as a step forward rather than a step backwards, because sharing material goods can be advantageous not only economically but also socially and environmentally. In turn, a sharing culture of this kind can help reverse the growing trend towards social isolation, turning the sharing of material goods into an excuse for sharing time together.

Today, these are some of the socio-economic aspects that are being addressed by designers in the housing arena. Eventually, new questions will arise, and new answers will need to be provided. That's why it's important to keep the flame of research, risk and curiosity very much alive. And design competitions are one of the main ways in which this is done today. It is the formula through which cities and governments can attract talent, encourage creative competition and, consequently, improve the quality of public housing. The resulting public housing developments have more nuanced, respectful relations with their context and with our contemporary times. They can serve as an example for private developers. And they can serve as an inspiration across our landscapes and beyond.

35 homes

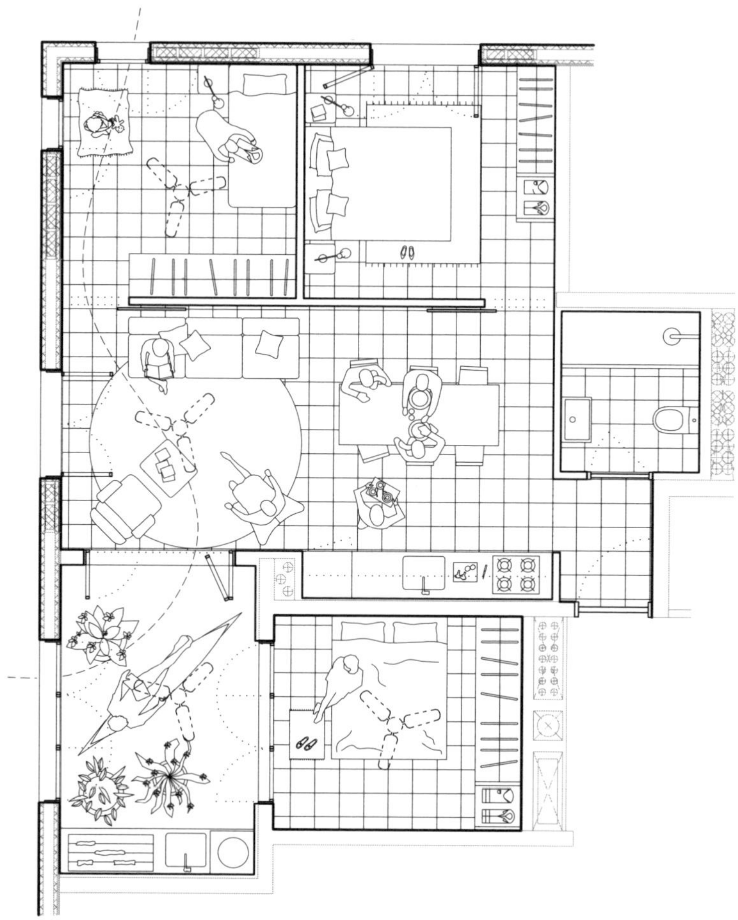

Housing unit type

METRONOM

2021—under construction

Open-plan kitchen

Generic rooms

Interconnecting rooms

Intermediate climatic spaces

Intermediate social spaces

Housing unit type – Aggregation
The proposed housing type is compact, and the entire useful floor area is habitable. The rooms are stripped of hierarchy and intercommunicate freely. The kitchen is the centre of the home, the heart of social life.
The apartment is flexible and adaptable to different realities of sharing and moments in life, and has a generous outdoor space. The most characteristic, singular room is the semi-exterior gallery: a space that can be converted into a terrace in the summer and a spectacular glazed balcony in the winter.

The tower-block typology allows four homes per floor, all of them corner units. There are three two-bedroom apartments and one with three, which fits into the layout thanks to the off-centre position of the stairway. At the centre of the tower in a cross-shaped formation are the building's server systems: communications, wet areas and installation conduits. The rooms in the façade are arranged around it in a ring.

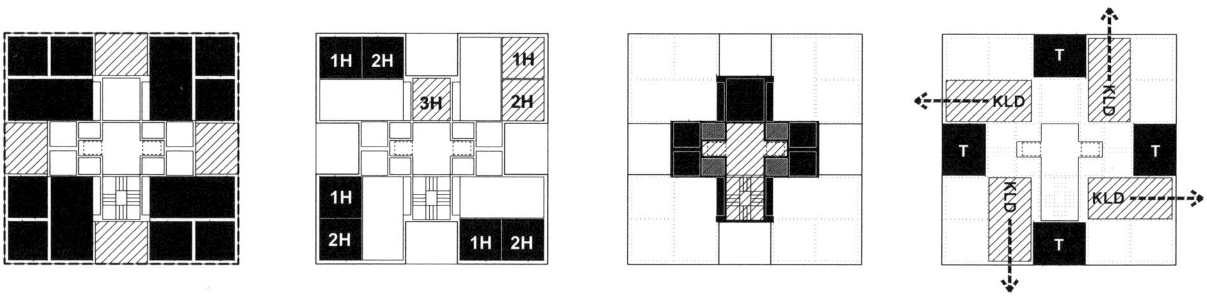

Floor plan diagrams

Section

0 2 5 10 20

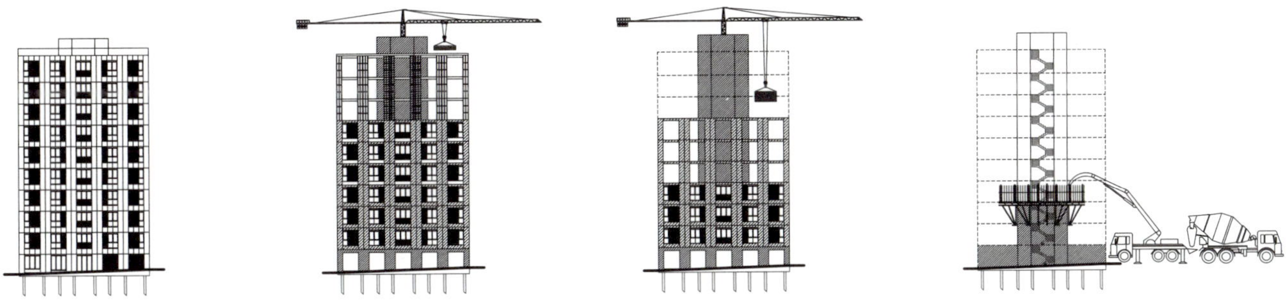

Building process

Urban context – Urban response
It is a tower block of GF+8, slightly turned from its neighbours and inserted in a sloping topography. The tower makes itself present not only in its immediate urban setting but also when seen from the railway lines. The orderly, forceful composition of the façades, despite the domesticity of their use, offers a strong response to this metropolitan scale. Entrance to the foyer of the apartments is from the busiest road. The vacant plot is organized and landscaped, giving continuity to the existing pedestrian network. A space for neighbourhood use is also created in the gardens to introduce activity onto the highest level of the plot.

Materiality
The tower has a prefabricated CLT structure. The façade comprises an abstract, rationalized, unifying mesh that simultaneously introduces the urban and metropolitan scale through the grids with their various openings, presenting a Mediterranean image that also responds to the typological singularity of the outer rooms that the project proposes for each home.

Energy strategy
- All the homes have cross ventilation.
- The semi-exterior balcony functions as a thermal buffer.

Energy certification: A.
- Non-renewable primary energy consumption: A (12.73 kWh/m^2 year).
- Carbon dioxide emissions: A (2.61 kg CO_2/m^2 year).

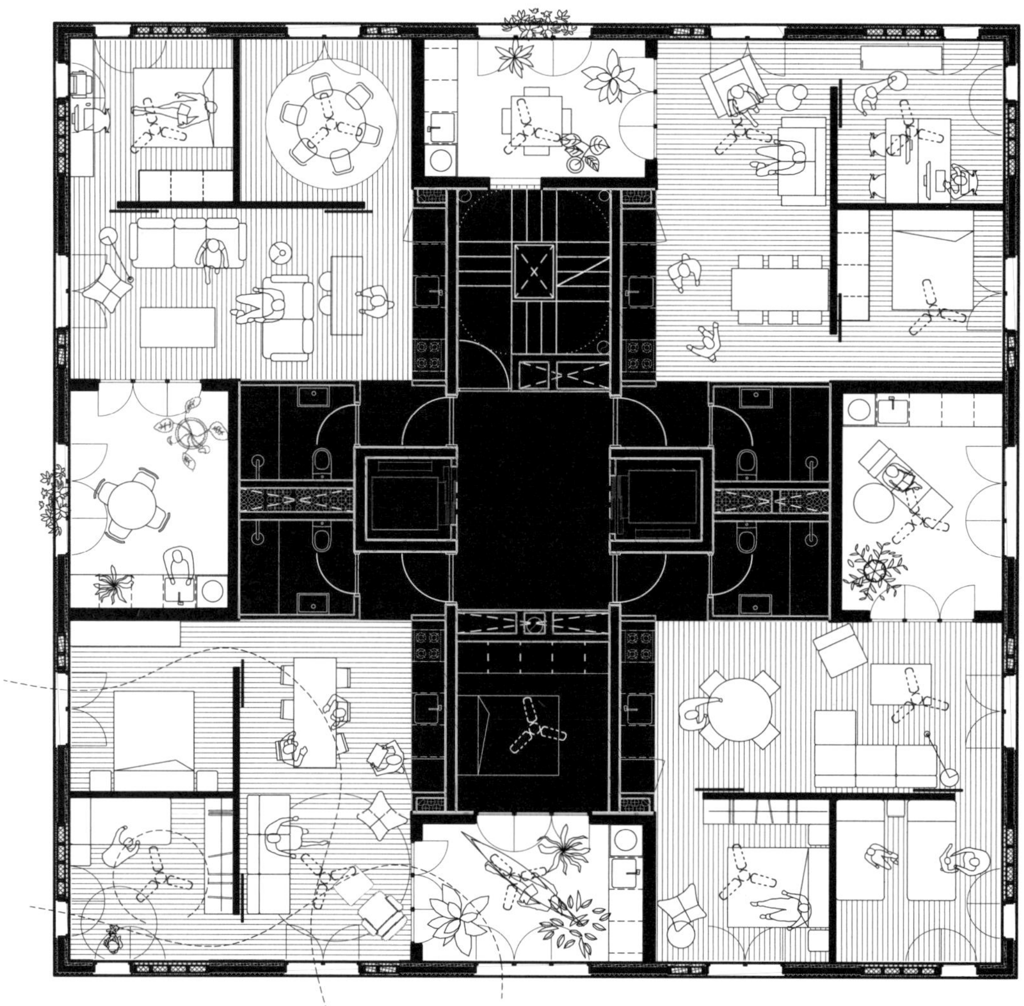

Typical floor plan

No. rooms	3	2
Total surface area (m^2)	68.45	60.55
Kitchen-living-dining room (m^2)	22.88	22.94
Semi-exterior glazed balcony (m^2)	8.57	8.57
No. homes	**9**	**26**

Architects: Maria Amat, Albert Casas, Frederic Villagrasa. Team: Cristina Requejo, Luisa Lisboa, Arnau Espona, Ludovica di Lernia. Works management: Francesc de Haro Macià, Francesc Xavier Aumedes Farré, Gemma Rius Macies (Arrevolt). Collaborators: Estudi M103 (structures), ELETRESJOTA (installations), Societat Orgànica (environmental consultancy), The Soundwich Project (acoustics), Jorge Suarez Kilzi (renders). Location: Avinguda Mancomunitat, 24. Floor area: 3,240 m^2. Construction budget: €3,760,609.50

Site

Location

Sant Andreu de la Barca

36 homes

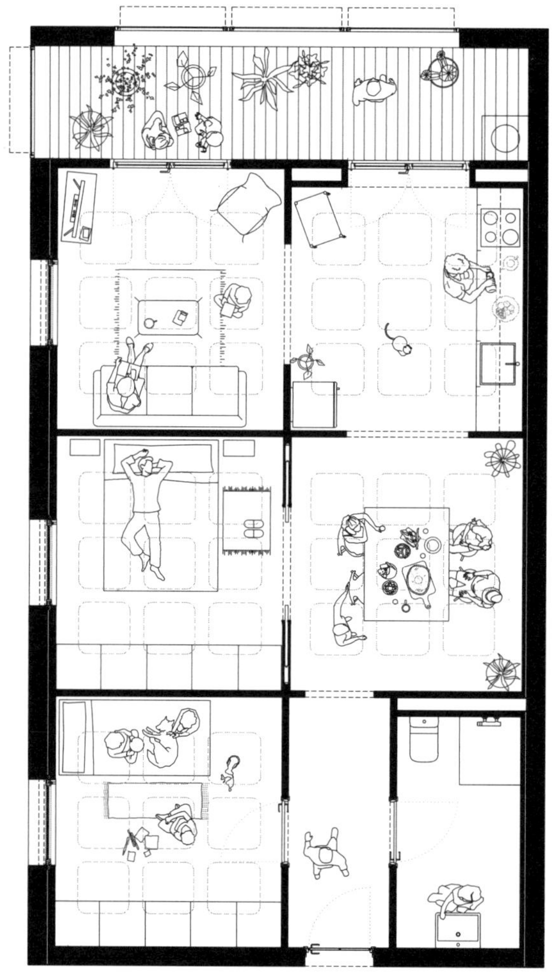

Housing unit type

0 1 2 3 4 5

Open-plan kitchen

Generic rooms

Interconnecting rooms

Intermediate climatic spaces

Intermediate social spaces

Housing unit type – Aggregation
The housing typology is based on a layout of cells of approximately 10 m^2 of useful surface, non-hierarchical spaces that can be used as a living room, dining room, bedroom or study, with multiple arrangements. The homes are made up of the aggregation of six or five and a half cells, and most have two bedrooms.

The project proposes a system of aggregation of apartments where each tower of GF+5 has its own communication shaft that organizes three apartments per floor. This minimizes the circulation spaces and lobbies both in the communal areas and inside the homes, and gives them all at least two façades facing different directions.

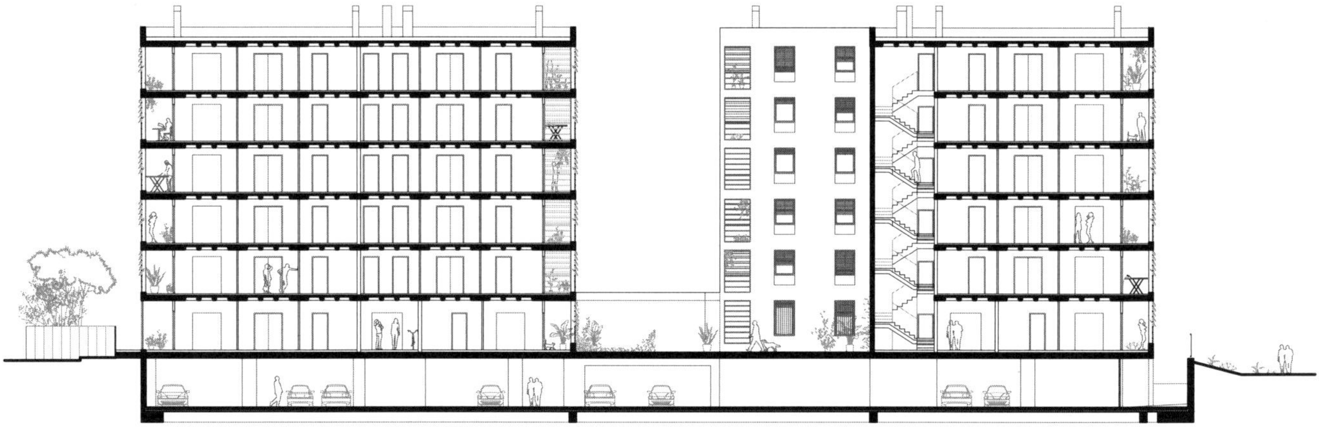

Longitudinal section

Urban context – Urban response
In response to its setting of unstructured volumes, the project proposes a building that is understood as one, with a continuous plinth, a single underground parking level and a ground floor that continues the street, Carrer Josep Pla. Then, on the first floor, it splits into two towers to avoid obstructing the views of the pre-existing building on the plot.

Materiality
The most determinant factor in the appearance of the two blocks is the structure of the building itself: concrete screens envelop all the volumes.
Inside the apartments, the structure also determines the condition of the spaces and each of the rooms. The concrete ribbed slabs are visible, and it is the ribs that mark the organization of the cells.

Energy strategy
- All the apartments have a glazed balcony that acts as a thermal buffer.
- All the apartments have cross ventilation and face two different directions.
- Inertia of the materials.

Energy certification: A.
- Non-renewable primary energy consumption: A (8 kWh/m^2 year).
- Carbon dioxide emissions: A (1 kg CO_2/m^2 year).

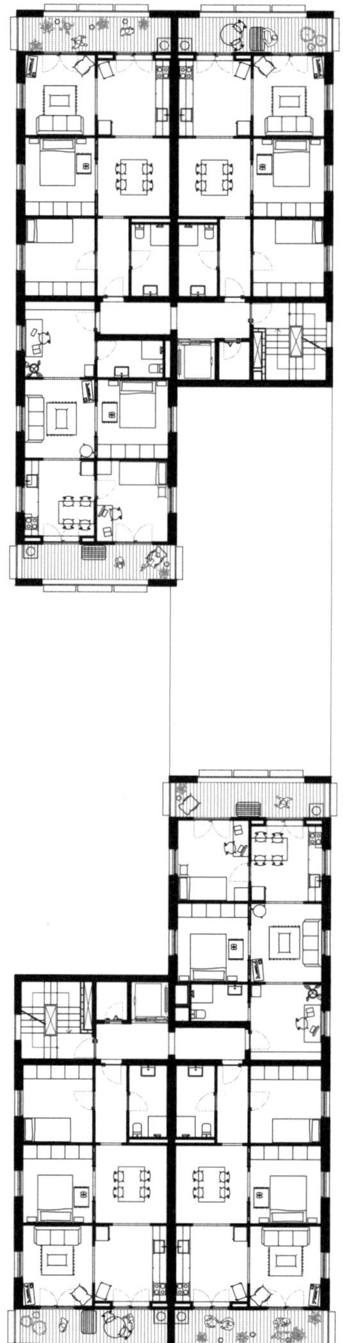

No. modules	6	5.5	4
Total surface area (m²)	60.00	54.42	40.00
Module/cell (m²)	10.00	10.00	10.00
Bioclimatic glazed balcony (m²)	9.60	9.60	9.60
No. homes	**24**	**10**	**2**

Typical floor plan

<u>Architects</u>: David Lorente, Josep Ricart, Xavier Ros, Roger Tudó.
<u>Team</u>: Montse Fornés, Anna Burgaya, Itziar González. <u>Works management</u>: Francesc de Haro Macià, Francesc Xavier Aumedes Farré, Gemma Rius Macies (Arrevolt). <u>Collaborators</u>: dsm arquitectes (structures), M7 Enginyers (installations), iA2 (acoustics).
<u>Location</u>: Carrer Josep Pla, 9-12. <u>Floor area</u>: 4,082 m^2.
<u>Construction budget</u>: €4,129,692.76

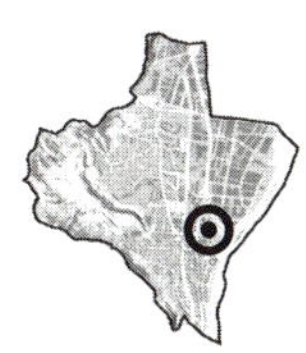

Site

Location

Montgat

39 homes

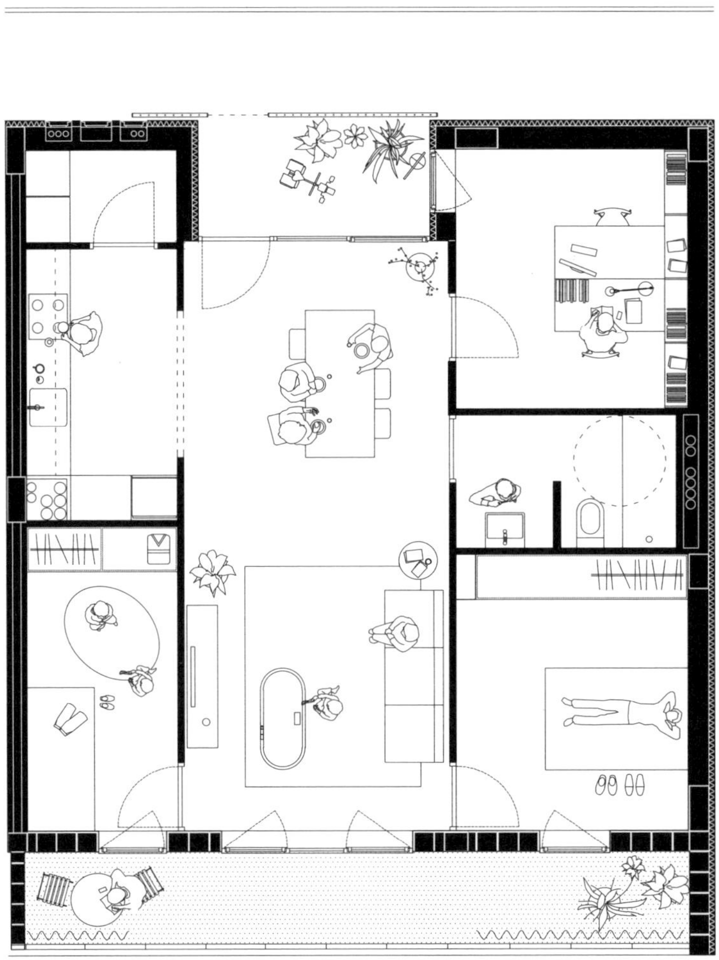

Housing unit type

|0 |1 |2 | | |5

Interconnecting rooms

Intermediate climatic spaces

Intermediate social spaces

Housing unit type – Aggregation

The project comprises a single type of housing that adapts to the different conditions of aggregation and geometry without losing its operational logic. Accordingly, the living-dining room, an abstract, rectangular through space, is laid out along the central axis of the home in contact with the entrance and the bioclimatic gallery via a large closable opening. To either side are the kitchen, bathroom and the bedrooms, which vary in number (two or three) and dimension depending on the depth of the volume.

Montgat

39 homes

The building is organized into two housing complexes with different entrances, one for each street. The volume in the upper street has 17 homes, laid out along a central corridor with six homes per landing, and a central stairway. In the street below, entrance to the apartments is via a stairway and lift shaft with sea views, positioned in the middle of a linear walkway that unites the two volumes, comprising GF+4, with five homes per landing and two on the ground floor.

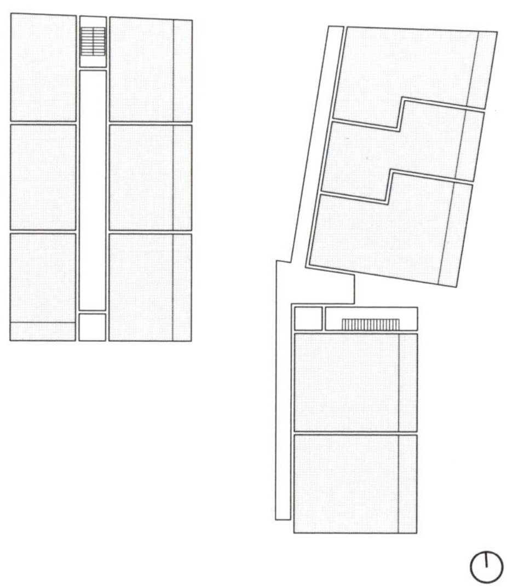

Aggregation diagram

Urban context – Urban response
The project takes advantage of the site's peri-urban condition and the steep 18-metre difference in level between the two streets to fragment the building, orienting and equipping the three volumes with heat-collecting façades, and introducing green space in the middle to improve views, sunlighting and cross ventilation.
To reduce earth movement on the site with its different rock strata, the project proposes an upper building with a 4.20 m overhang that minimizes the foundation; buildings on the lower part without basements, and surface parking and housing on the ground floor, in direct contact with the Parc de les Bateries.

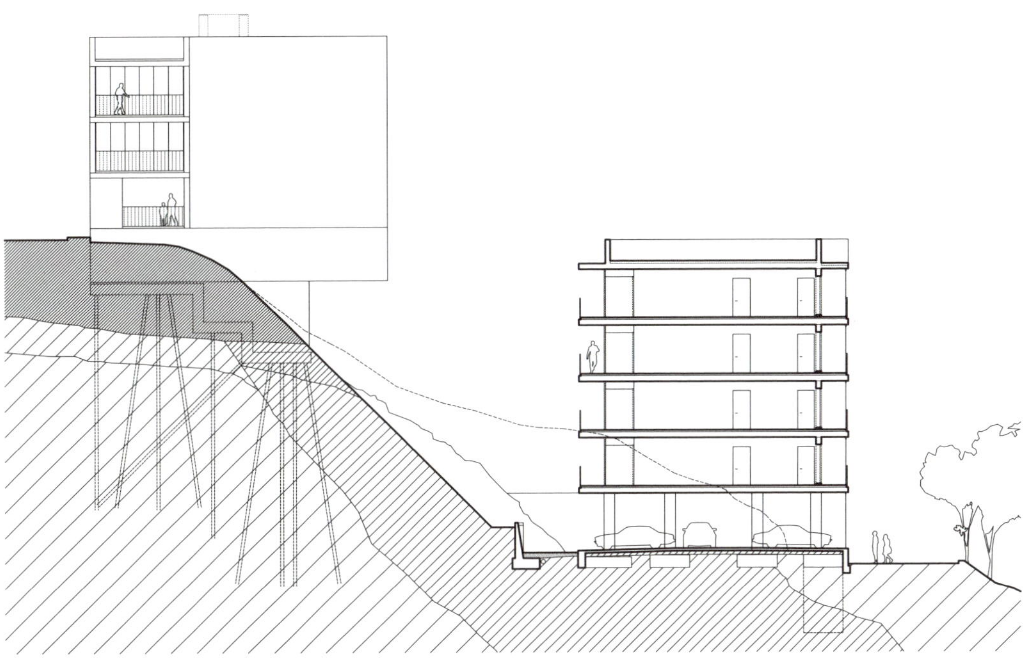

Cross section

Materiality
The concrete is left bare in all the structural elements, in its meetings with the ground, the pavements and the ceilings, taking advantage of the material's texture, durability, impermeability and inertia in each case. The concrete contrasts with the rocky ground and vegetation of the surroundings. The wooden joinery contrasts with the grey of the plastered façades. The project updates and modernizes the traditional Mediterranean enclosed balcony by giving it a sliding, fully retractable glazed system, with constant ventilation and no visible frames.

Energy strategy
The bioclimatic galleries have five main functions:
- Solar capture, which allows the temperature of the glazed balcony to be transmitted through the façade to the home.
- Micro-ventilation of the homes through the glazed balcony, reducing ventilation losses for health reasons.
- Reduction of thermal bridging.
- A thermal buffer that increases insulation of the homes and preserves indoor heat for longer.
- Simplified sun control by means of a basic curtain and the projection of the floor slab when everything is open.

Sun control using textiles.
Cross ventilation in all the homes.

Energy certification: A.
- Non-renewable primary energy consumption: A (23 kWh/m^2 year).
- Carbon dioxide emissions: A (4 kg CO_2/m^2 year).

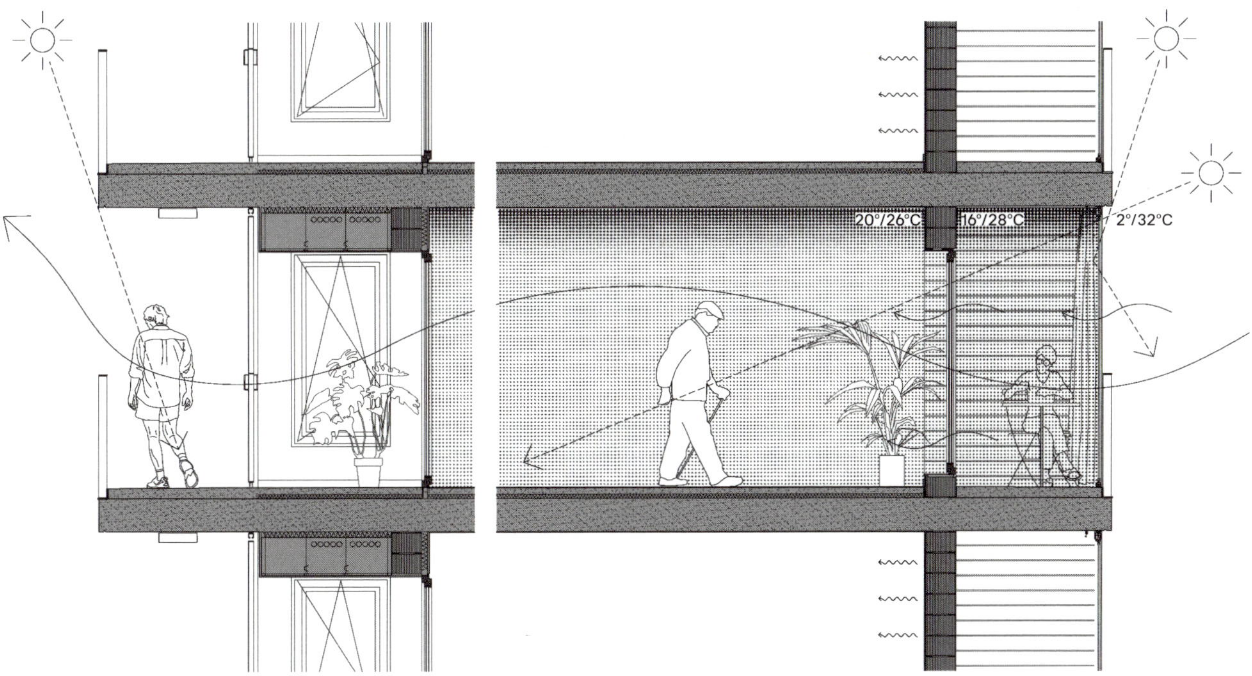

Climatic section

39 homes

Typical floor plan

No. rooms	3	2	1
Total surface area (m^2)	84.85	57.13	47.55
Living room-diner (m^2)	35.09	21.28	25.26*
Intermediate space (m^2)	4.60	4.60	4.60
Bioclimatic glazed balcony (m^2)	12.56	13.39	13.39
No. homes	**16**	**21**	**2**

* Kitchen-living-dining room

Architects: Claudi Aguiló, Albert Domingo, Xavier Vendrell. Team: Pau Cornellana, Ileana Manea, Andrea Rodríguez. Works management: Eulàlia Aran i Corbella. Collaborators: Manuel Arguijo y Asociados (structures), ELETRESJOTA (installations), Societat Orgànica (environmental consultancy).
Location: Carrer Sant Feliu, 17 and Camí de les Bateries, 24-26.
Floor area: 4,784.44 m^2. Construction budget: €3,944,031.54

Site

Location

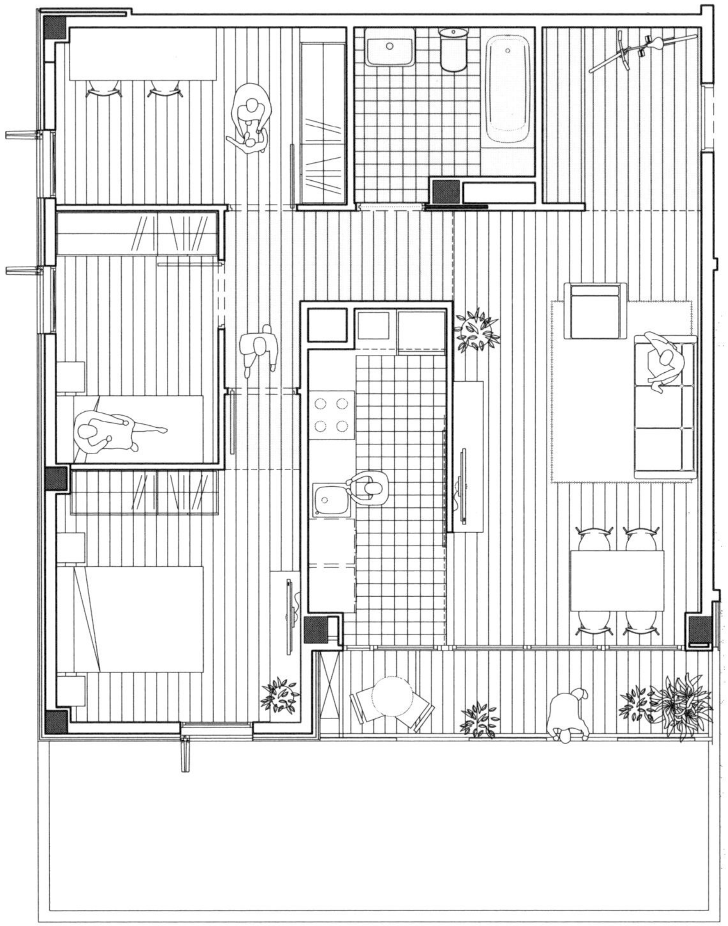

Housing unit type

Housing unit type – Aggregation
The proposed home combines the living room and dining room into one that gives directly onto the outdoor space. A terrace with unitized glazing that occupies the height and width of the room increases the inside-outside relationship and the feeling of spaciousness and brightness inside the homes. The server spaces are positioned against the party wall, thereby locating the rooms in the façade.
The 40 apartments, of which one has two bedrooms and the rest three, are arranged in eights in a length-wise block with a continuous façade onto the street. To minimize the effects of communal space on the homes, two communication shafts are created, each with four homes per landing. The shafts are located at the end of the block to ensure that the stairways receive natural light.

Urban context – Urban response
The brief occupies the entire 18-metre depth of the plot that allows the volume of GF+4 to fragment into two bodies in the façade that overlooks the green space. This creates greater development of the façade, and enables good orientation and cross ventilation of the homes without the need for lightwells.

Aggregation floor plan

Materiality
The façade, with its bare concrete plinth, is a ventilated cement-panel façade that incorporates into its modulation the balcony doors of the bedrooms, with folding aluminium blinds, and the long balconies of the rooms, with sliding aluminium blinds for sun control.
The façade combines different greys—the concrete, the cement panels, the anodized frames, the grey of the railings and finishing profiles (linings of jambs, edges of floor slabs and weather boarding of balcony doors) and the paint of the shutters—to create a uniform tone that coexists gently with the green of the park.

Energy strategy
- Good orientation of all the homes.
- Cross ventilation.
- Sun control systems.

Energy certification: B.
- Non-renewable primary energy consumption: B (43 kWh/m^2 year).
- Carbon dioxide emissions: B (7 kg CO_2/m^2 year).

Montgat

40 homes

Typical floor plan

0 2 5 10 20

No. rooms	3	2
Total surface area (m^2)	71.60	66.49
Living room-diner (m^2)	29.00	28.90
Terrace (m^2)	5.85	16.80
No. homes	**39**	**1**

Architect: Isabel Bennasar. Team: Corina Dindareanu, Nilton Paes. Works management: Xavier Badia (VINCLAMENT). Collaborators: Bernuz-Fernández Arquitectes (structures), MI ENGINYERIA (installations). Location: Ronda Països Catalans, 8 and Carrer Joanot Martorell, 1-5. Floor area: 6,241.19 m². Construction budget: €2,472,608.21

Site

Location

Sant Feliu de Llobregat 40 homes

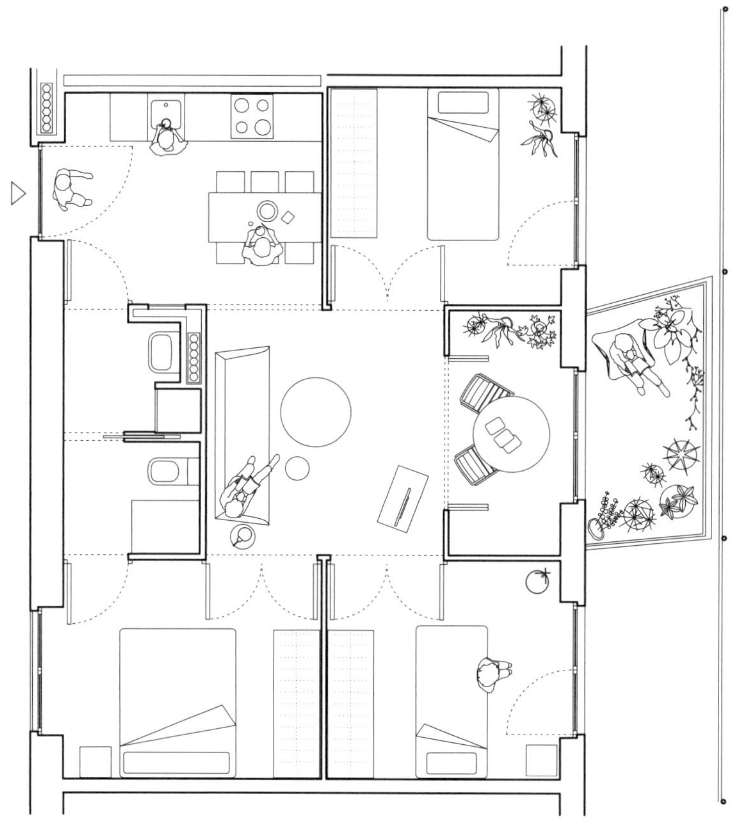

Housing unit type

Open-plan kitchen

Generic rooms

Interconnecting rooms

Intermediate climatic spaces

Intermediate social spaces

Housing unit type - Aggregation

The apartments are made up of generic spaces with no hierarchy. They are flexible, adaptable spaces of similar dimensions, shunning a housing layout in which spaces are predestined for a specific use or a single family model. Entrance to the homes is via the kitchen, which, like the rest of the spaces in the apartment, is laid out around a central area which opens onto a semi-exterior space that functions as a catchment area. The project expands the exterior surface area of the apartments to the maximum allowed, creating large outdoor spaces. The 40 homes (30 with three rooms and 10 with two) are grouped in fours around the two communication shafts arranged in the central lengthwise courtyard, making a total of eight homes per floor. The courtyard, together with the building's compact volume, maximizes the number of external rooms.

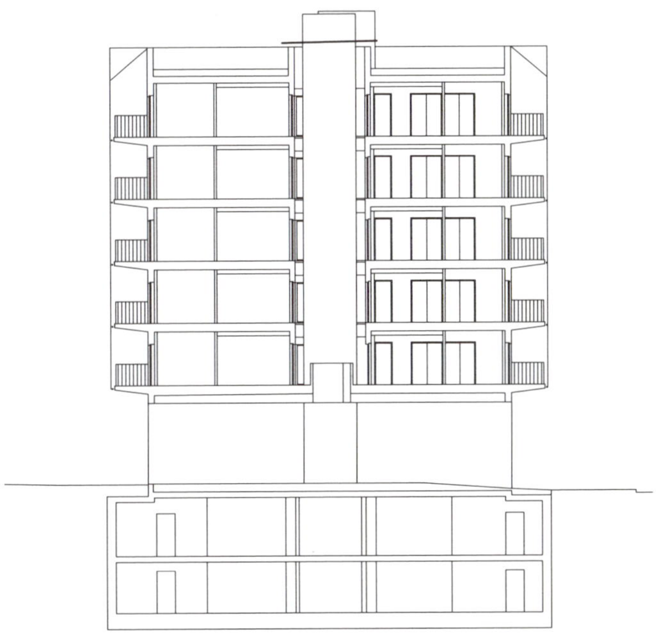

Cross section

|0 |2 |5 |10

Urban context – Urban response
The plot is bordered to the northeast by industrial buildings, to the northwest by a street, Carrer Anselm Clavé, and to the southeast and southwest by the green community areas of a neighbouring apartment building. The ground floor forms a passageway that connects the street and the park, providing connectivity and integration of the two urban areas, while dividing the space into two enclosed areas for commercial and public uses. Its shape, a five-floor, compact, orthogonal parallelepiped, follows the nature of its setting for optimum integration, and its finishes facilitate accessibility and maintenance.

Communal space
On the ground floor, in addition to two shops, is the entrance to the two communication shafts, spaces for communal installations and a large foyer. This foyer incorporates space to park bicycles and, potentially, space for the community, and generates a physical and visual connection with the green urban area beyond. The roof is accessible for community use.

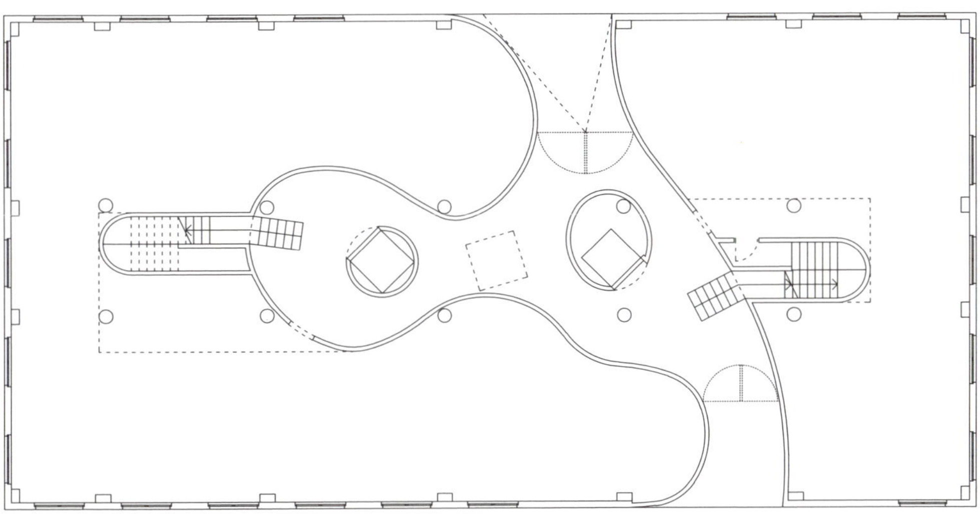

Ground floor plan

28

STOP

Materiality
The project prioritizes dry construction and industrialization with pre-assembly, such as lightweight structures and standardized openings. The façade incorporates a light structure that serves to house the solar protection system and the large balconies, while using the minimum necessary material by decreasing the section of the slab. The ETICS-type façade is installed overlapping part of the frames; in this way, thermal loss is further reduced and windows in the façade are maximized, etc.

Energy strategy
- All the homes are cross ventilated.
- The central court is covered but ventilated and serves to regulate the temperature.
- The large openings in the façade have textile curtains for sun control.

Energy certification: A.
- Non-renewable primary energy consumption: A (25 kWh/m² year).
- Carbon dioxide emissions: A (4 kg CO_2/m² year).

Sant Feliu de Llobregat

40 homes

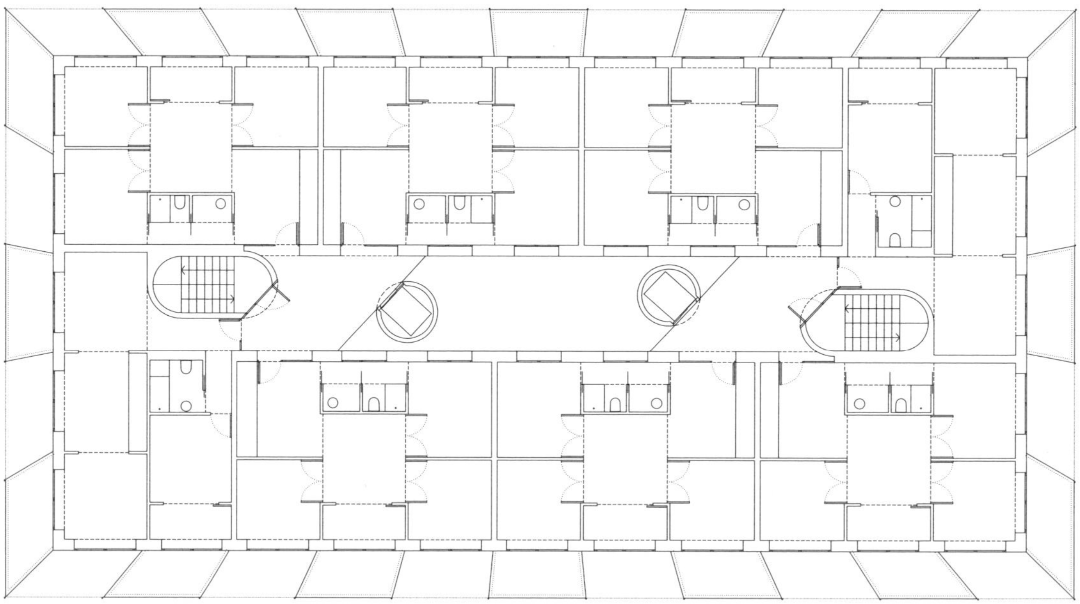

Typical floor plan

No. rooms	3	2
Total surface area (m^2)	63.39	63.40
Central space (m^2) *	10.92	10.92
Semi-exterior space (m^2) *	4.82	4.82
Balcony (average) (m^2)	12.17	15.15
No. homes	**30**	**10**

* Unit type

Architects: Anna Puigjaner, Maria Charneco, Guillermo Lopez, Alfredo Lérida. Team: Martí Amargós, Julio Sánchez. Works management: DALMAU-MORROS TÈCNICS. Collaborators: MASALA (structures), Font i Armengol (installations), AIGUASOL (energy consultancy). Location: Carrer Anselm Clavé, 21-27. Floor area: 5,366.03 m². Construction budget: €3,686,720.18

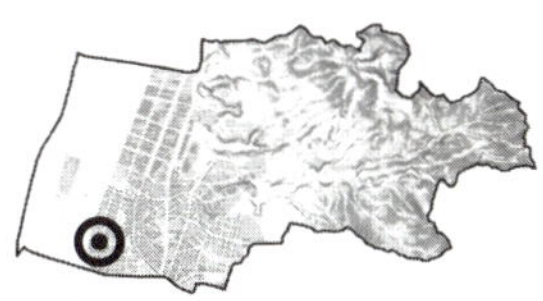

Site

Location

Perceiving and dwelling: the home as experience in the digital era

Technology has changed our lives radically; however, its impact on our way of living is not always that obvious. The home as experience is more than a place for events and activities; it is an intangible continuum in which the body and its movements, through the senses, interact and intertwine with objects and the environment that surrounds us. The philosopher Merleau-Ponty, in *Phenomenology of Perception,* writes that we do not perceive the world from a distance, but rather that we are immersed in it, concluding that perception is an act of inhabiting the world, not just observing it from the outside. If technology is capable of affecting our perception, then it influences the way we live. The gaze moves from the object—the home—to the subject—the inhabitant—to explore how technology has influenced our behaviour, modifying our relationship with space, the way we share it, and our conception of intimacy.

With technological advances, especially in the digital sphere, our interaction with the physical world and our bodily experience are transformed. This affectation becomes more complex when, over and above technological devices, we contemplate the new environments that technology offers us. From *augmented reality*, which adds layers of digital information—visual, auditory and even tactile—to the real environment, to *virtual reality*, which generates a completely virtual space that replaces the physical environment. Between these extremes emerges an intermediate alternative, *mixed reality*, which encourages immersion in scenarios where real and virtual elements interact in real time and in three dimensions, becoming integrated into the physical environment, superimposing a layer of digital information that reconfigures the immediate space. For example, RoomAlive is a mixed-reality technology in which, by means of projectors, using motion sensors to map the environment, images and interactive elements are projected onto real surfaces. This technology makes for an immersive experience in which the real body interacts naturally and directly, with no need for individual portable devices or wearables specific to each user. RoomAlive merges the physical and the digital worlds, transforming any room into a shared interactive experience.

The result of these new environments will probably be another form of appropriation of space, no longer limited exclusively to the objects that surround us and that acquire a symbolic value in the process of dwelling. The house will not only be occupied by real objects, it will also behave as a setting that offers and accumulates experiences. These new immersive environments can transform our experiences, freeing them from physical limitations and things that alter our perception of space and the body.

Constant connection and interaction through screens can change the way we experience physical presence and human interaction. It is cause for concern that we are witnessing a growing splitting of our self, between *real self* and *virtual self*, proportional to the time spent in social networks and the way we present ourselves on them. Our physical room is no longer the place where we keep things we do not want to share with anyone; technological devices have for the most part monopolized that space of intimacy. The intimacy of the person, previously associated with the solid privacy of their room, now seems more liquid when it is limited to the vicinity of the body, within that area of *personal distance* encompassed by our arms, whether to access our personal computer or to hold our mobile phone in our hands. We only have to remember

Marta Peris is an architect and lecturer (ETSAB). She gained her PhD in 2016 with the thesis *The Japanese House in the Cinema of Yasujiro Ozu*, published in 2019 with the title *La casa de Ozu*. She is co-founder of PERIS+TORAL ARQUITECTES, a studio that won the CSCAE Spanish Architecture Award in 2022 and was a finalist in the EUmies Award 2022, among others. Her projects and articles have been widely published in national and international journals and media.

the feeling of intrusion when someone looks at our computer or mobile screen while we are connected.

At the same time, we are beginning to have more perspective on the consequences of social exposure on the Internet, leading to greater awareness of the need to preserve privacy. Intimacy is a concept that began to develop in the age of the Enlightenment, characterized by emphasis on individual reason and a new appreciation of private and personal life, and it progressively evolved with society, directly influencing the home. From the large shared public room of the Middle Ages to the Renaissance model of rooms interconnected in an *enfilade*, to the consolidation of the corridor and the individual room in the nineteenth century, in the modern world the home is the result of the conquest of privacy.

According to Robin Evans, the development of the corridor was a significant change in architectural design as it allowed more efficient circulation. With the introduction of corridors, rooms could be arranged so that they were accessed independently from a common hallway. Paradoxically, by facilitating necessary communication, it decreased chance communication, reducing contact between occupants (Evans, 2005: 95).

If intimacy moves from physical to virtual space, even if we retain some link with the *room of one's own,* perhaps it will cease to be the place of independence and individuality. Faced with the challenge of technological dependence, instead of closed, self-contained rooms, which in themselves encourage isolation, the historical process could be reversed and return to a layout of communicating rooms that encourage interdependence and social interaction. Or even, taking this argument to the extreme, perhaps we could return to one large room as the physical setting of the virtual universe, in the event that the metaverse triumphs, the act of dwelling intensifying in the same neutral space, sparsely furnished and with few belongings.

When rooms are interconnected and the house becomes porous to the gaze, the perception of space changes significantly, and the traditional room is deconstructed. Self-contained, clearly defined, separate rooms give way to places or zones within a larger, more fluid space, where the traditional boundaries between rooms are blurred, creating a feeling of spaciousness and continuity.

This continuity allows different routes, so that the house multiplies in the mind of the inhabitant. Because each different route establishes new relationships with the body that moves, with the objects with which it interacts, and the interior and exterior views that it combines. Juhani Pallasmaa (2007: 14) says that we necessarily inhabit two houses: the physical, material home and the interior home of the mind. The porous house therefore encourages more nomadic behaviour in the inhabitant: from tracing out fluid routes that inflame the senses and imagination, to finding corners for introspection, concave areas into which we lean to preserve personal distance and our virtual intimacy. These small technological windows are, then, reversible, and allow us to look out and expose us to the Internet. In terms of social exposure, the home becomes both a refuge and a stage, since technology has made the public/private dichotomy reversible at a click.

Designating specific areas for entertainment, work and rest creates a psychological separation between different activities, without the limits of walls or doors, that can coexist in the same room. This helps to avoid multitasking and the sensory overload associated with the constant use of technology, as well as greater awareness of the time dedicated to leisure and technology.

The significance of objects in our memory processes is the main reason why we like to surround ourselves with familiar or peculiar objects, regardless of their utilitarian function. Consciously linking certain objects to these specific areas can activate healthy habits by acting as signs of commitment that regulate a good use of technology. Habits are actions that the brain automates without the person needing to actively think about them. This is part of the brain's efficiency in managing routine tasks. For example, leaving bottles of water around the house encourages us to hydrate more often. Likewise, the simple action of putting a clock in a specific place can remind us of the importance of limiting screen time. Objects can therefore act as signals that condition our behaviour almost unconsciously.

Maximizing the size of the room is essential in this ambivalent way of dwelling, which promotes both the appropriation of personal places and fluid movement around the home. Increasing the size of rooms extends their porosity. As well as connecting, when they open, large-format doors add rooms, expand space, and combine interior and exterior views. Then, when they close one after the other, the space retracts, like a telescopic device, to preserve the privacy of the room.

Since the standards for the surface area of social housing are unlikely to change significantly, to maximize space in the flexible, non-hierarchical home that our times call for, it may be necessary to give up some of the traditional rooms. It seems unlikely that the kitchen, rooted in our evolutionary memory and linked to fire and the hearth, will disappear from the home. However, it may be transformed into the familiar kitchen-dining room, a perfect place for sociability, or reduced to a kitchenette, depending on needs and ways of dwelling. However, technology has diversified options of access to digital platforms and individualized consumption of information. This means that the living room, traditionally a meeting place around the fireplace of yesteryear or the television, is increasingly regarded as anachronistic, losing its original function. It would not be unreasonable, then, to consider the eventual disappearance of the living room, redistributing its surface area to other rooms in the house. The question is, then, what is the right surface area of the room in a gender-free, non-hierarchical, undifferentiated, hyperconnected and porous house?

I close with two citations from Robin Evans that seem to me to be more pertinent than ever:

"Certainly it would be foolish to suggest that there is anything in a plan which could compel people to behave in a specific way towards one another [...]. It would be still more foolish, however, to suggest that a plan could not prevent people from behaving in a particular way, or at least hinder them from doing so." (Evans, 1997: 89).

" [...] there is surely another kind of architecture that would seek to give full play to the things that have been so carefully masked by its antitype; an architecture arising out of the deep fascination that draws people towards others, an architecture that recognises passion, carnality and sociability. The matrix of connected rooms might well be an integral feature of such buildings." (Evans, 1997: 90).

Bibliographic references

EVANS, Robin. "Figures, Doors and Passages." *Translations from Drawing to Building and Other Essays*, 1997.

PALLASMAA, Juhani; BLAS, Javier; FERNÁNDEZ APARICIO, Carmen. "Alojar el alma." *Espacios para habitar. Fondos de la Colección permanente*. Museo Nacional Centro de Arte Reina Sofía, 2007, p. 14.

El Masnou

40 homes

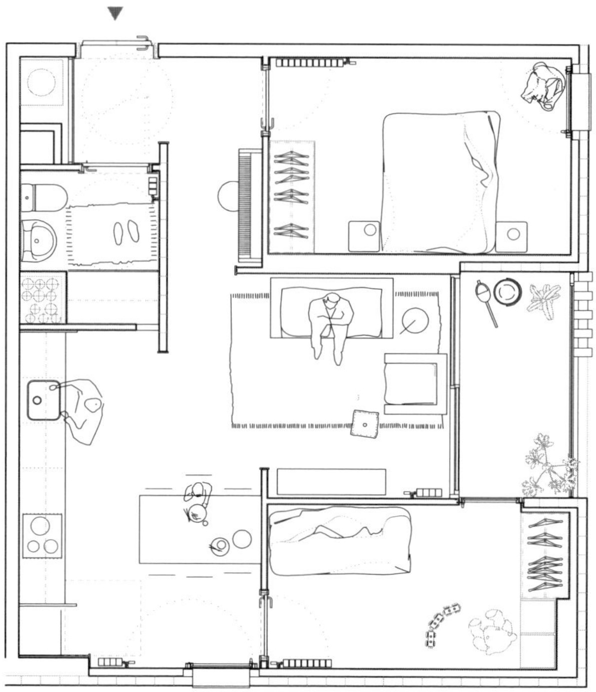

Housing unit type

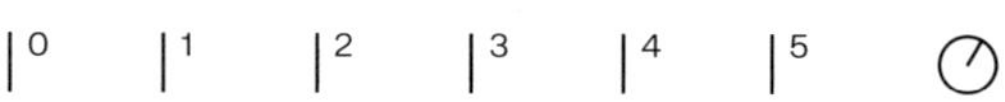

Open-plan kitchen

Interconnecting rooms

Intermediate climatic spaces

Intermediate social spaces

Housing unit type – Aggregation

The typological proposal is based on the strategy of grouping the bathroom, kitchen and installation ducts beside the party wall, freeing up the rest of the floor plan. The kitchen, dining room and living room form a single space that overlooks the intermediate space, an enclosed outdoor area that is large enough to be inhabited. The rooms, all the same size, are located against the outer façade of the apartment and, according to their layout in the floor plan, offer three different ways of living.

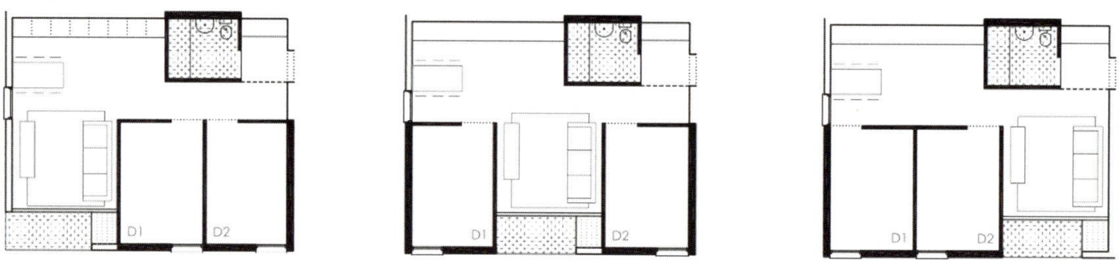

Typologies

The complex with its 40 homes is made up of three aggregation units of three and four apartments per landing, optimizing the communication shafts and circulations. Although the building is divided into two parts—a long block with two nucleuses and another, more compact block with one—they are connected by a plinth.

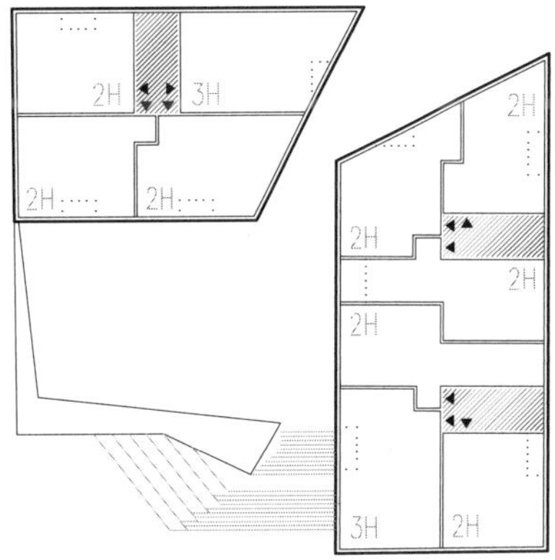

Aggregation diagram

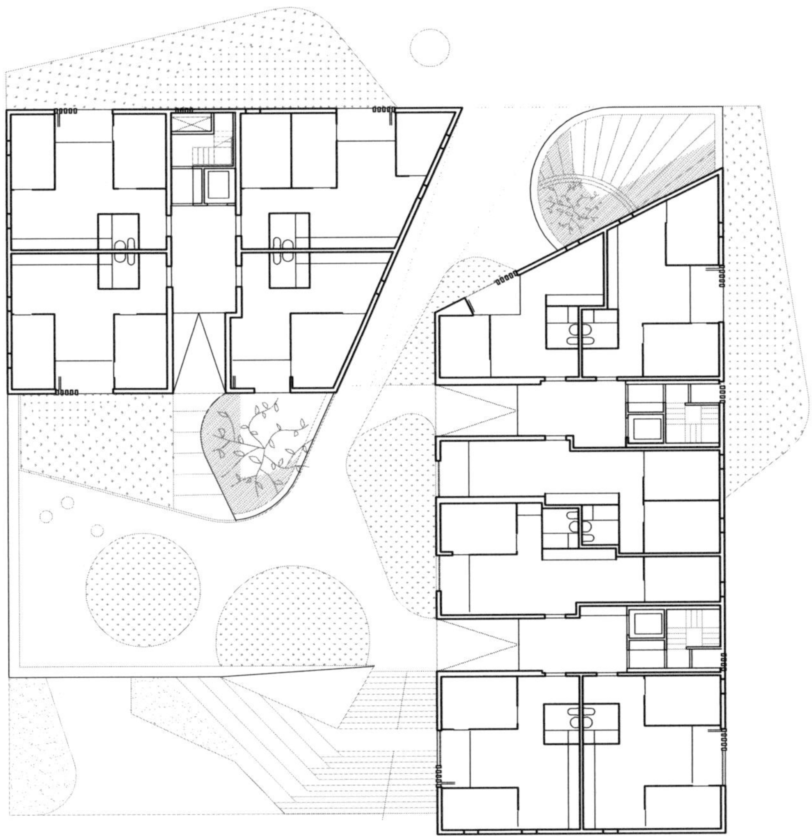

Ground floor plan

Urban context – Urban response
The volume incorporates and extends the street layout of Carrer de Ciutat Reial, emptying the northern corner of the building to connect the new square with its surroundings. A gently sloping ramp separates the entrance from the level of the adjacent streets; in this way, entry to the lobbies is not directly from the street, but from the observation deck above the plinth that houses the installations and the commercial premises, connected by a stairway with Plaça U d'Octubre.

The void in the volume not only picks up the traces of the site, it also improves the orientation of the least favourable façades to receive more sunlighting. From certain points of view, the building is perceived as two parts, reducing the scale of the intervention in a setting where the small grain of single-family housing prevails. However, the proximity between the buildings and the plinth produces a unitary intervention.

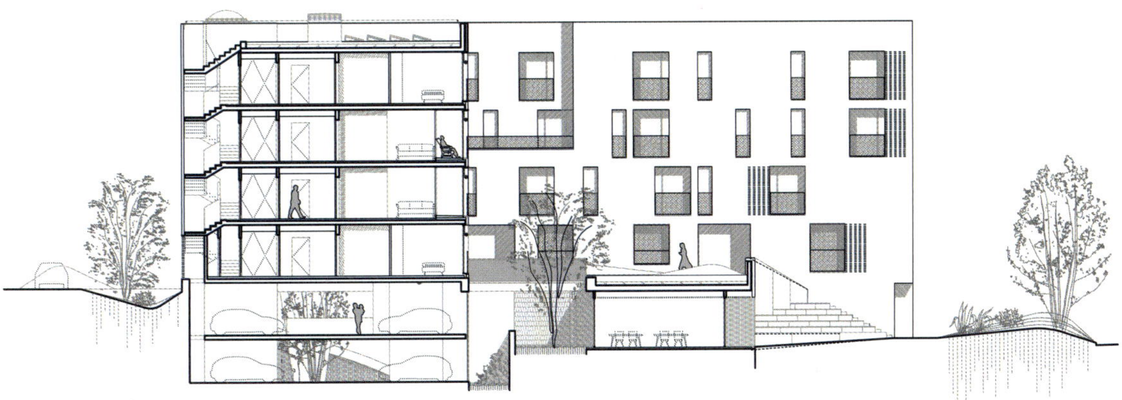

Cross section

0 2 5 10 20

Energy strategy

- All the homes have dual orientation and cross ventilation through the living room.
- The terraces incorporate a double closure that functions as a heat buffer and collector gallery in the winter and allows cross ventilation in the summer.

Energy certification: A.

- Non-renewable primary energy consumption: A (26 kWh/m^2 year).
- Carbon dioxide emissions: A (4 kg CO_2/m^2 year).

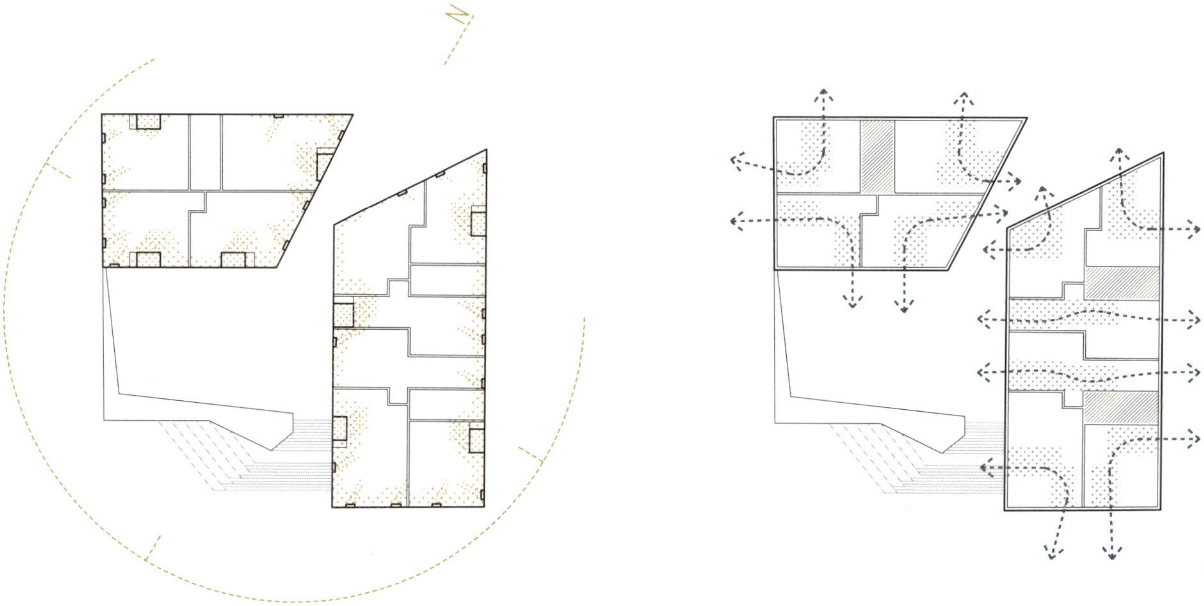

Heat capture and buffering / Cross ventilation

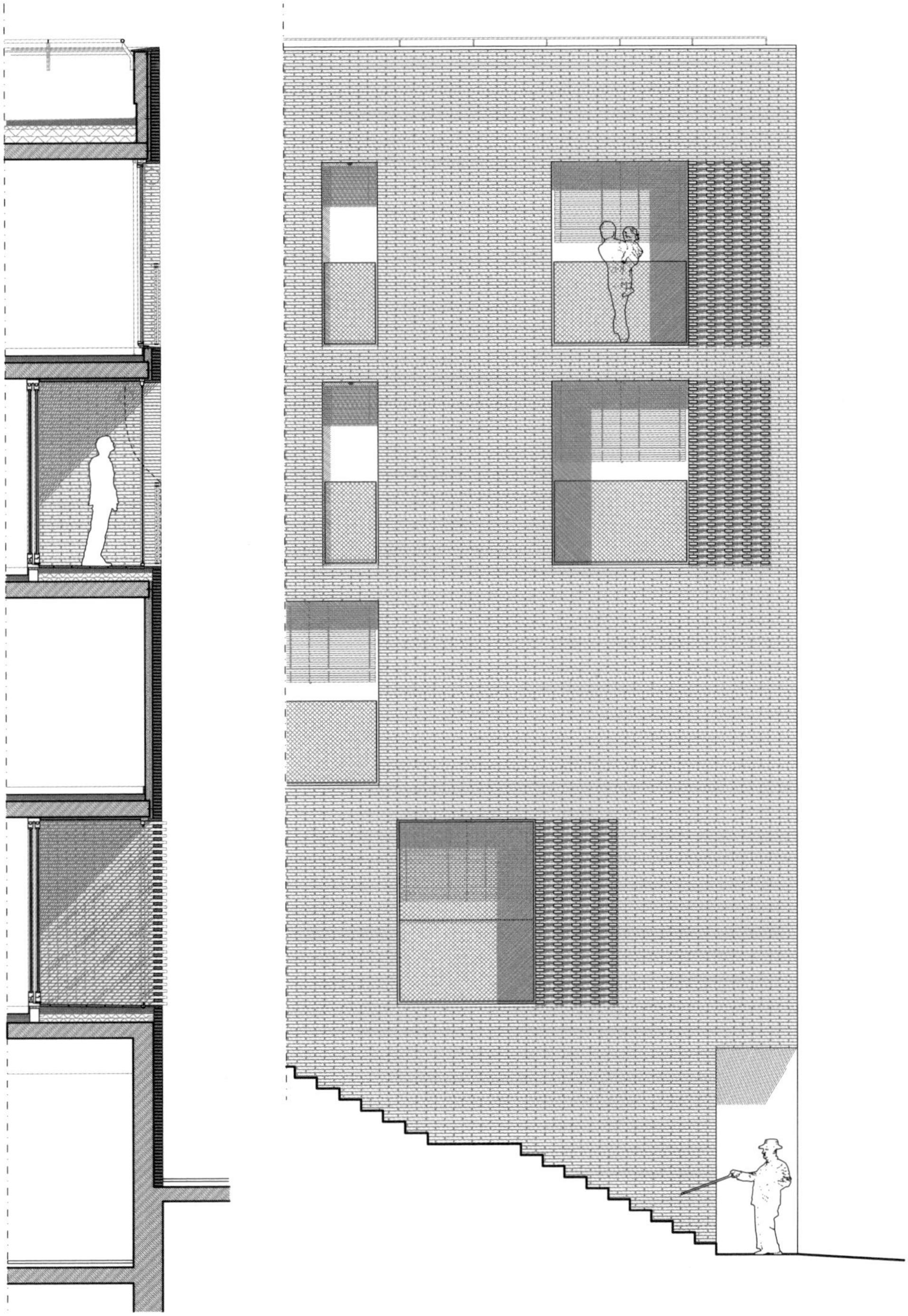

Façade detail

40 homes

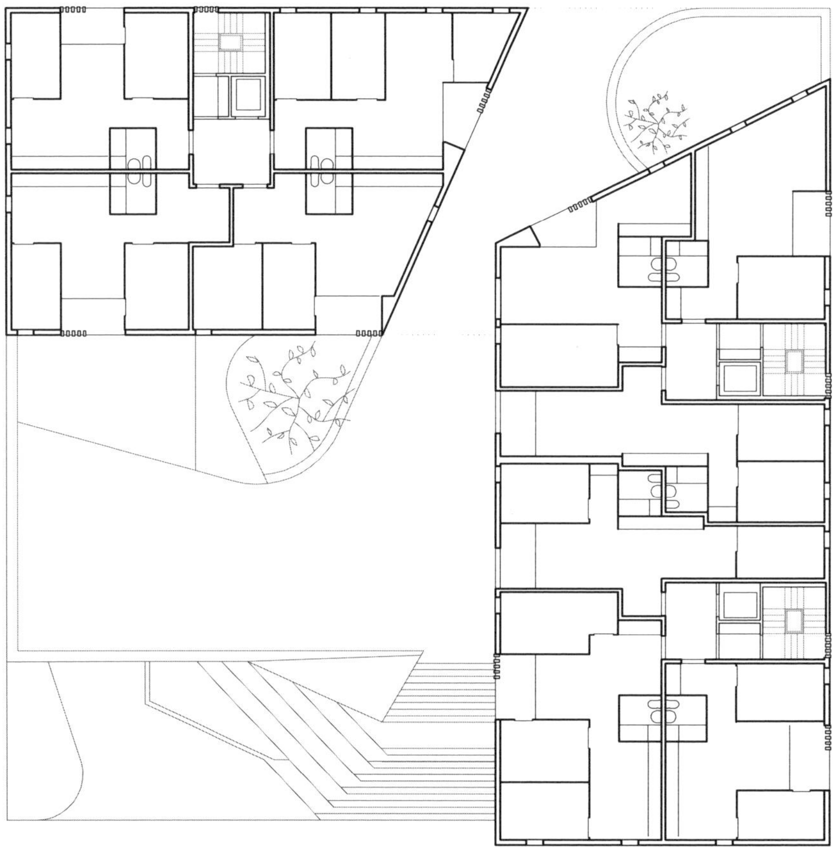

Typical floor plan

No. rooms	3	2	1
Total surface area (m²)	68.16	55.35	44.61
Kitchen-living-dining room (m²)	23.75	42.61	24.30
Bioclimatic glazed balcony (m²)	3.92	4.45	5.33
No. homes	**5**	**31**	**4**

Architects: Marta Peris, José Manuel Toral. Team: Ana Espinosa, Izaskun González, Guillem Pascual, Maria Megías, Cristina Porta, Miguel Bernat, Rita Martins Alves. Works management: Joan March i Raurell. Collaborators: Bernuz-Fernández Arquitectes (structures), ELETRESJOTA (installations), Societat Orgànica (environmental consultancy). Location: Plaça U d'Octubre. Floor area: 4,923.86 m^2. Construction budget: €4,433,539.29

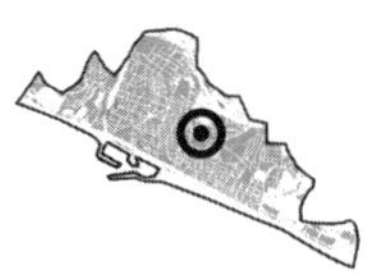

Site

Location

Sant Boi de Llobregat

42 homes

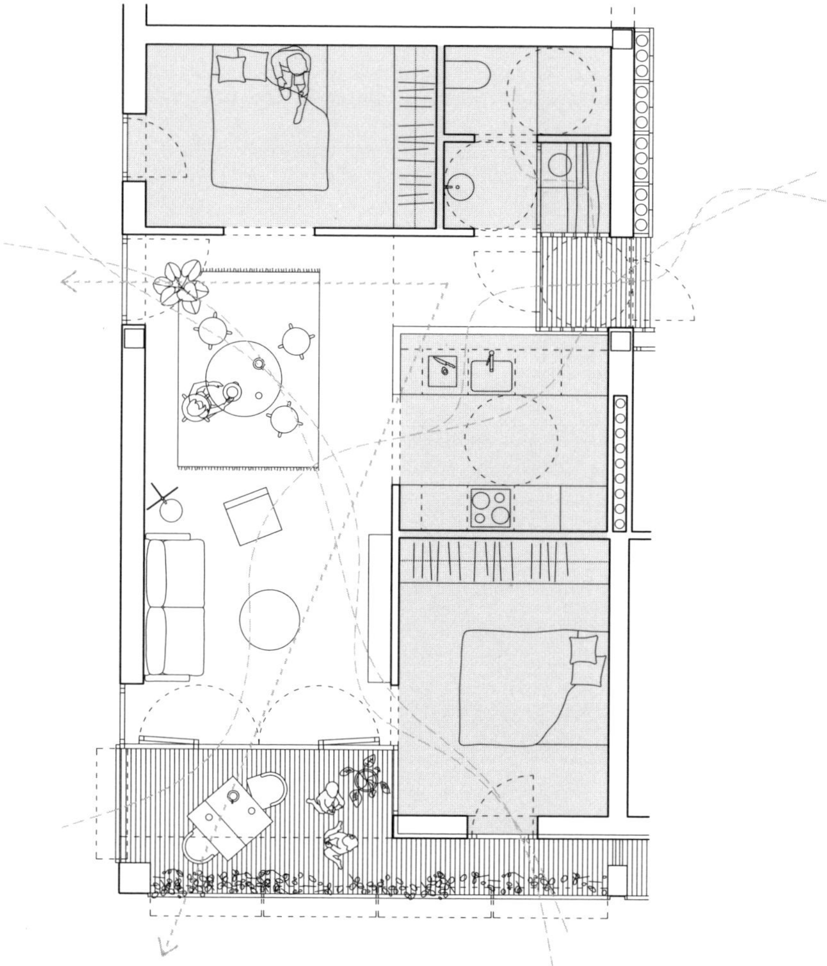

Housing unit type

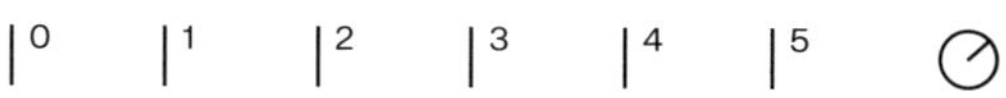

Generic rooms

Interconnecting rooms

Intermediate climatic spaces

Intermediate social spaces

Housing unit type - Aggregation
The dining room is the central part of the home and organizes the rooms, which are turned to the exterior. The living room opens onto a glazed balcony with adjustable shutters. The kitchen is open plan, with the possibility of separating it from the communal space. The project proposes a flexible configuration system that organizes the 42 homes around the central atrium using a system of concentric rings that organize the servant wet strip in relation to the served dry strip.

Communal spaces
The central atrium defines a garden on the ground floor and, on the other floors, organizes the entrance walkways, offering quiet, airy and sunny areas and spaces for neighbourly relations, which also guarantee natural lighting and ventilation in all the homes. The entrance to the building makes its way through a sequence of open thresholds and porches that define spaces for social contact.

Energy strategy
- The building's morphology is designed to maximize energy gains in winter and heat dissipation in summer.
- The central atrium functions as a thermal chimney.
- The apartments have cross ventilation.
- The glazed balconies, which function as thermal buffers, have adjustable solar protection to reduce solar radiation in the interiors.

Energy certification: A.
- Non-renewable primary energy consumption: A (24 kWh/m^2 year).
- Carbon dioxide emissions: A (4 kg CO_2/m^2 year).

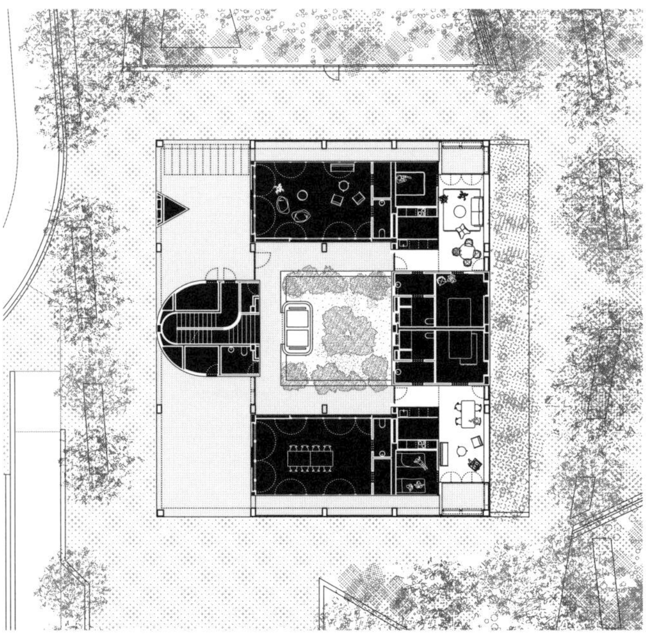

Ground floor plan

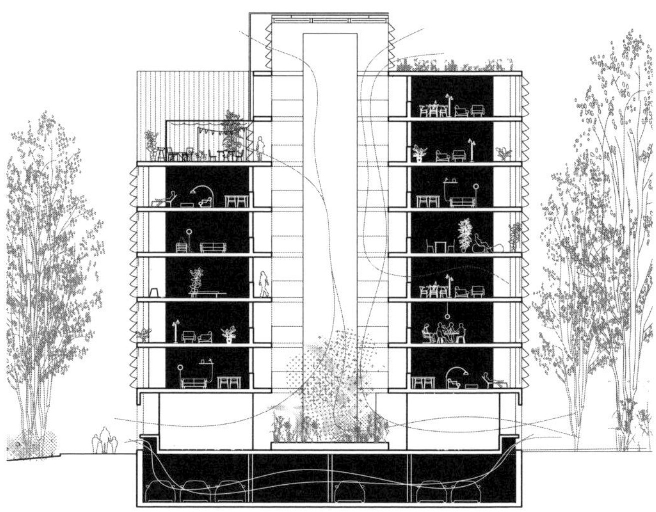

Section

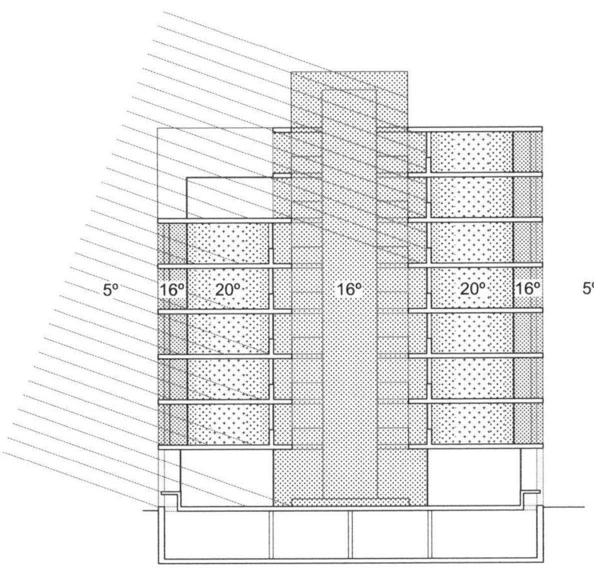

Winter

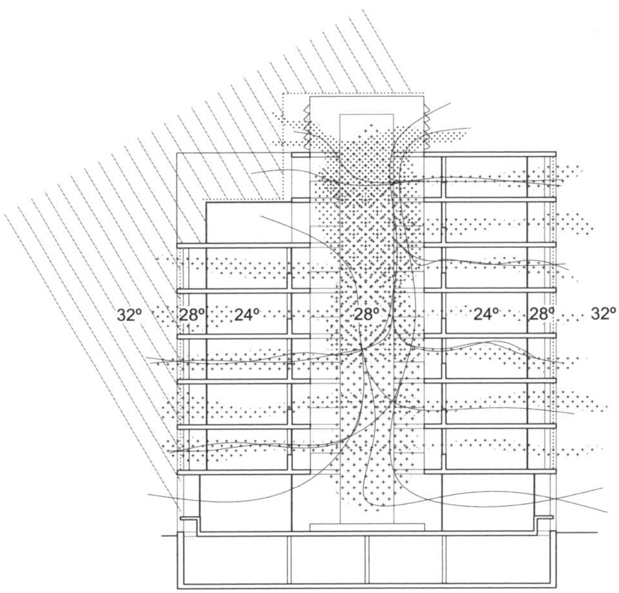

Summer

0 2 5 10 20

Sant Boi de Llobregat

42 homes

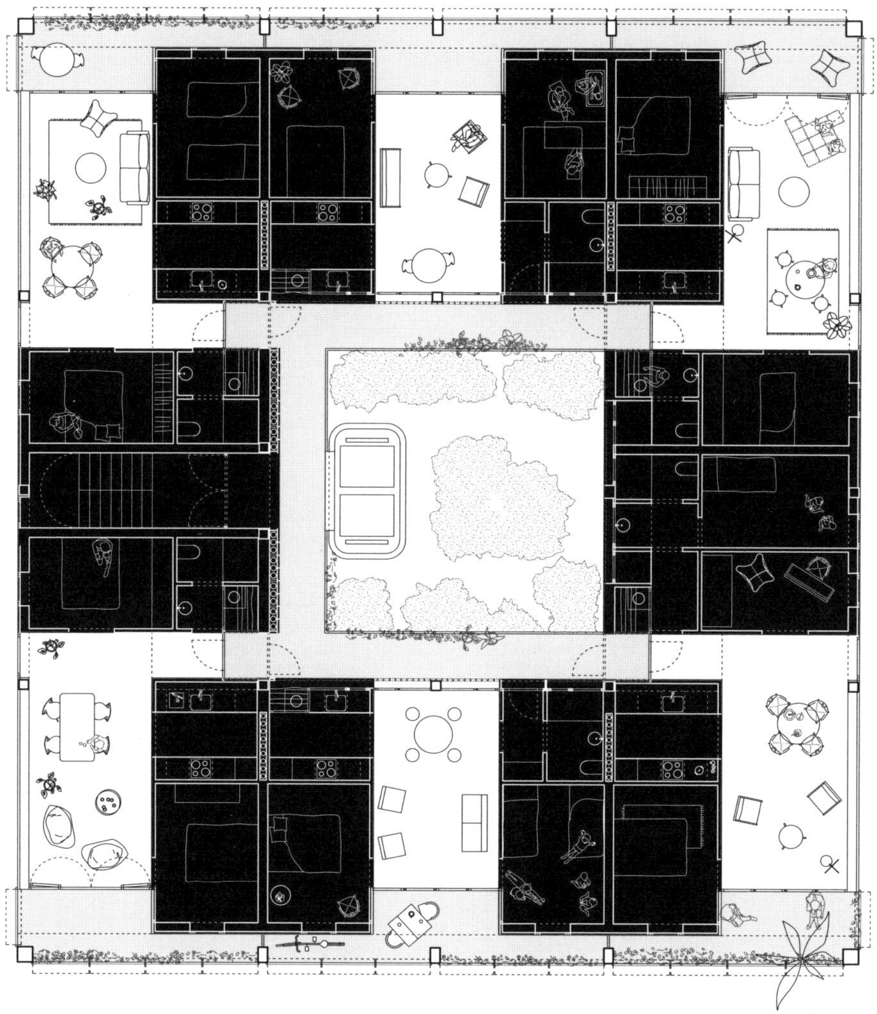

Typical floor plan

0 1 2 5 10

No. rooms	3	2	2
Total surface area (m²)	72.45	56.92	58.31
Living room-diner (m²)	31.05	25.25	27.07
Boclimatic glazed balcony (m²)	8.02	10.55	8.04
No. homes	**7**	**12**	**23**

Architects: Aixa del Rey, Tomeu Ramis. Team: Luis Tresaco, Itziar Cabo, Alberto Espinosa, Arnau Reventós, Maria López. Works management: Brufau Cusó estudi d'arquitectura. Collaborators: otherstructures (structures), Societat Orgànica (environmental consultancy), ELETRESJOTA (installations), Ivanna Rossell (acoustics), SomEnginy (BIM), Anfibio (3D). Location: Carrer Isaac Albéniz, 95. Floor area: 4,600 m^2. Construction budget: €4,285,713.79

Site

Location

Molins de Rei

44 homes

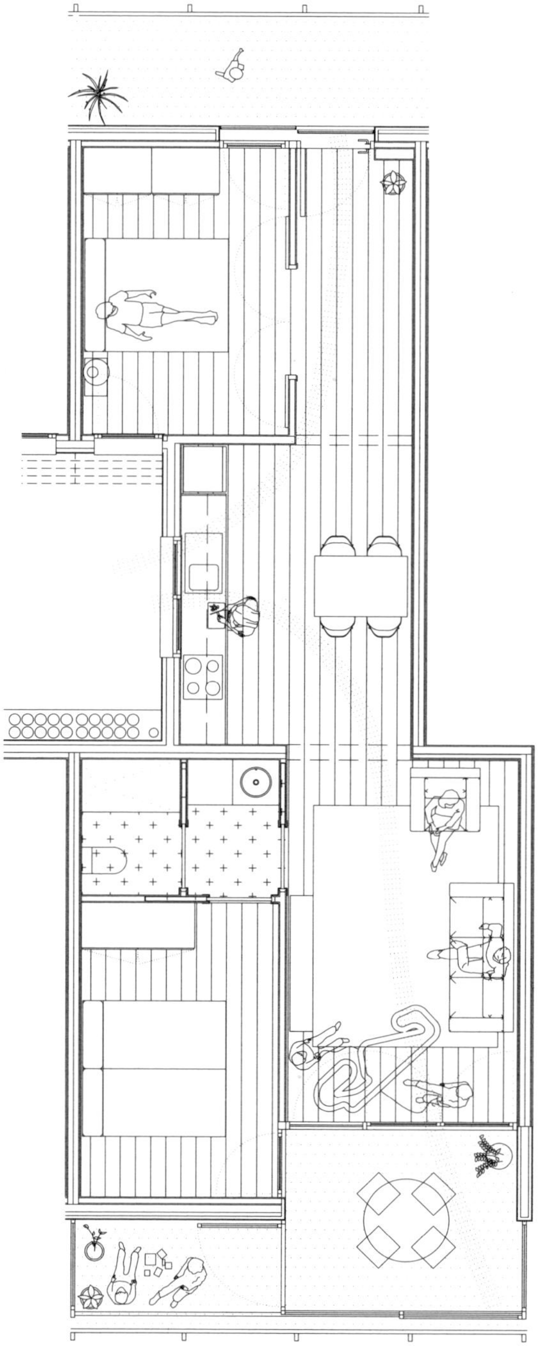

Housing unit type

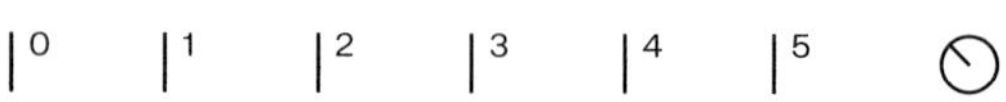

Carlos Valls Arquitectura —
AAAR Arquitectes

2021—under construction

Open-plan kitchen

Generic rooms

Intermediate climatic spaces

Intermediate social spaces

Housing unit type – Aggregation
The project proposes homes that are fluid; the concatenation of spaces emerges naturally from the desire to perceive the light from the south via the terrace, from the north-facing entrance. In the centre, illuminated by the inner court, is the living centre of the home: the kitchen-dining room. The flows are simple and functional, and all the spaces have long lines of sight, creating a sense of spaciousness. All the apartments are inclusive and the rooms have the same dimensions, with no spatial hierarchy. Of the 44 apartments, 33 have two bedrooms and 11 have three.
A neutral block with a single communication nucleus and distribution along a walkway in the northeast façade, on the street side, addresses the aggregation of nine homes per floor on the four upper floors and eight on the ground floor.

Urban context – Urban response
Since the proposed built mass is sufficiently forceful, the building is intended to be very neutral. This formalization helps to structure the street and add to the city. This is why the façades on the street and in the interior of the street block are conceived visually with the necessary opening-up to be able to lighten the mass of wall in the façades: the communicating walkways are on the street side and there are large terraces on the inside.

Communal spaces
At the only entrance to the ground floor, a 40 m^2 communal space offers views of the community garden at the centre of the street block. The communal activities that take place in this space will be decided by community participation.

Energy strategy
- 100% of the homes are cross ventilated and give onto the inner court.
- The courts act as thermal chimneys.
- The form factor is modelled to offer the greatest permeability.
- The façade is protected thanks to the dimensions of the eaves and terraces, and Barcelona rope blinds.
- 82% of the homes receive direct sunlight in the living room between 10 a.m. and 2 p.m.
- A gallery is incorporated into the south-facing terraces in order to create a buffer.

Energy certification: A.
- Non-renewable primary energy consumption: A (9 kWh/m^2 year).
- Carbon dioxide emissions: A (1 kg CO_2/m^2 year).

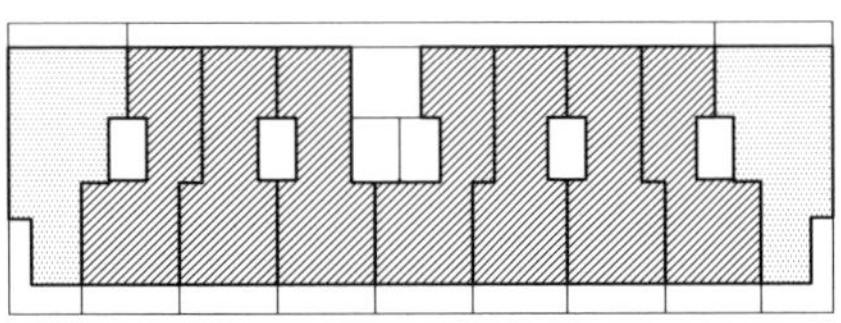

Typical floor plan

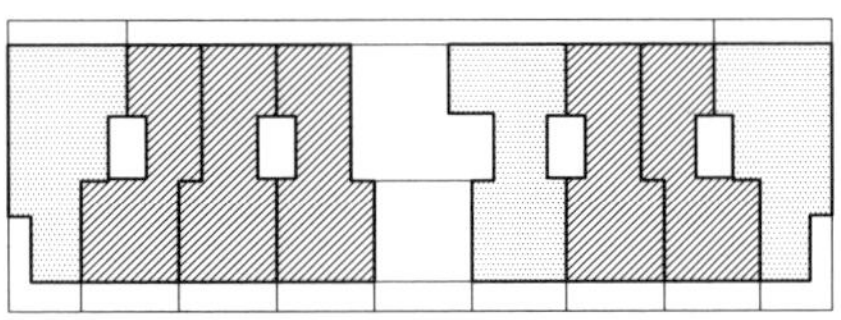

Ground floor plan

Diagrams of typological aggregation

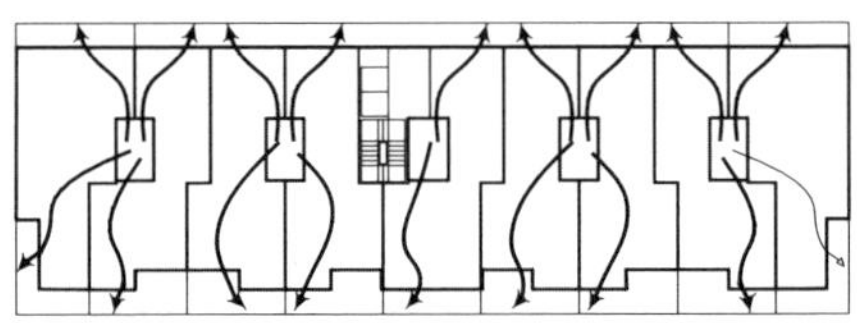

Summer

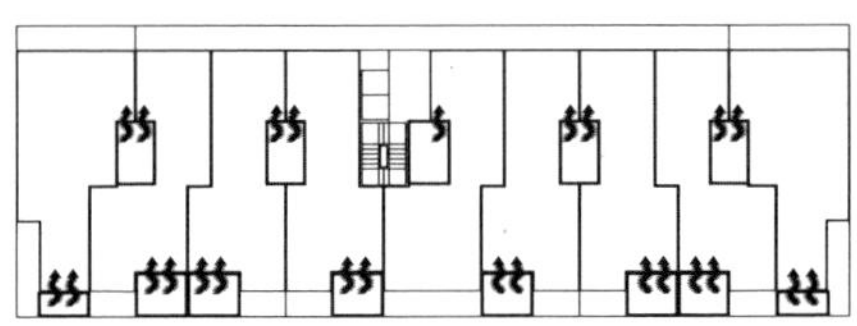

Winter

Passive energy efficiency systems

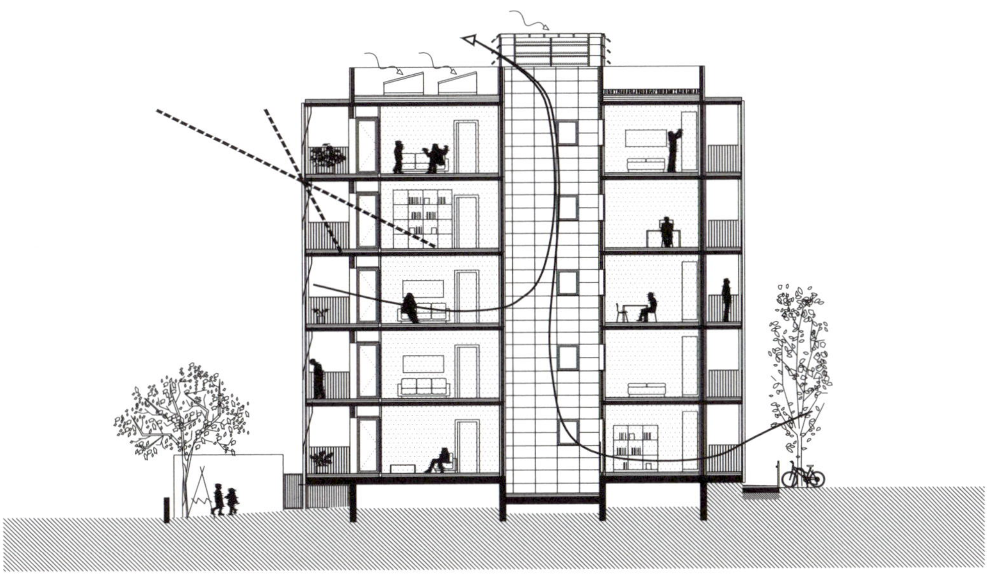

Cross section

|0|1|2| | |5 |10

44 homes

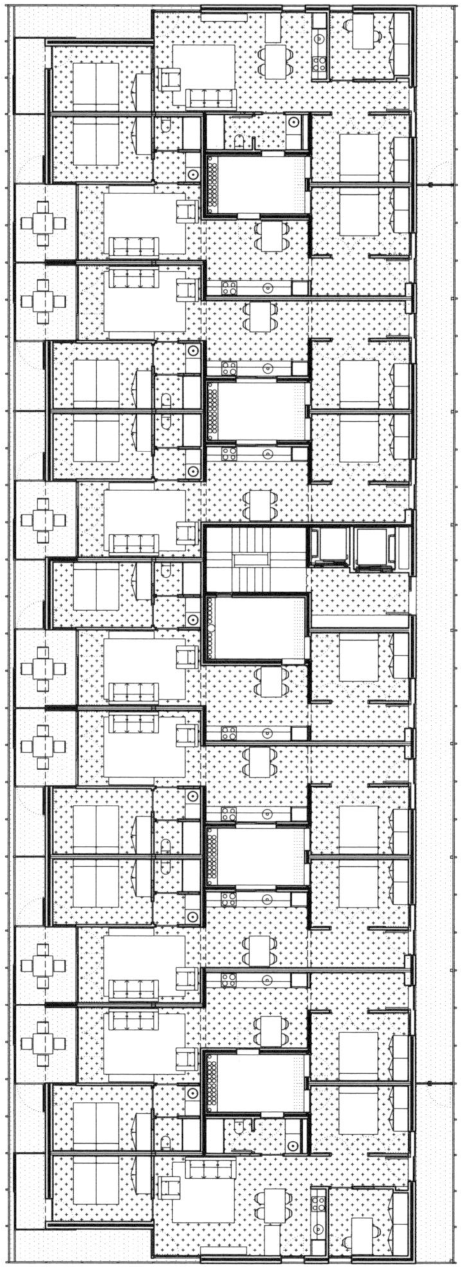

Typical floor plan

No. rooms	3	2
Total surface area (m²)	70.19	63.06
Kitchen-dining room (m²)	13.10	12.06
Bioclimatic glazed balcony (m²)	8.08	8.08
No. homes	**11**	**33**

Architects: Carlos Valls, Sergi Raventós, Jordi Altabàs. Works management: Brufau Cusó estudi d'arquitectura. Collaborators: S4 Arquitectes (structures), JSS efficient engineering (installations), Societat Orgànica (environmental consultancy), David Casadevall (acoustics). Location: Carrer Turó del Mulei, 10-12. Floor area: 3,776.40 m². Construction budget: €4,285,713.79

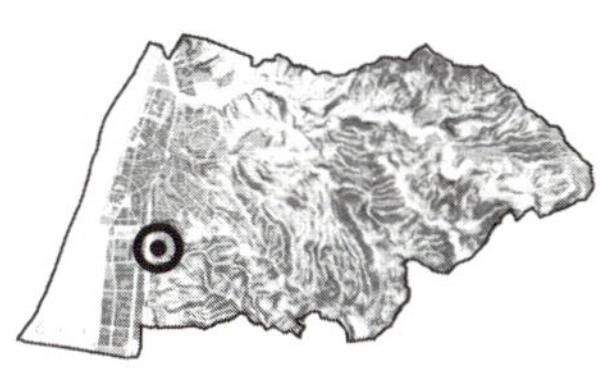

Site

Location

Cornellà de Llobregat

51 homes

Housing unit type

|0 |1 |2 |3 |4 |5

Open-plan kitchen

Generic rooms

Intermediate climatic spaces

Housing unit type – Aggregation
The housing typology is based on the premise of integrating the kitchen into the living-dining room in a single space linked to the terrace, which is set back from the line of the façade. The typology rotates according to its position in the floor plan, to always turn this intermediate space towards the greatest possible sunlighting. The project envisages 51 apartments with one, two or three bedrooms; the wet spaces are positioned in the interior, and the rooms are arranged in the façade, with views.
The homes are arranged in a swastika shape, four by four, around a vertical communication shaft comprising two scissor staircases and two lifts.

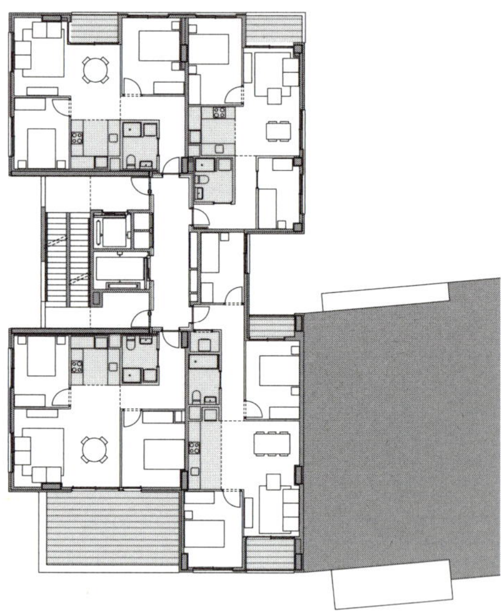

Third floor plan

|0 |2 |5 |10

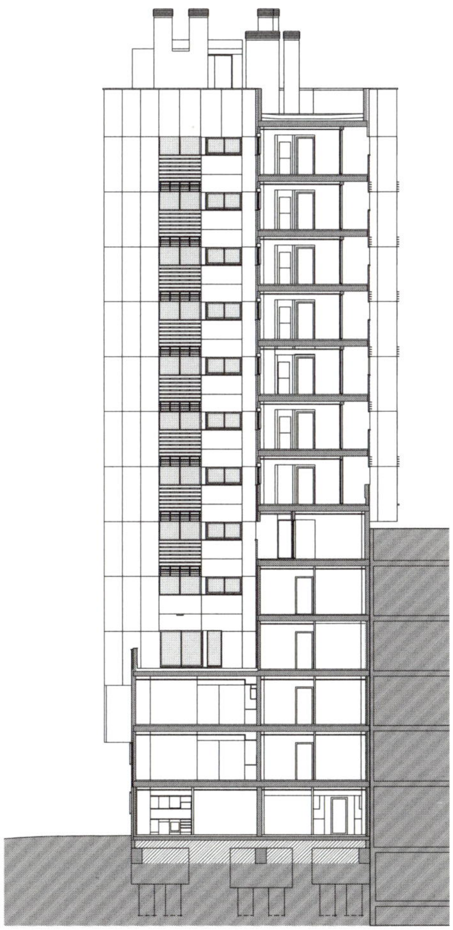

Cross section

0 2 5 10

Urban context – Urban response
The GF+12 volume changes as it rises according to its orientation, integrates into the complex setting and adapts in height to neighbouring buildings, and is partially set back from the alignment of the plot on the south-west side to allow for windows. The building shares a party wall with the adjacent plot up to the fourth floor, but from the fifth floor up it is freestanding.

The 1.5-m terraces are set back from the façade to offer shelter from the wind, which becomes more noticeable above a certain height.
The interplay of volumes, the easement of view with regard to the other blocks and the changes in typology serve to create a simple yet dynamic compact volume, while maintaining the image of naturalness with façades of sliding windows and set-back terraces.

Communal space

The entrance foyer to the apartments is situated on the ground floor, connecting two public spaces and freeing up the footprint of the building, which forms the end of the street block.

Energy strategy

- All the houses are located at a corner, thereby guaranteeing cross ventilation.
- Thanks to its depth, the set-back terrace acts as a solar regulator in the summer and a heat collector in the winter.

Energy certification: A.
- Non-renewable primary energy consumption: A (23 kWh/m^2 year).
- Carbon dioxide emissions: A (3 kg CO_2/m^2 year).

Cornellà de Llobregat

51 homes

Typical floor plan

No. rooms	3	2	1
Total surface area (m²)	72.90	59.25	47.85
Kitchen-living-dining room (m²)	26.15	25.50	22.90
Terrace (m²)	6.39	4.63	3.94
No. homes	**12**	**34**	**5**

Architects: Ana Pérez Lázaro, Joan Casanovas Miñán. Team: Pablo Palomar Gonzalo. Works management: Francesc de Haro Macià, Francesc Xavier Aumedes Farré, Gemma Rius Macies (Arrevolt). Collaborators: Bernuz-Fernández Arquitectes (structures), ELETRESJOTA (installations), 3D leap (BIM), DEKRA (energy rating).
Location: Carrer de l'Oliverar, 7. Floor area: 4,637.94 m^2.
Construction budget: €4,696,860.66

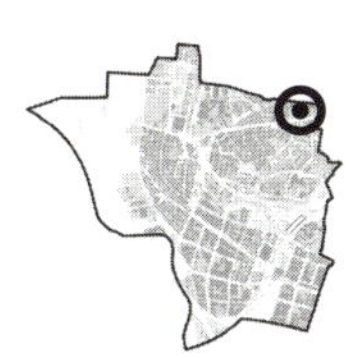

Site

Location

Sant Adrià de Besòs 58 homes

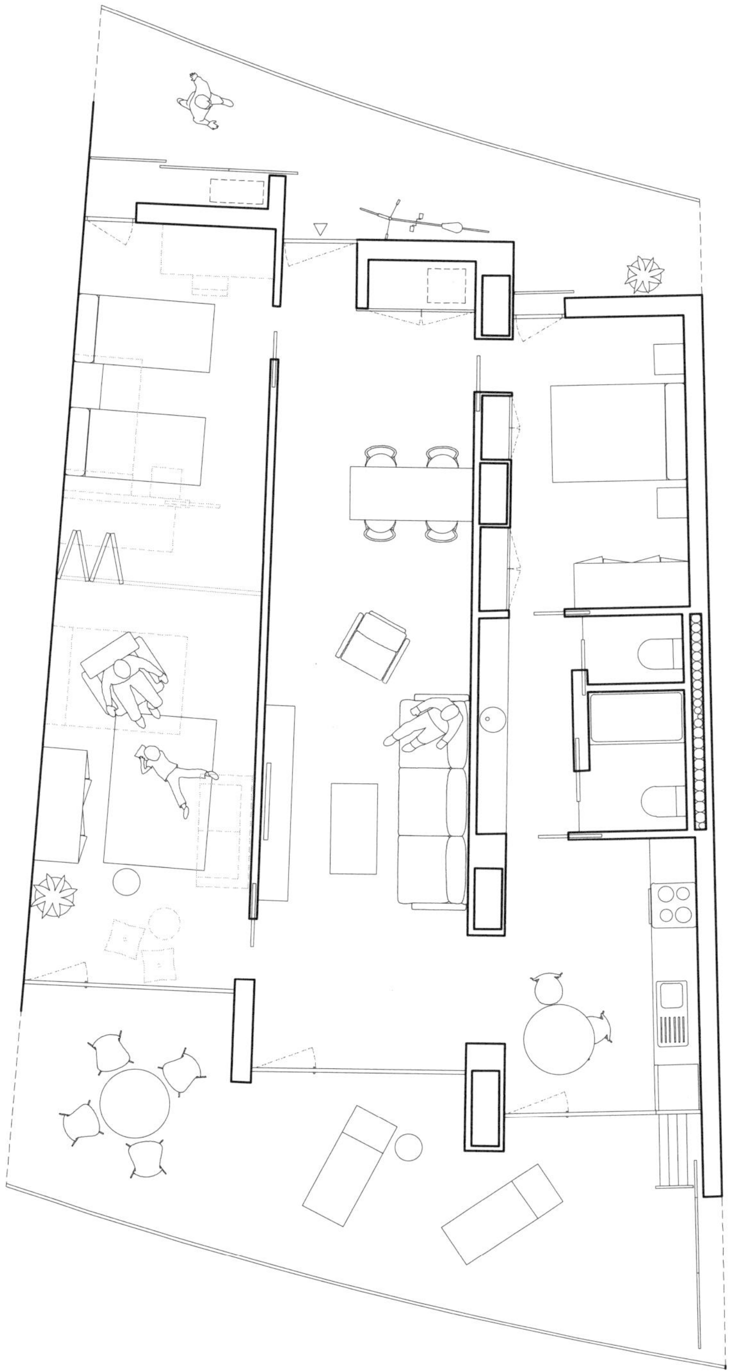

Housing unit type

Generic rooms

Interconnecting rooms

Intermediate social spaces

Housing unit type – Aggregation
This project presents a flexible typology that organizes the housing brief in three through spaces that flow out towards the terrace: two served spaces that can be arranged in different ways, as two, three or four spaces, and a servant space where the kitchen and the toilets are situated. The terrace is seen as an extension of the home that is large enough to be considered a cool, shady room—a terrace-dwelling or a terrace that is a dwelling.

The apartments are grouped in a fan layout, in a curved, south-facing linear block with a single communication shaft around which seven homes are arranged per floor. A north-facing walkway leads to the apartments. The terraces mark out the horizon of the homes, and crosswise divisions and the open curve of the façade provide the necessary privacy for each.

Urban context – Urban response
The building is an urban fan that unfolds before the straightness of the city fabric and rebels against the inert straight line. It is a gentle movement that closes the space at the centre of the block, at the same time opening up to sun and wind. It is a gentle curve that leads to the sea, looking out at the chimneys of the Besòs power plant cut out against the intense blue of the Mediterranean. The GF+9 block rises up wide and transparent at its base and narrows as it nears the top.

Communal space
The communications shaft stands in a dominant position at the eastern end of the block, facing the horizon, where the blue of the sea can be seen in the distance. This position is used by all residents, as they all pass by at some point during the day, with 180° views over the landscape to share and enjoy.
The nucleus open to the horizon is landscape, and the terraces are its extension. Its surroundings are the corridors, like streets, between public and private, wide enough to provide access and give the homes the necessary degree of privacy.

Materiality
The fan structure of reinforced concrete portal frames matches the linearity of the partitions. Four pillars easily span the building's largest bay and give the spaces inside the homes their flexibility.

Energy strategy

- All the homes are protected from the sun's rays by the overhangs of the terraces and a system of awnings.

Energy certification: A (emissions), B (consumption).

- Non-renewable primary energy consumption: B (34.74 kWh/m^2 year).
- Carbon dioxide emissions: A (6.05 kg CO_2/m^2 year).

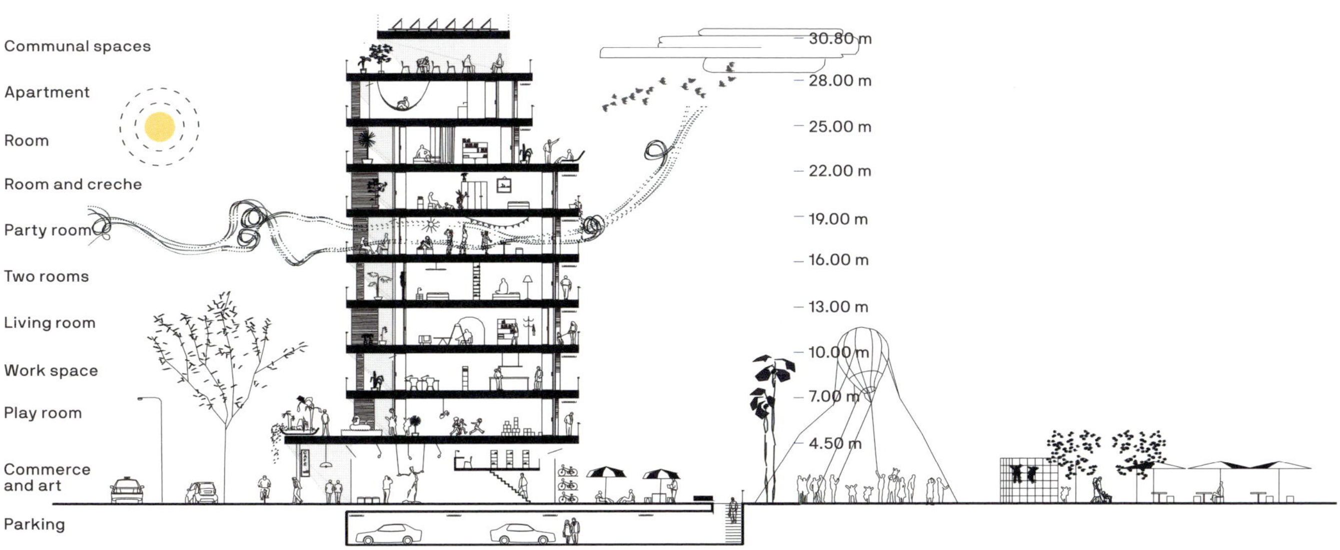

Section with solar incidence

Sant Adrià de Besòs

58 homes

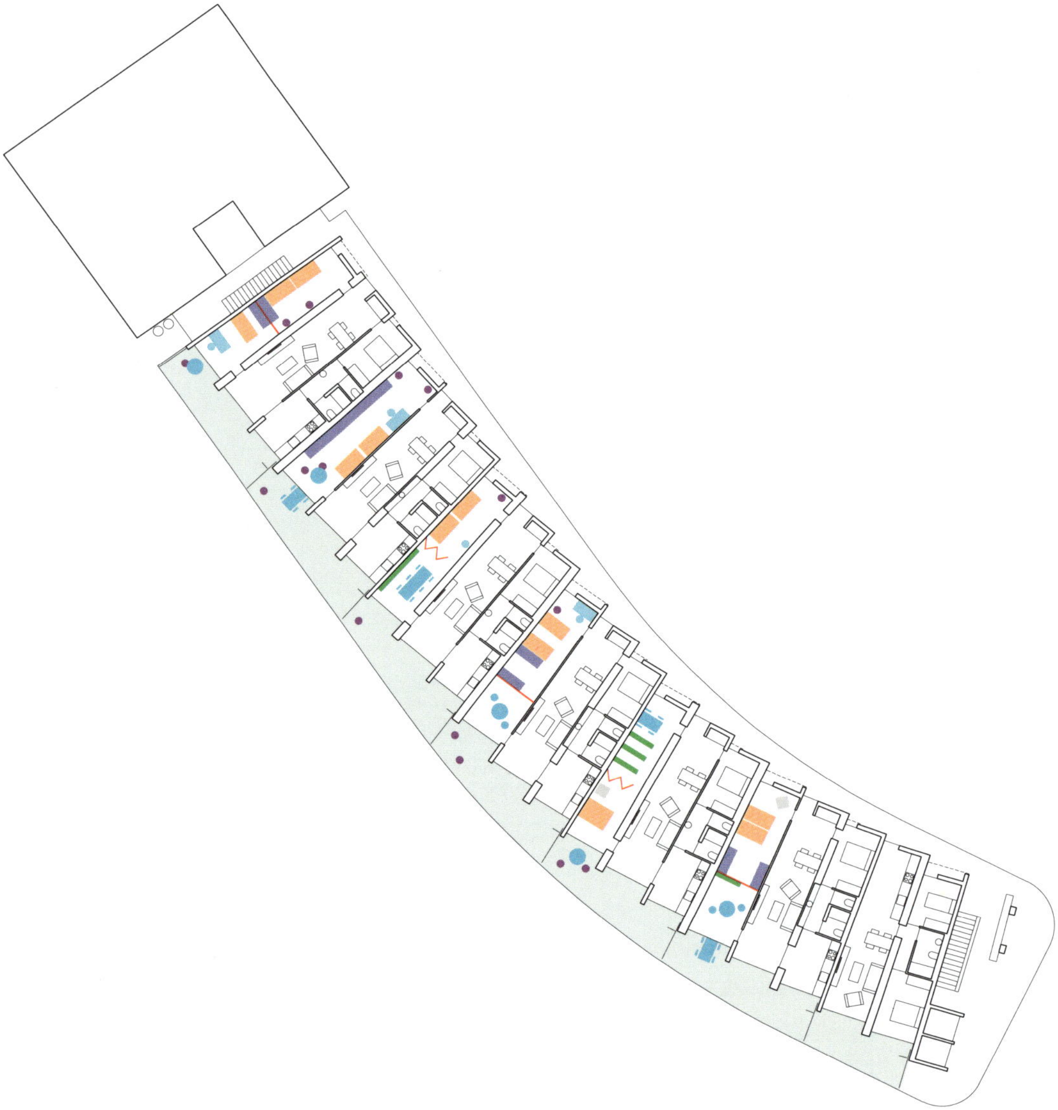

Typical floor plan

No. spaces	3	2
Total surface area (m²)	89.93	72.90
Through space (m²)	30.00 (× 3)	30.00 (× 2)
Terrace (m²)	21.90	13.47
No. homes	**47**	**11**

Architectss: José Durán Fernández, Daniel Moreno Ruiz. Team: Clara Latorre Zorzano, José Manuel Pérez Quereda, Paula Castellanos Ayala. Works management: Marc Serrano Rosón. Collaborators: Windmill Structural Consultants (structures), Adypau (installations).
Location: Avinguda La Catalana, 200. Floor area: 6,198.49 m^2.
Construction budget: €6,643,354.91

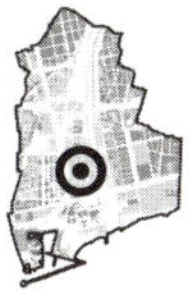

Site

Location

62 homes

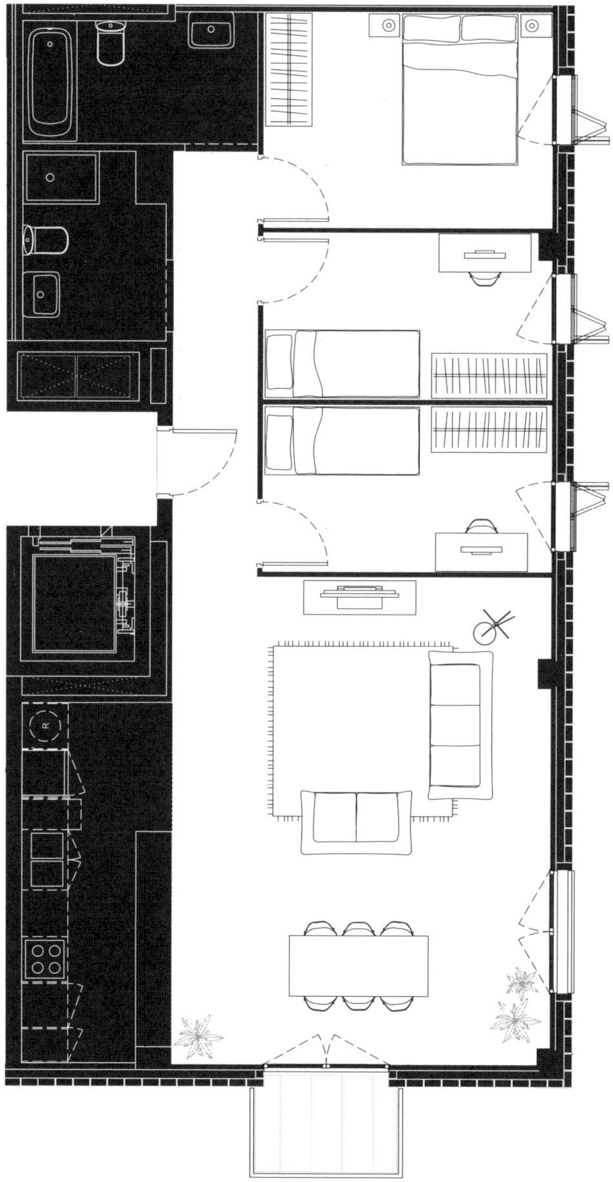

Housing unit type

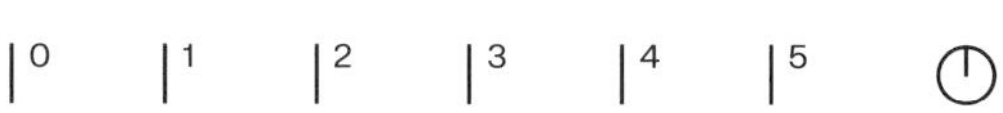

Open-plan
kitchen

Housing unit type – Aggregation
The project proposes a highly functional home in which the day- and night-time areas are clearly differentiated. The main rooms—living-dining room and bedrooms—are situated in the façade, with sea views, while the wet areas are located in the innermost ring of the building, looking onto the 3-metre-deep inner court. The kitchen is open to the living-dining room and is turned to face the views.
The building is organized in a single volume comprising a bar (GF+4) and a tower (GF+6) with three communication shafts; on each landing there are three or four homes. The typology adapts to the geometry of the floor plan.

Communal space
Entrance to the homes is organized in three nucleuses with two distinct foyers that lead to the inner courts of the volume. Entrance to stairways A and B is from Avinguda Can Serra, and to stairway C from Carrer de Joanot Martorell.

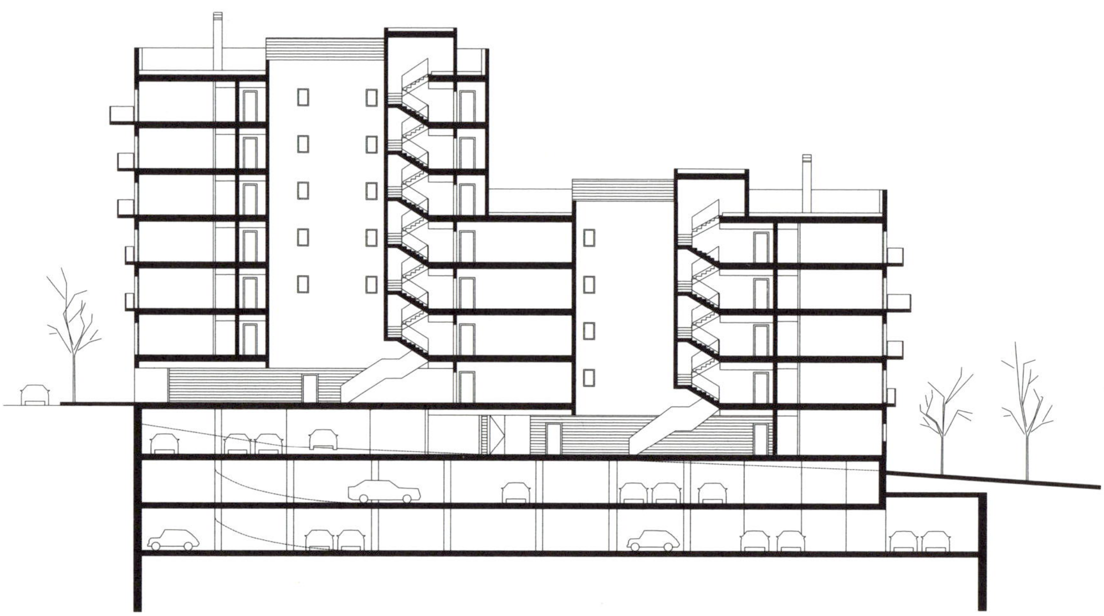

Longitudinal section

0 2 5 10 20

Materiality

The outer façades are double-layer red clinker brick masonry in the typical floor plans, while on the ground floor they are single-layer green glazed units.
The façade uses an innovative Halfen-type construction system that allows the brick to pass whole in front of the edge of the slabs; since the typical queen closer is not used, no cracks, fissures or detachments can occur. For spaces that need ventilation from the outside, such as the car park, a special perforated green enamel unit was designed that allows ventilation via open work.
Sun control in the main rooms is provided by hinged shutters painted with fire retardant in the same colour as the brickwork, creating movement in the façade depending on whether the shutters are open or closed.

Energy strategy

- All the homes have cross ventilation.
- Shade elements are used to provide solar protection.
- The materials used require little maintenance.

Energy certification: B.

- Non-renewable primary energy consumption: B (40.31 kWh/m² year).
- Carbon dioxide emissions: B (8.22 kg CO_2/m² year).

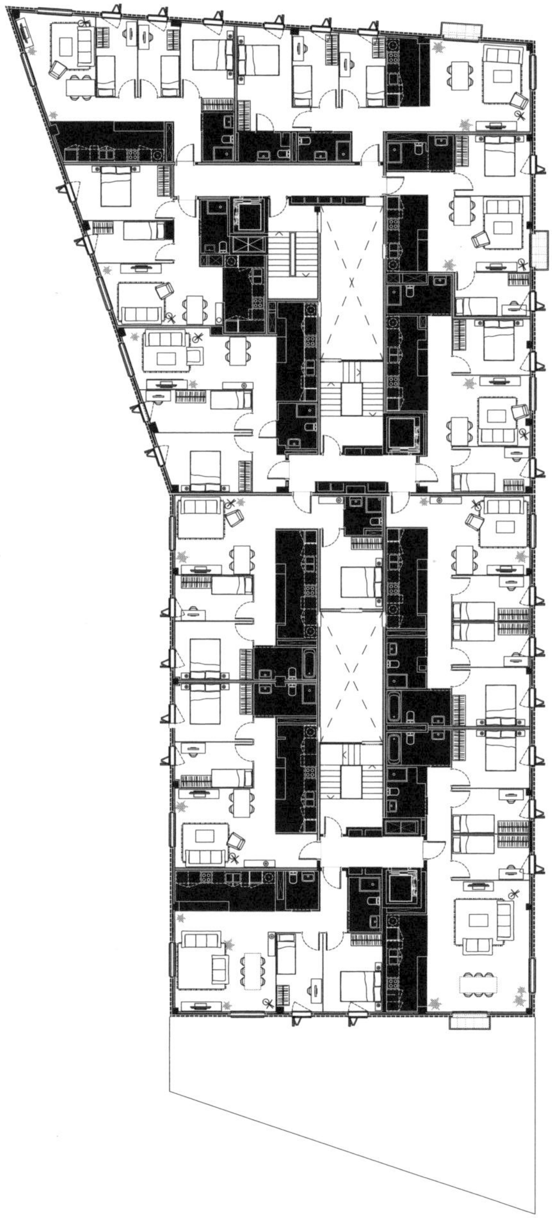

Typical floor plan

No. rooms	3	2
Total surface area (m^2)	85.80	55.02
Kitchen-living-dining room (m^2)	40.02	25.75
No. homes	**26**	**36**

Architects: Franc Fernández, Jordi Sancho Fortuny. Works management: Jordi Albors (a3AT). Collaborators: Base Dos Professional d'Arquitectura (structures), Carles Subirats (installations).
Location: Avinguda Can Serra / Carrer Joanot Martorell.
Floor area: 8,249.99 m². Construction budget: €5,031,250.90

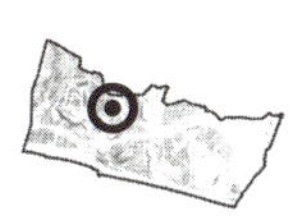

Site

Location

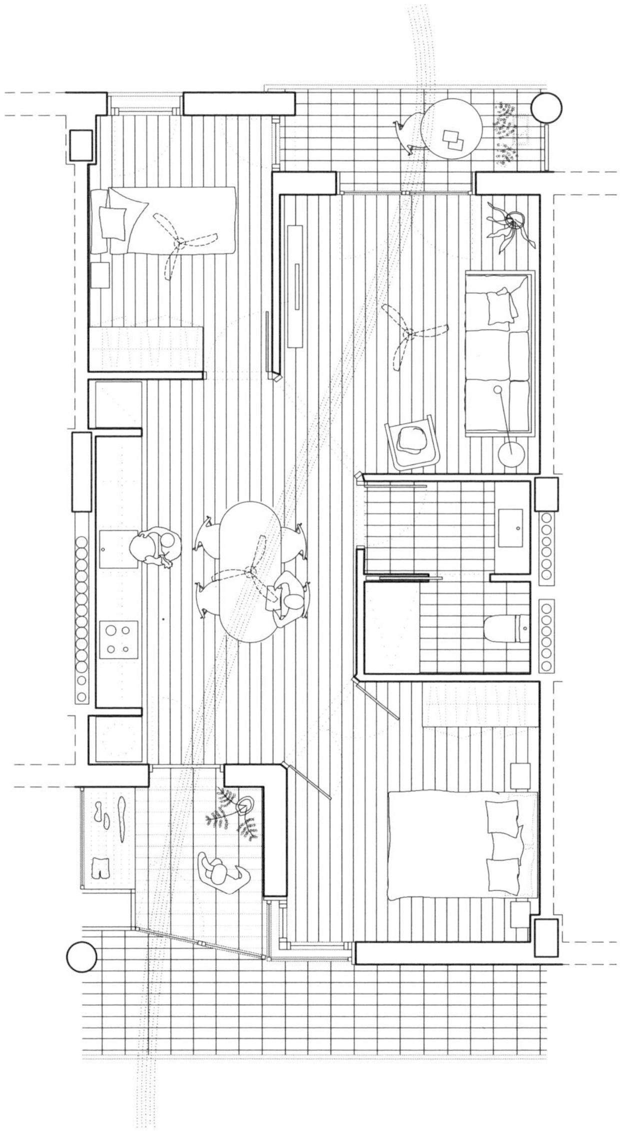

Housing unit type

|0 |1 |2 |3 |4 |5

Open-plan kitchen

Interconnecting rooms

Intermediate social spaces

Housing unit type – Aggregation

The typology proposed defines the kitchen-dining room as the nerve centre of the home, becoming its most social and stimulating part. The layout of the other rooms diagonally from the kitchen breaks with the traditional day-time/night-time arrangement. The wet areas are situated in the centre of the floor plan, and living areas are turned towards the outside. Access to the homes is through a gated space that provides privacy and ensures ventilation.

A mother typology of two bedrooms (A) produces the three variants in the building: (C) addresses the home at the corner; (B) marks the transition from (A) to (C); and (A'), with its three bedrooms, forms the meeting point with the entrance nucleus. The apartments, 14 per landing, are laid out in lines to either side of the communication nucleus at the centre of the inner court on the plot.

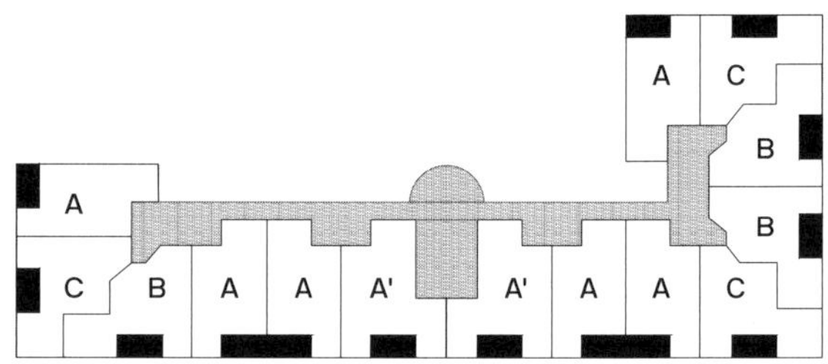

Longitudinal section

0 5 10 20

Urban context – Urban response

The urban implementation strategy consists of occupying the perimeter of the plot to create a large, lengthwise communal courtyard and respond to the three levels of public space that mark out the plot.

The building represents the longest façade on the plaza, and therefore uses a composition that breaks up its great length and makes the whole vibrate thanks to the different treatment of the balconies. In this way, the homogeneous composition of voids is broken up by the appearance of two vertical strips of open balconies.

On the ground floor, meanwhile, the horizontal rhythm of the porch continues the urban connections at different levels.

Energy strategy

- Natural cross ventilation in 100% of the homes.
- Planting of vegetation to promote a cool microclimate in the inner courtyard.
- Protection from the sun provided by projections and moveable awnings.
- Concrete structure with high thermal inertia.

Energy certification: A.

- Non-renewable primary energy consumption: A (17 kWh/m^2 year).
- Carbon dioxide emissions: A (3 kg CO_2/m^2 year).

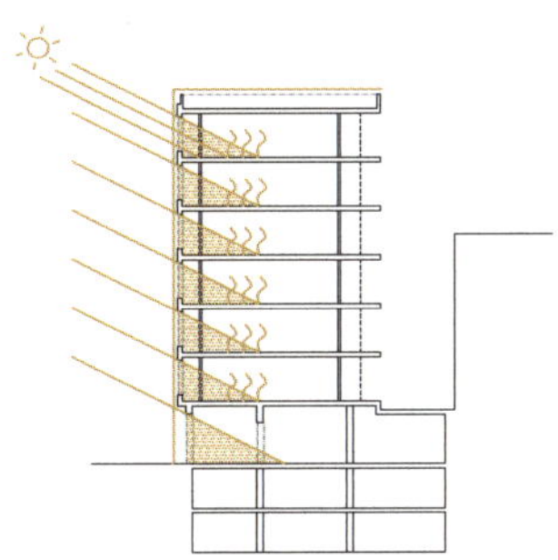

Winter

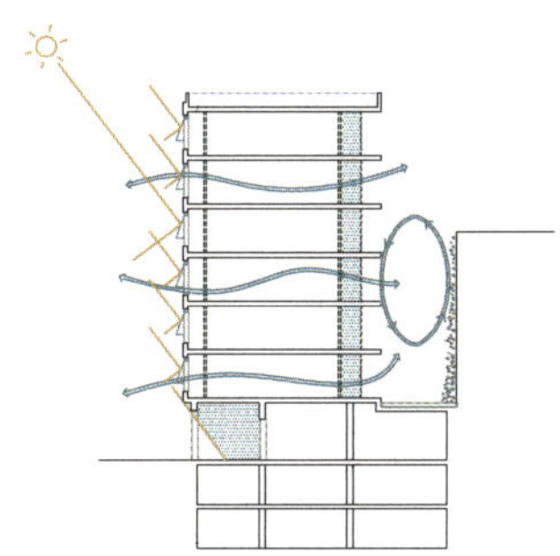

Summer

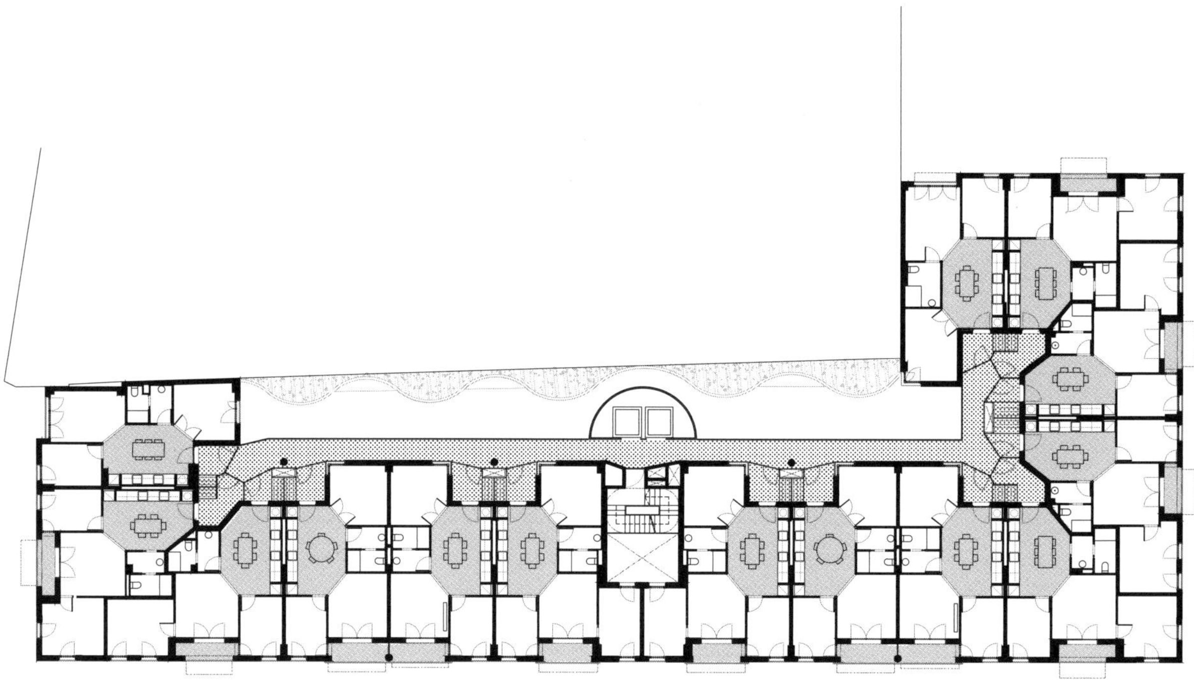

Typical floor plan

No. rooms	A	B	C	A'
Total surface area (m^2)	55.58	57.02	57.43	64.72
Kitchen-dining room (average) (m^2)	28.00	28.00	28.00	28.00
Intermediate space (m^2)	4.66	3.37	5.29	4.41
Balcony (m^2)	3.21	2.78	2.47	2.1
No. homes	**31**	**12**	**12**	**12**

Architects: Marta Benedicto, Ivet Gasol, Carlota de Gispert, Anna Llonch, Lucia Millet and Clara Vidal (Cierto Estudio), Franc Llonch. Team: Jesús Fajer. Works management: Betarq Group. Collaborators: Bernuz-Fernández Arquitectes (structures), ELETRESJOTA (installations), Societat Orgànica (environmental consultancy).
Location: Carrer Itàlia, 5 / Plaça Nova de les Dones del Tèxtil, 13.
Floor area: 8,656.81 m². Construction budget: €8,361,796.18

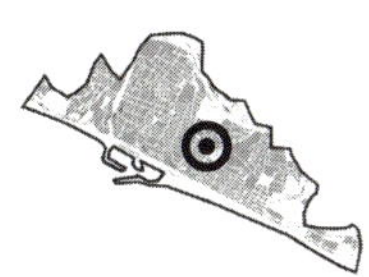

Site

Location

Castelldefels

72 homes

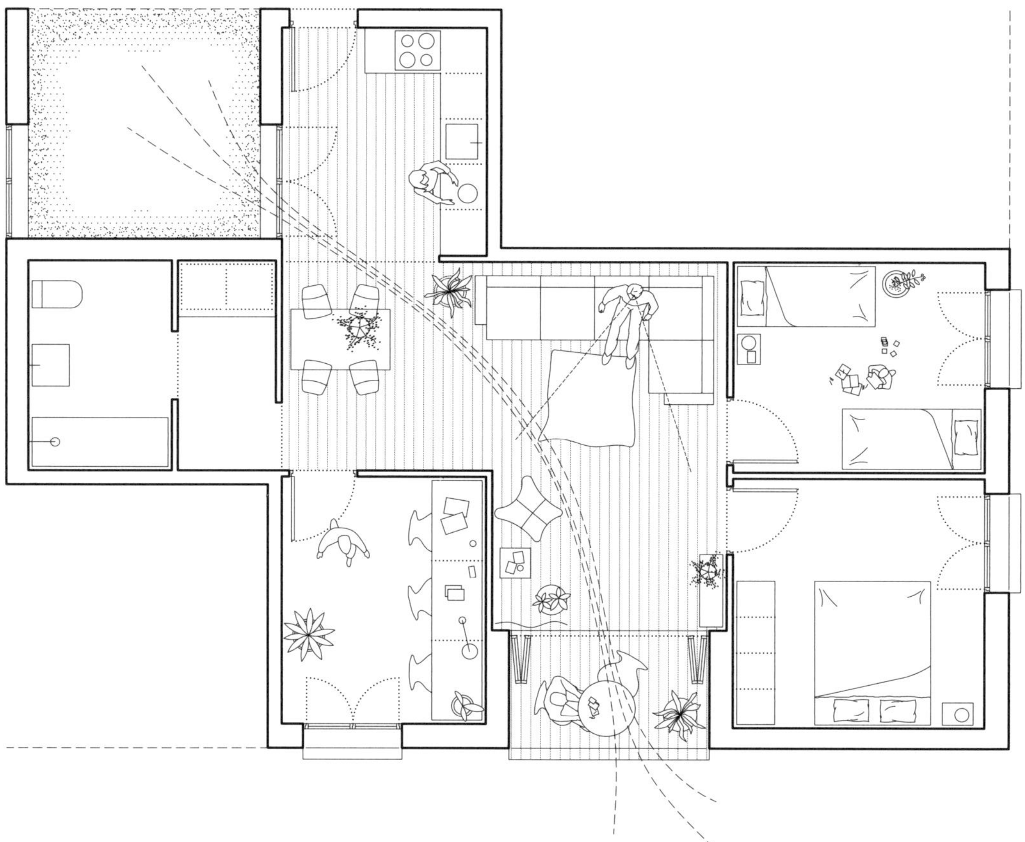

Housing unit type

Carles Enrich Studio

2019—under construction

Open-plan kitchen	Generic rooms	Interconnecting rooms	Intermediate climatic spaces	Intermediate social spaces

Housing unit type – Aggregation
The housing brief is laid out in rings. The central ring houses the wet areas, and the outer one the rooms, giving them views of the natural surroundings to reinforce the idea of living in a park. The kitchen and the living-dining room form a single unit that connects directly with the outside space, the terrace. There are three types according to the number of rooms: (A) with three, (B) with two and (C) with one. The apartments situated at the corner are laid out as a sum of concatenated spaces.
The design strategy sets out to maximize the total number of residential units, and the useful surface area of each, thereby producing a total of 72 homes that are organized in two volumes of GF+4, with eight homes per floor around a compact central nucleus formed by circulation spaces and four courtyards.

Urban context – Urban response
With the aim of integration into the natural setting and respecting the heritage value of the historic castle complex close to the plot, the project divides the volume proposed by planning into two equal compact parts. The two parts separate to generate a two-level porched space that functions as a doorway to the foyers, a permeable area that continues the public space.

Communal space
The central nucleus is given great spatial quality thanks to the introduction of four linked courtyards that provide natural light and ventilation. Community space thereby becomes a semi-outdoor space that also contributes to the energy strategy of the complex.

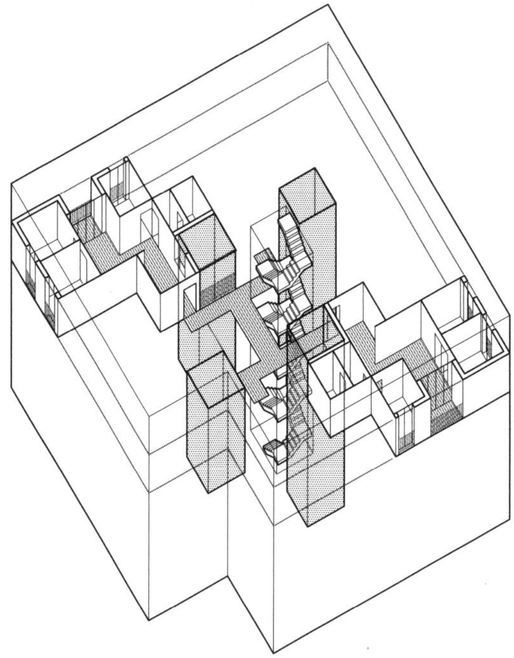

Energy strategy
- Cross ventilation in all the housing units thanks to the arrangement of the inner courts.
- Solar protection is provided by filters such as roller blinds.
- External insulation with lime mortar, which improves the hygroscopic conditions of the façades.

Energy certification: A.
- Non-renewable primary energy consumption: A (23 kWh/m^2 year).
- Carbon dioxide emissions: A (3 kg CO_2/m^2 year).

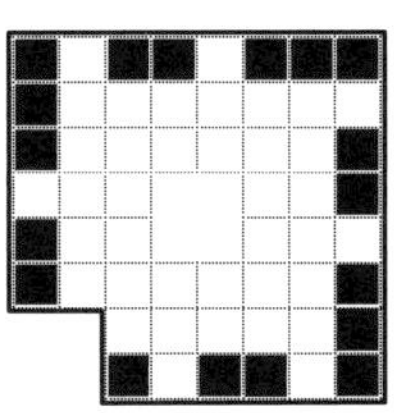
Rooms

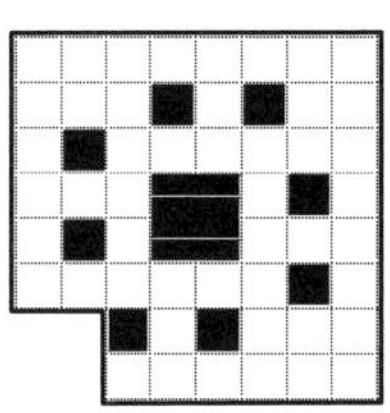
Wet areas

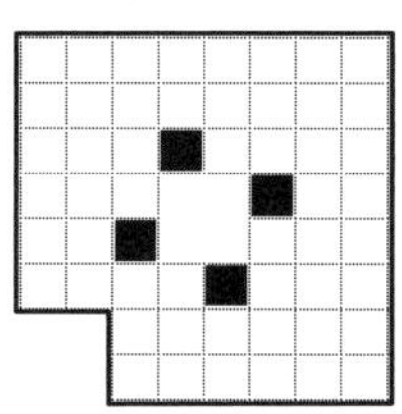
Courtyards

Project diagrams

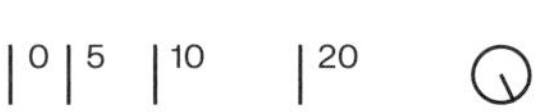

Cross section

0 2 5 10 20

72 homes

Typical floor plan

No. rooms	4	3	2	1
Total surface area (m2)	80.52	69.72	59.54	42.77
Kitchen-living-dining room (m2)	30.55	30.55	28.38	21.55
Terrace (m2)	2.89	2.89	2.89	2.89
No. homes	**1**	**26**	**28**	**17**

Architect: Carles Enrich Studio. Works management: Brufau Cusó estudi d'arquitectura. Collaborators: BBG Estructures (structures), SJ12 Enginyers (installations), Praxis Resilient Buildings (sustainability), QIEstud (acoustics).
Location: Carrer de Jesús Romo, 1. Floor area: 7,195.05 m².
Construction budget: €7.359.318,57

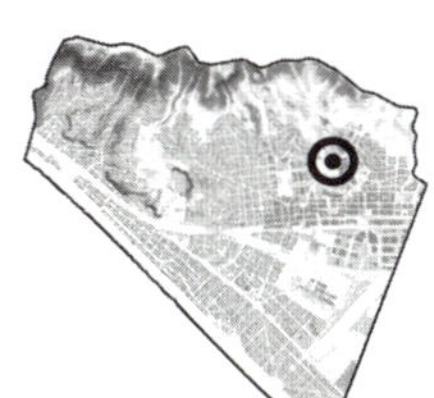

Site

Location

Good bioclimatic citizens

Habitability, understood as the quality given to a space to be inhabited according to cultural and legal conditions, involves management that goes beyond the mere physical arrangement of materials, extending to include society and energy, and constituting a much wider metabolism.

In his *Essai sur l'architecture*, Marc-Antoine Laugier presented the notion of the primitive hut as an exploration into the anthropological relationship between human beings and their natural environment, and established a fundamental basis for architectural creation. Laugier suggested that the essence of architecture lay in the simplicity and purity of natural forms, such as a cabin built using simple elements found in the environment.

However, as history has advanced, with the industrialization of our society, this idyllic vision of architecture has faced ever greater challenges. The notion of *abundance* that emerged with industrialization and mass urbanization has led to an unbridled, unsustainable approach, with buildings consuming large amounts of energy and materials, and contributing to environmental degradation.

In today's context, marked by overlapping social, political and climate crises, architecture faces the great responsibility of rethinking and adapting our architectures to respond to the changing complexities of life.

In *We Have Never Been Modern*, Bruno Latour warns of the extractive mentality, which sees nature as an unlimited font of resources to be exploited, depletes natural resources, and undermines the ecological systems and local communities that depend on them.

This transition from the primitive hut of Rousseau's "good savage" interpreted by Laugier to Latour's critical awareness of technological abuse implies a paradigm shift in the way we understand, practise and inhabit architecture. This shift goes beyond mere aesthetics or the application of materials; it calls for a proactive attitude and transforms inhabitants into good bioclimatic citizens, prepared to adjust their comfort threshold to a conscious practice of global responsibility and thereby, activating eminently passive measures and willing to share certain resources, to address the complicit complexities and interconnections—why not?—between architecture, environment and society.

In the effort to move towards a new, holistically sustainable model, the challenge of decarbonization stands out as a commitment that encompasses all areas of production and consumption. We are aware that construction, in particular, has a significant influence on the emissions of gases that contribute to global warming, both during the process and in the resources needed to maintain the liveability that it aims to provide.

However, we cannot focus solely on reducing energy demand or the environmental impact of materials and waste, their circularity and life cycle; we need to address the crucial task of reconstructing the values that guide our societies. This means a metamorphosis, ideally from individualism to the common, and from unlimited growth to the fair, sustainable management of resources. In this process of reconstruction of values, architecture takes on a central role, transcending its physical function and becoming a means to foster a more equitable, sustainable society.

Sustainability has mostly been addressed from a technical perspective, with the emphasis on standards and seals based on various regulations. While these technical tools can be valuable for guiding more sustainable practices, they have also led to a fragmented perception of sustainability, often focused on excessively specific aspects and lacking

Mariona Benedito is an architect and co-founder of Arquitectura MIM-A studio (2007-2020). As a researcher, she forms part of the winning curatorship team for UIA26, "Becoming. Architectures for a Planet in Transition". She is working on a thesis on residential architecture in Barcelona between 1940 and 1960. She teaches classes and workshops on architectural projects at several national and international universities.

a deeper understanding of the interconnections between society, economy and environment.

When questioning the processes and methods of the culture of energy abundance, an understandable reaction is to move from high-tech to low-tech, to the vernacular. This perhaps romantic look back to a primeval pre-industrial moment may have the merit of recovering lost or discarded techniques and materials, but it could be accused of picturesqueness and, above all, it is unable to cope with growing demand.

It seems more pertinent to reach further and address more committed issues, with a dynamic, collaborative approach that makes the most of technology, research and creativity to come up with a material and architectural vocabulary that creates alliances with industry and updates traditional construction systems in a relationship based not on romanticism but on efficiency and decarbonization.

We have to recognize that bioclimatic decisions directly influence the geometry and appearance of our built environment, and have the potential to deploy alternative tectonic approaches that seek beauty and wonder in construction, and empower us to create and foster an improved coexistence on Earth.

Despite the restrictive regulatory context, there is room for evolution and, fortunately, we have environmental experts and building performance simulation tools that allow us to evaluate innovative strategies and justify decisions that look beyond regulatory restrictions. This commitment is reflected in the incorporation of bioclimatism and its management to achieve optimal energy efficiency, reduce energy demand and move closer to a zero net energy approach. We have to make the most of climatic conditions, taking into account factors such as orientation, compactness of design and envelope systems that adapt to the seasons, as well as taking on a new commitment to adjust the comfort threshold, with the recovery in this case of certain pre-industrial practices. Sustainability cannot be fully effective if it is limited to a technical framework; it has to be a cultural change that redefines our practices and values in relation to our environment and society.

It is not surprising that some of these solutions become precedents, but the fact that the impetus towards this paradigm shift has been led by the public sector is exemplary. This committed government, with the help of responsible architecture studios, and despite serious budgetary limitations, has been able to create a catalogue of very high quality architecture that explores and innovates in terms of typology, materials and bioclimatic performance of buildings. It has also implemented a solid management and pedagogy protocol for the systems used.

The impact of this comprehensive approach is felt across the board, making a mark on society but also at domestic level, reflected in lower energy bills; in this way it not only facilitates access to housing and improves the quality of life of the inhabitants, it also contributes significantly to long-term sustainability and energy efficiency.

Bibliographic references

LATOUR, Bruno (Porter, Catherine, transl.). *We Have Never Been Modern*. Harvard University Press, 1993.

LAUGIER, Marc-Antoine. *An Essay on Architecture*. Hennessey & Ingalls, 1977.

ROUSSEAU, Jean-Jacques (Johnston, Ian, transl.). *Discourse on the Origin and the Foundations of Inequality Among Men*.

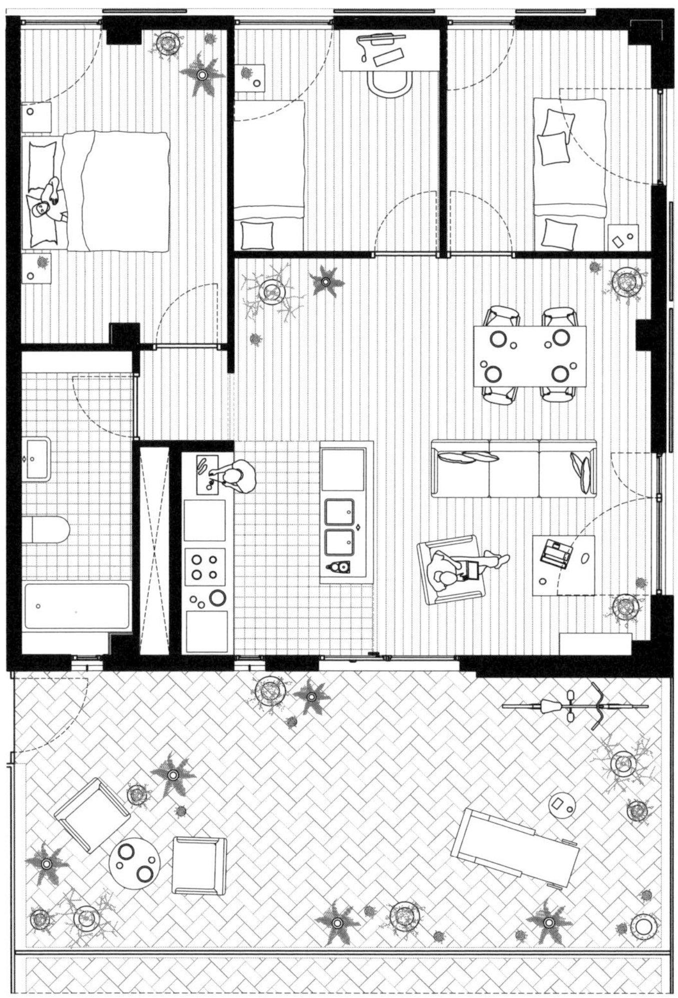

Housing unit type

Open-plan kitchen

Intermediate climatic spaces

Intermediate social spaces

Housing unit type – Aggregation
The proposed home unifies the living and dining rooms, which become the common space of the home onto which the kitchen opens to encourage domestic life and avoid gender roles. The rooms are exterior, while the kitchens, bathrooms and entrances give onto the access walkways, one for every three apartments. Since planning does not allow protruding elements, inside the homes the door and window frames have 40-cm sills and reach almost to the ceiling to create a balcony effect that significantly extends indoor space. The apartments, 12 per floor, are organized around a through hall, with a single central nucleus equipped with two intertwined stairways, two lifts and two installations shafts, accessible both from the street and from the public space. This arrangement is repeated on the seven floors of the building, creating five apartments that give rise to two subtractions from the volume, of great plastic value and notable environmental effects.

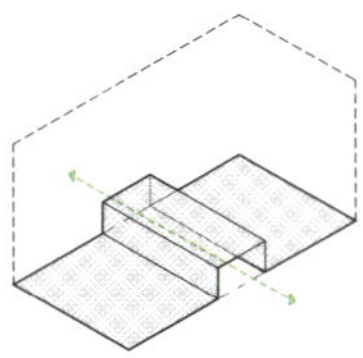

THROUGH LOBBY
Street-park connection

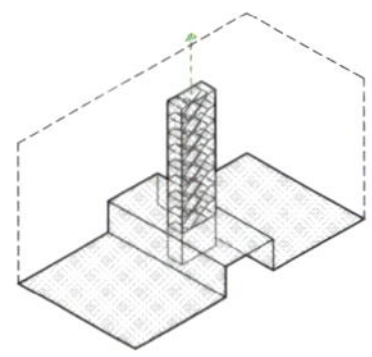

2 INTERTWINED STAIRWAYS
Single central nucleus

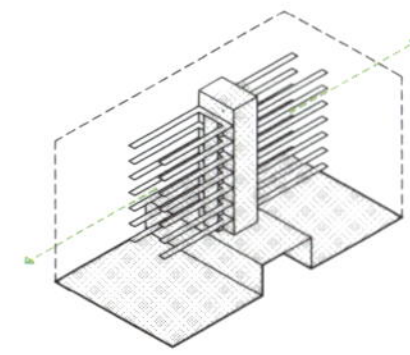

OUTDOOR WALKWAYS
Diagonal sightlines

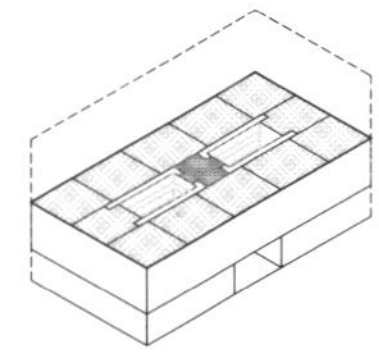

12 HOMES PER FLOOR
Cross ventilation and daylight

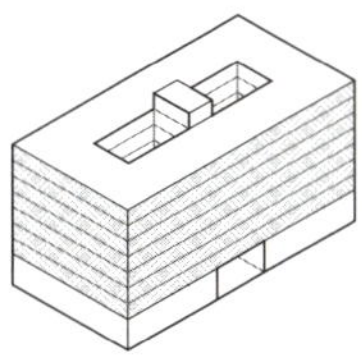

SOLIDIFICATION OF THE VOLUME

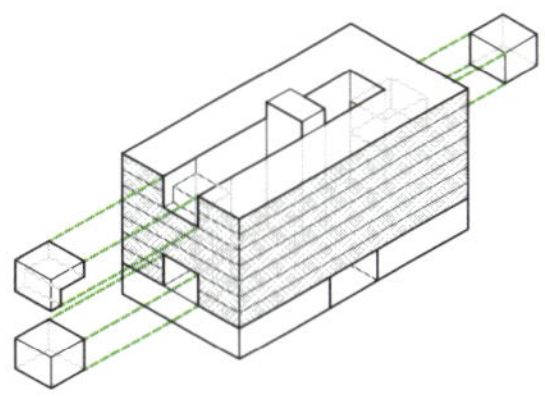

SUBTRACTION OPERATIONS
Lightening of the density

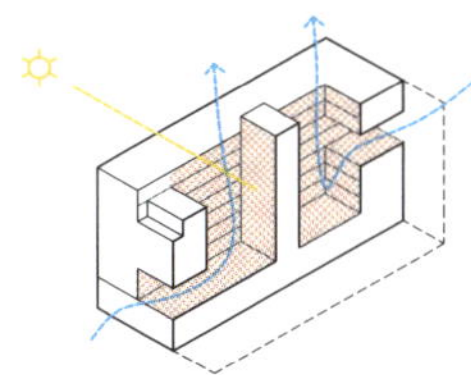

INSIDE MATERIALS
Warm tones of user-friendly materials

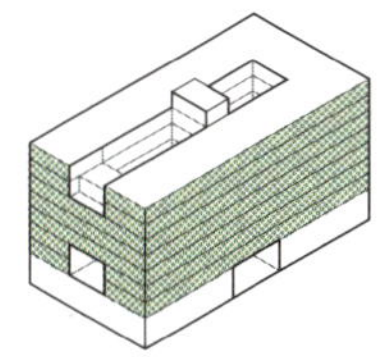

OUTSIDE MATERIALS
Massed industrial materials

Urban context – Urban response
The Caragol (Snail) building is an invitation to rethink the concept of periphery. It is the same distance by bike from the old town, the vegetable production areas on the banks of the river Llobregat, the beach and Barcelona-El Prat airport. Perhaps a context like this, where residential blocks blur with industrial warehouses, presents a centrality with access to a variety of contexts and scales that are not accessible from the conventional centre. The arrangement of volumes produced by planning based on large entities results in a pragmatic volume that responds to the conditions of the context.

Longitudinal section

0 2 5 10 20

Communal spaces
The building aims to be an optimistic expression of the ideal of living together with its typological scheme of a courtyard with glazed balconies that function as spaces to meet and socialize. The volumes cut out of this construction generate a new morphology with generous communal and individual terraces that enable cross ventilation, diagonal views and a lightening of the original density, which turn the building towards its most attractive landscapes, offering them to the community.

sorigue

Materiality

The outer façades, made of ventilated industrial panels, are repetitive. Large groupings of windows simplify the image, accentuate the horizontal dimension and give the volume an almost monumental status. Colour is an important ingredient in this characteristic silhouette, and an interplay of green tones responds to the possibilities of the surroundings.

The façades of the courts and walkways are very light and bright, and combine two similar tones to create a vibration that accentuates their cheerfulness. The materialization makes it almost picturesque with its use of lattices, tiles and paving in a herringbone pattern reminiscent of Mediterranean tradition.

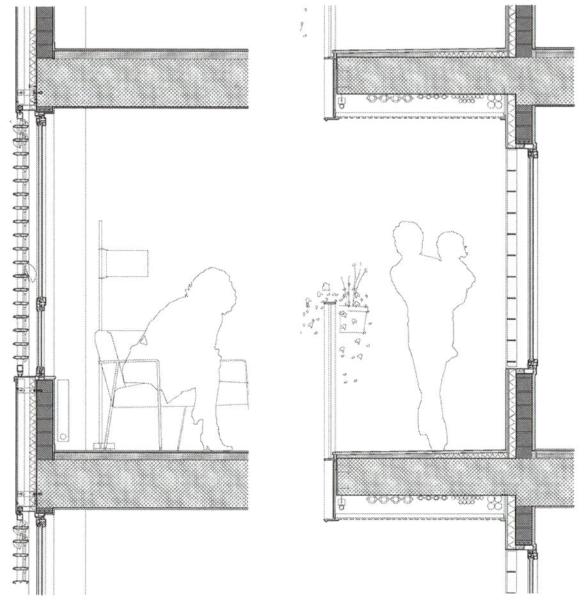

Façade details

Energy strategy
- Ventilated façades.
- Adjustable solar protection.
- Cross ventilation in all the apartments.
- Maximum use of daylight.

<u>Energy certification:</u> A (emissions), B (consumption).
- Non-renewable primary energy consumption: B (28 kWh/m^2 year).
- Carbon dioxide emissions: A (4 kg CO_2/m^2 year).

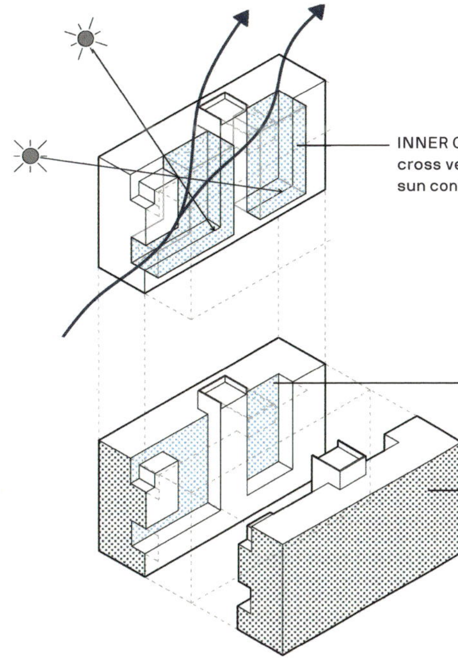

Bioclimatic diagram

Sant Boi de Llobregat

79 homes

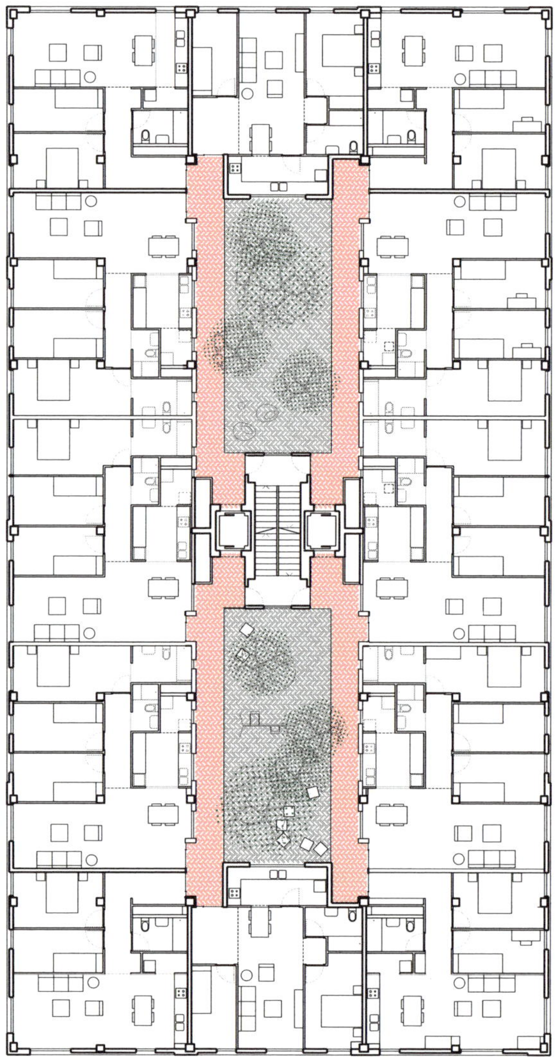

Typical floor plan

0 2 5 10 20

No. rooms	3	2	1
Total surface area (m²)	81.51	63.85	47.37
Kitchen-living-dining room (m²)	27.67	28.60	21.80
No. homes	**48**	**30**	**1**

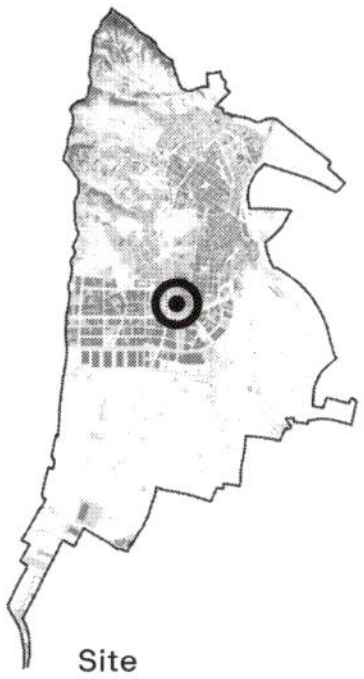

Site

Location

Architects: Juan Herreros, Jens Richter; Mariona Benedito, Martí Sanz. Team: Abraham Piñate, Martha Sosa Días, Verónica Meléndez, Paola Simone, Carmen Antón, Filippo Sapienza, Xavier Isart, Clara Vidal, Ignasi Agustí, Ignasi Navàs. Works management: Eulalia Aran. Collaborators: Manuel Arguijo y Asociados (structures), PGI Engineering & Consulting (installations).
Location: Carrer Baldiri Net i Figueres, 5-7. Floor area: 12,500 m^2.
Construction budget: €6,972,435.93

Cornellà de Llobregat

85 homes

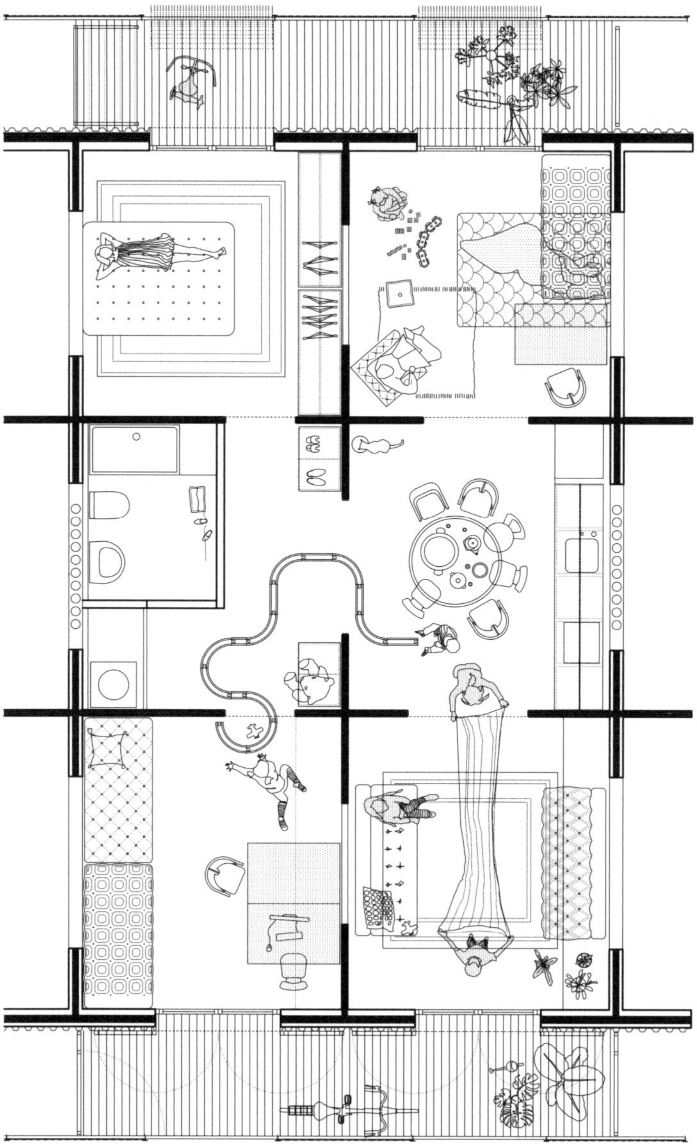

Housing unit type

|0 |1 |2 |3 |4 |5 ⊖

Open-plan kitchen

Generic rooms

Interconnecting rooms

Intermediate climatic spaces

Intermediate social spaces

Housing unit type – Aggregation

The homes are made up of modules/spaces of approximately 13 m². According to the type of apartment (two- or three-bedroomed), the groupings comprise four and a half, six or six and a half modules. The dimension of the module allows flexibility based on the ambiguity of use and functional indeterminacy, and on an optimal bay for the wooden structure with which the volume is built. The strategy of placing an inclusive open-plan kitchen at the centre of the home makes it the nexus of the home, as well as visibilizing domestic tasks, thereby breaking with gender roles.

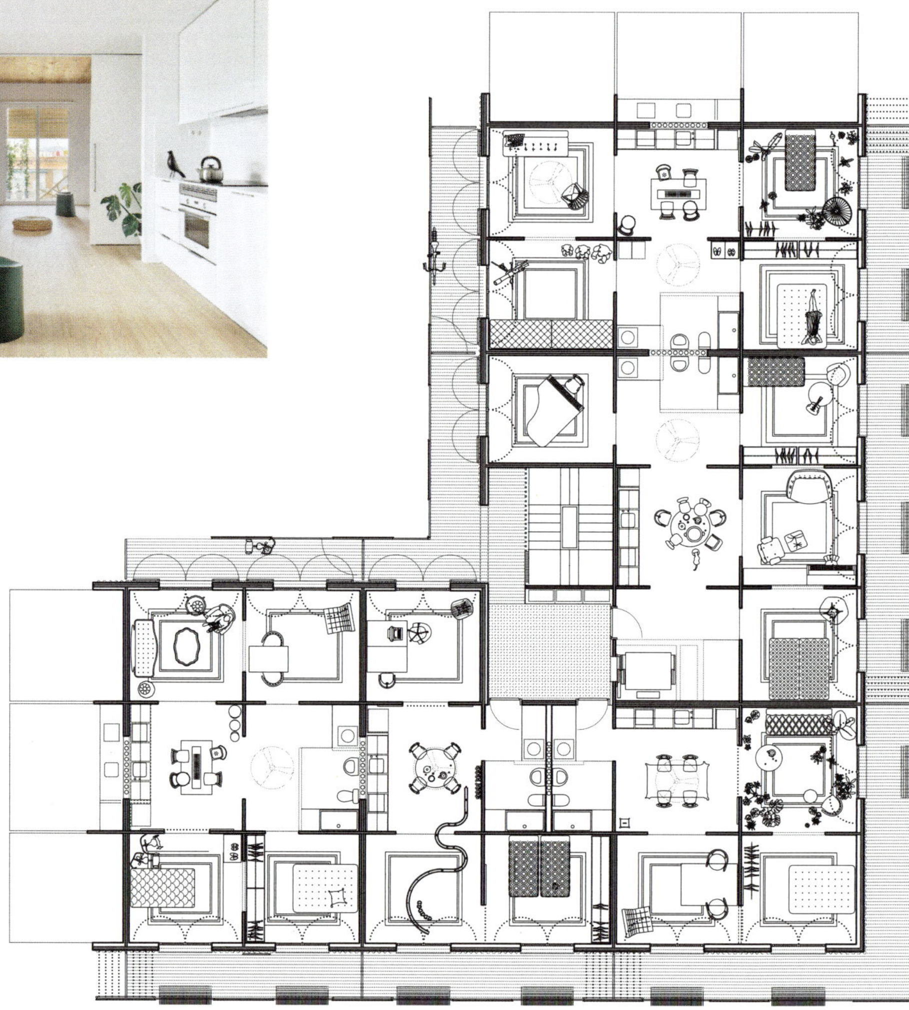

Aggregation diagram

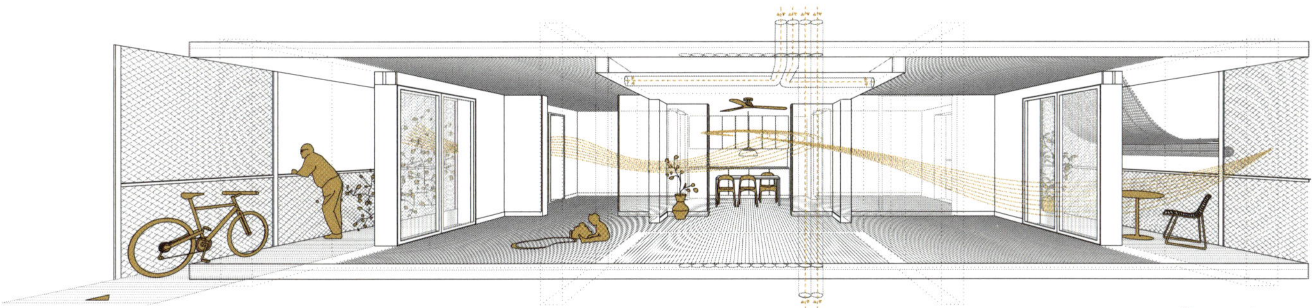

Apartment section

The building is organized as a matrix of communicating rooms: 114 modules/spaces per floor, of similar dimensions that eliminate both private and communal corridors to make the most of the floor area. The server spaces are laid out in the central ring of the matrix and the rest of the generic rooms run along the façade, offering different forms of dwelling. Another terrace in the outer ring completes the spatial sequence, the enfilade of spaces interconnected by large openings, permeable to the air, the gaze and movement.
The 114 spaces per floor form 18 homes and four circulation shafts around which four or five homes are arranged.

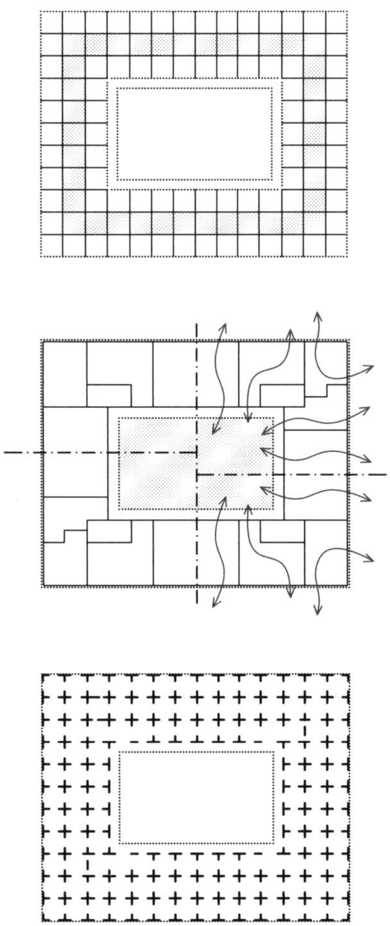

Diagrams

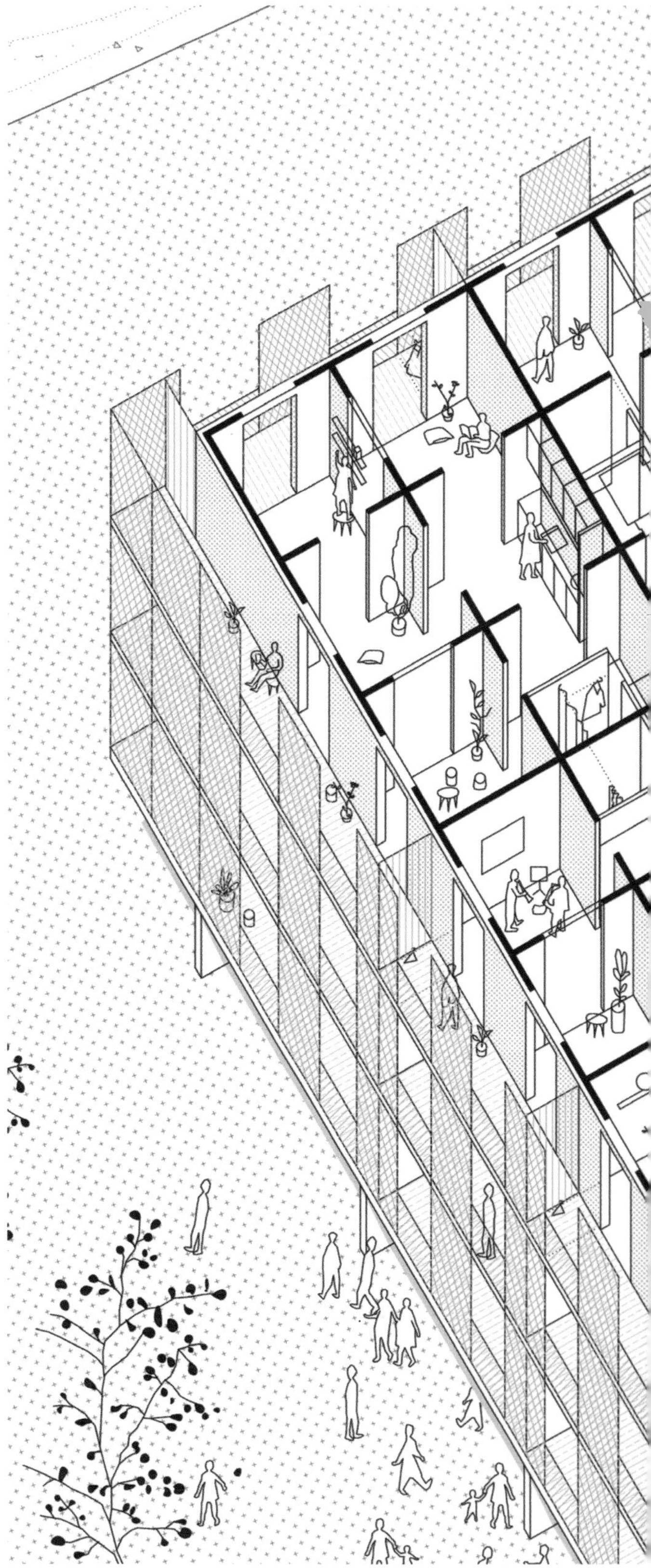

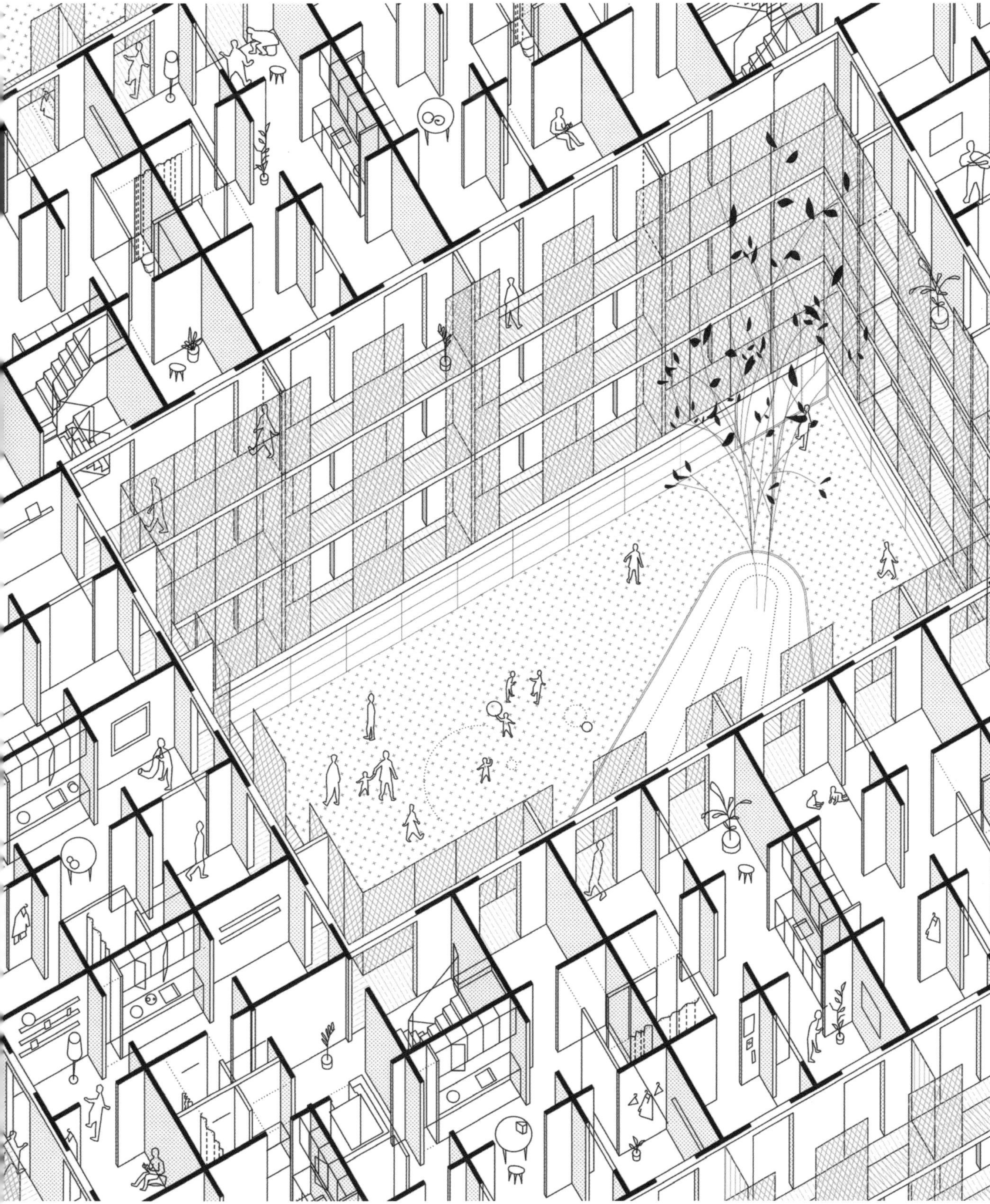

Urban context – Urban response
The project is located on a site formerly occupied by Cornellà's historic Pisa Cinema, a rectangular plot that regulations required to be filled in with GF+5 around a central courtyard. In response to the prerequisites of the plot, the strategy of the project is to arrange the commercial premises on the ground floor, open to the street; the amenity in the basement, with street access, and the entrance to the four communication hubs of the apartments through the central communal courtyard.

Communal space
The central courtyard organizes a sequence of intermediate spaces. On the ground floor, a portico open to the city anticipates the doorway of the building and filters the relationship between public space and the resident's courtyard that acts as a small plaza for the community. Instead of directly and independently entering each lobby of the building from the exterior façade, the four communication shafts are located at the four corners of the courtyard, where all the residents converge and meet in the courtyard-plaza that therefore offers a safe space from a gender perspective. Access to the apartments is via this nucleus and from the private terraces that form the outer ring that gives onto the courtyard.

Cornellà de Llobregat

Materiality
The project, defined by the steel mesh and the warmth of the natural pine, chooses a wooden structure for its performance in terms of hygrothermal capacity (regulating humidity) and its ability to absorb odours, as well as its ideal adaptation to the structural spans of the proposed housing type. The structure composes the space. To achieve the economic viability required by social housing, the volume of wood needed per square metre of construction has been optimized, requiring 0.24 m^3 per square metre of built surface area.

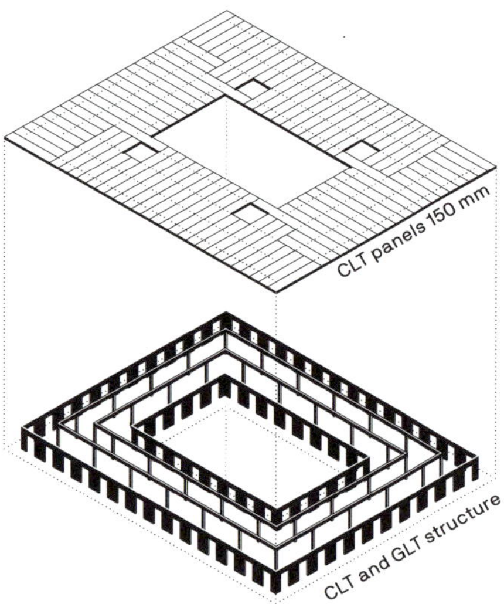

Structure diagram

0 0,25 0,5 1

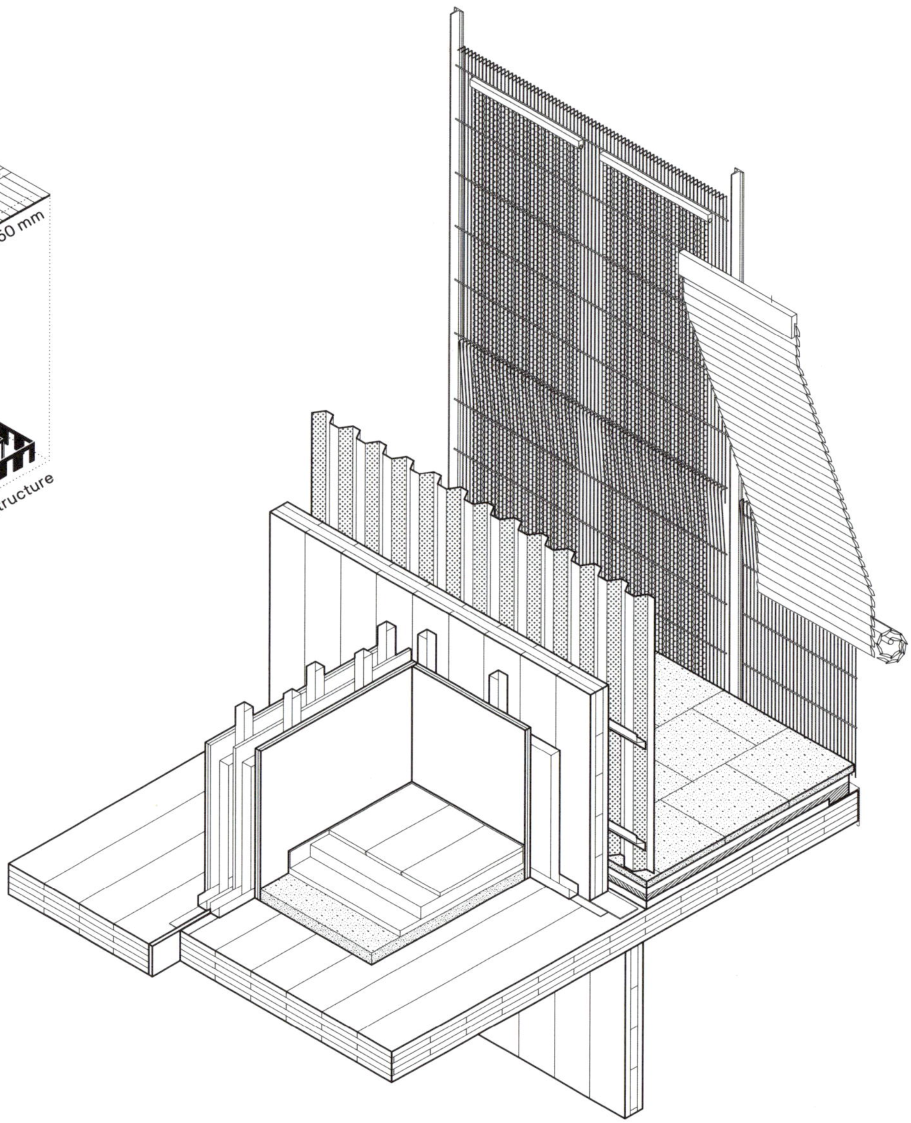

Construction detail

Energy strategy

- All the apartments have cross ventilation and face two directions.
- Sun control is provided by various filters in the façade and the creation of intermediate spaces outside the homes.
- Materials used in a biospheric state (such as wood) or recycled (such as steel and aggregates) reduce the building's carbon footprint by 55%.

Energy certification: A.

- Non-renewable primary energy consumption: A (20 kWh/m^2 year).
- Carbon dioxide emissions: A (3 kg CO_2/m^2 year).

Cornellà de Llobregat

85 homes

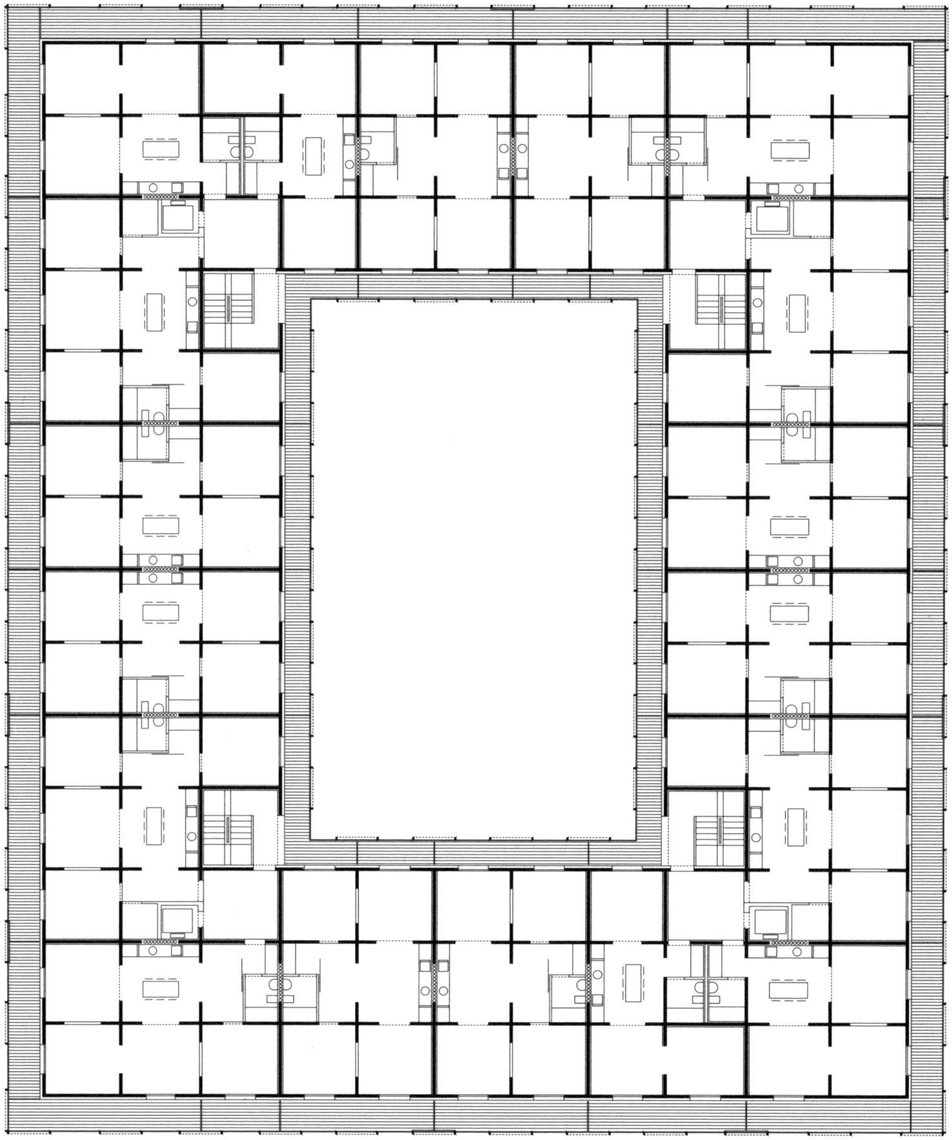

Typical floor plan

No. modules/spaces	6.5	6	4.5
Total surface area (m²)	90.00	82.50	63.00
Module (m²)	13.00	13.00	13.00
Intermediate space (m²)	16.50	20.32	11.00
No. homes	**20**	**47**	**18**

Architects: Marta Peris, José Manuel Toral. Team: Ana Espinosa, Leticia Soriano, Izaskun González, Guillem Pascual, Maria Megías, Cristina Porta, Miguel Bernat. Works management: Joan March i Raurell. Collaborators: Bernuz-Fernández Arquitectes (structures), ELETRESJOTA (installations), Societat Orgànica (environmental consultancy), Àurea Acústica (acoustics).
Location: Avinguda de la República Argentina, 21. Floor area: 12,815.55 m^2. Construction budget: €9,383,293.66

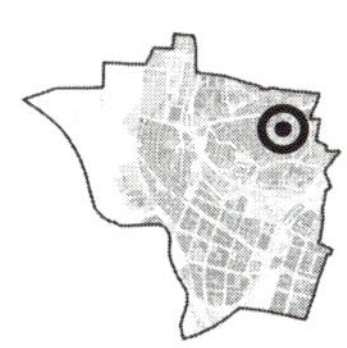

Site

Location

Molins de Rei

117 homes

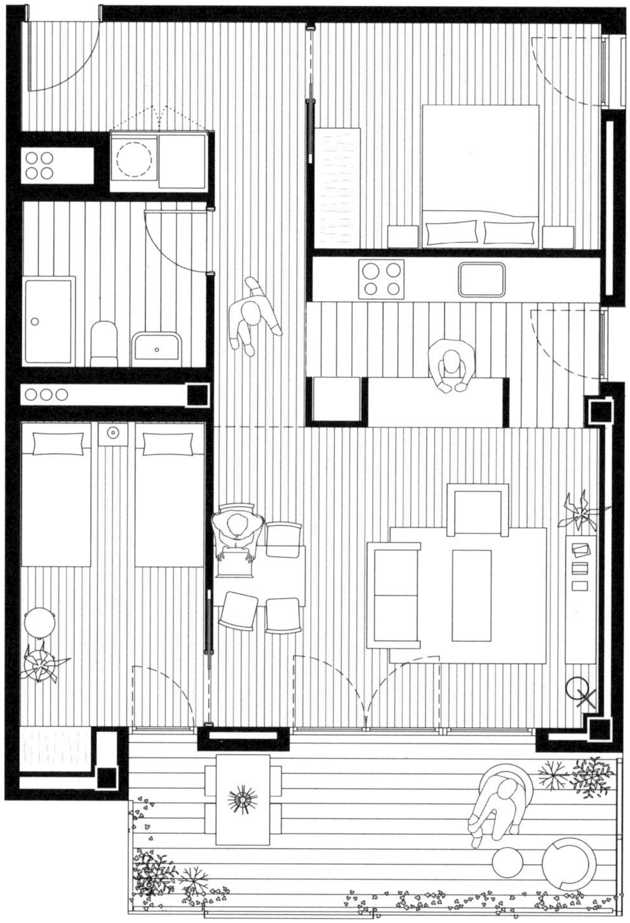

Housing unit type

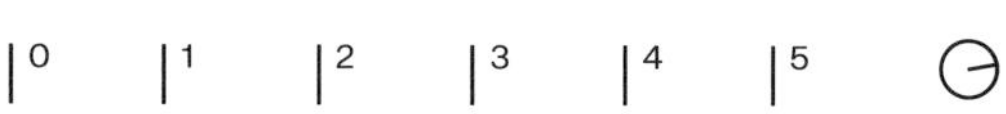

Open-plan kitchen

Intermediate social spaces

Housing unit type – Aggregation
The proposed typology sets out to increase the sense of space of the apartments by introducing diagonal views and interconnected spaces. The kitchen is integrated into the living-dining areas to avoid segregation of uses. The only fixed parts of the homes, the wet areas, are positioned in such a way to enable modification of the spatial layout over time. Generously sized terraces are proposed, up to 2.20 m deep, seen as outdoor rooms or extensions of the interior. The complex offers 56 homes with three bedrooms, 51 with two and 10 with one bedroom.
The overall complex of 117 homes has just eight communication shafts, which improves the relationship between useful surface and built surface, and increases the surface area of the homes. The project consists of four freestanding buildings, each with two communication shafts. The buildings facing Avinguda de la Mancomunitat and Carrer Puig d'Olorda have aggregations of four and five homes per floor, while the two buildings on Carrer Torrent d'en Benet comprise an aggregation of two through apartments per floor.

Urban context – Urban response
Sectoral planning for this street block proposed the construction of three volumes following the street layout in order to complete, alongside the existing buildings, a block that frees up the central space to house a landscaped area and a small municipal facility. The slope of Carrer Torrent d'en Benet, greater than 6.5%, made it advisable to fragment the volume that stands there to avoid the appearance of a staggered building. This improves the adaptation of the volumes to the slope of the street and the connection between the spaces at the centre of the street block and the landscaped public spaces around them.
The design and construction of the project was carried out in two phases. The development consists of a first phase with 56 homes intended for sale and a second phase with 61 homes intended for rent.

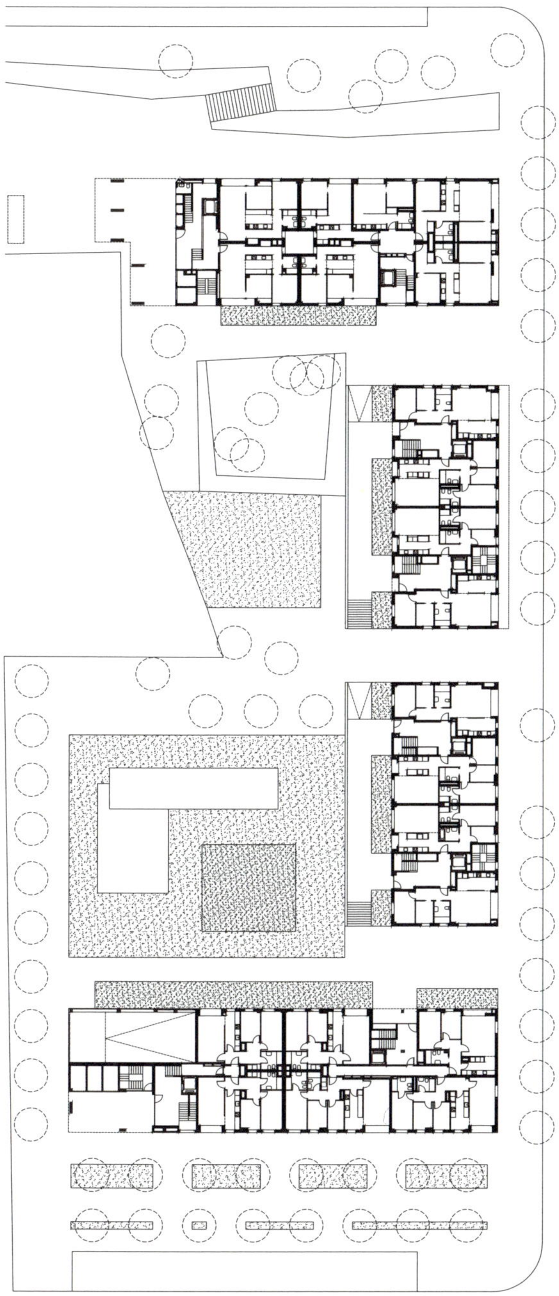

Ground floor plan

Communal space

The project aims to promote the use of the landscaped public space at the centre of the street block, which leads to the entrance foyers of the apartments. The idea is that this landscaped community space with a children's play area will provide a neighbourhood meeting place, facilitating routes between the homes and the surrounding streets.

Energy strategy

- Cross ventilation in practically all the typologies.
- Application of optimized insulation thicknesses to minimize unwanted energy losses and gains.
- Use of light colours in the most exposed horizontal planes, both roofs and pavements, to reduce the heat island effect.

Energy certification: A.
Phase I:
- Non-renewable primary energy consumption: A (26 kWh/m^2 year).
- Carbon dioxide emissions: A (4 kg CO_2/m^2 year).

Phase II:
- Non-renewable primary energy consumption: A (19 kWh/m^2 year).
- Carbon dioxide emissions: A (3 kg CO_2/m^2 year).

Materiality

Bearing in mind the volume of the buildings, it was decided to use bare masonry for the façades with non-uniform clinker-type bricks. The texture of the material and the combination of colours of the bricks and the mortar joints give the complex great expressivity. The choice of this material also guarantees the durability of the envelopes, with almost zero maintenance costs.
This traditional material has been used on site with a self-supporting system (GHAS), in which the bricks are supported directly by the crown of the foundation or metal dentils rather than the slabs of each floor, thereby preventing the usual pathologies caused by deformation of the structure. The stretches of brick in the façades pass whole in front of the floor slabs and are attached to the structure by stainless steel fixings to avoid horizontal movements. This system provides continuous thermal insulation of the façade, covering the edges of the slabs and avoiding thermal bridges.

Molins de Rei

117 homes

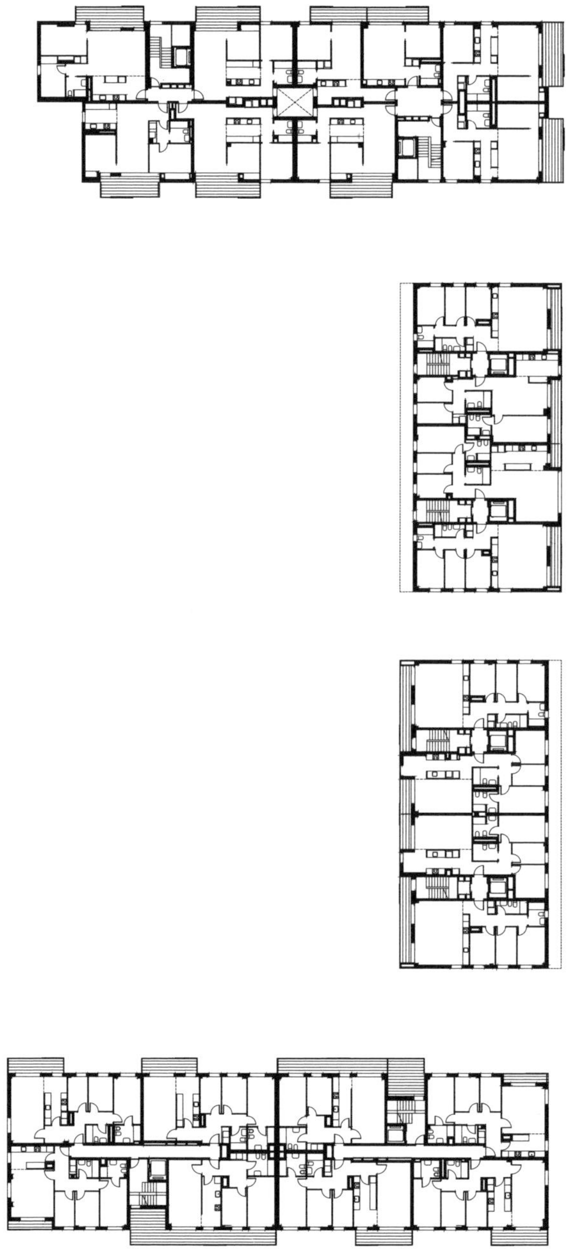

Typical floor plan

0 5 10 20 50

No. rooms	3	2	1
Total surface area (m^2)	80.48	72.05	49.15
Terrace (m^2)	6.45	10.75	7.50
No. homes	**55**	**52**	**10**

Architects: Joan Pascual, Ramon Ausió, Cristóbal Fernández. Team: Pilar Enjuanes, Javier Sanz, Manuel Salas, Júlia Viñeta, Mónica Braña. Works management: Ferran Pelegrina, David Prera (FPA). Collaborators: BAC Arquitectura e Ingeniería. Location: Passatge Mossèn Ignasi Mora Terrats, 2 / Carrer del Torrent d'en Benet, 1-3-5-7-9-11 / Carrer Puig d'Olorda, 4. Floor area: 11,980.43 m^2. Construction budget: €11,447,361.28

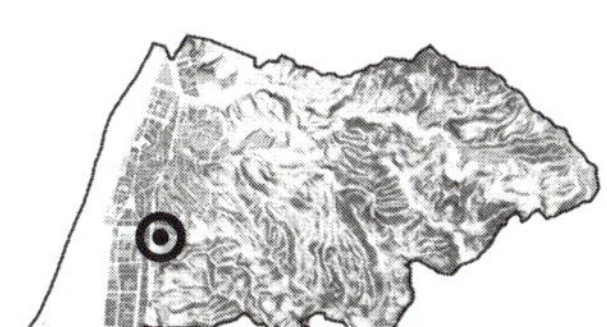

Site

Location

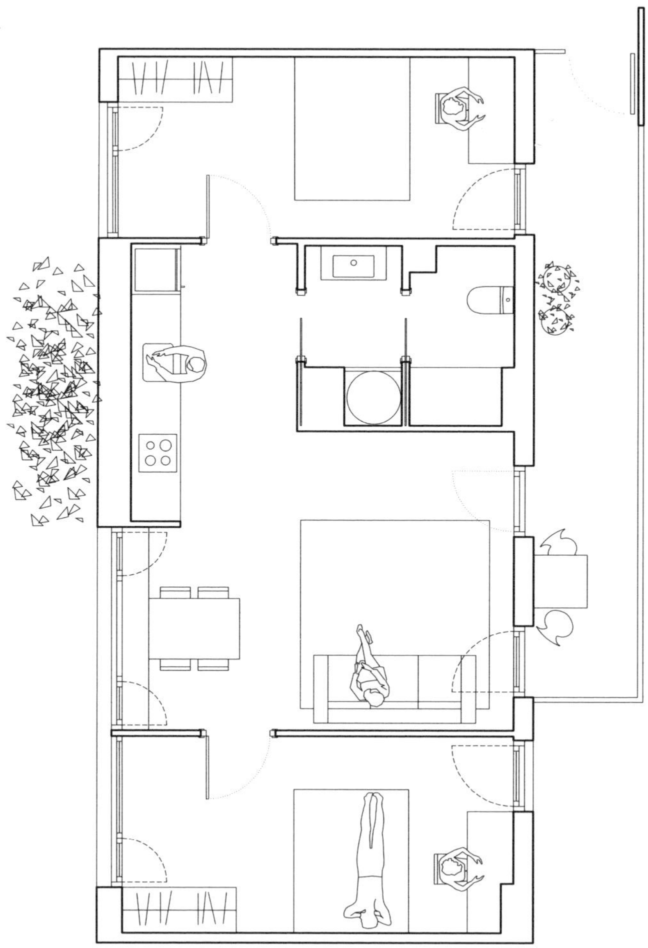

Housing unit type

Open-plan kitchen

Generic rooms

Interconnecting rooms

Intermediate climatic spaces

Intermediate social spaces

Housing unit type – Aggregation
The proposed typology brings together the living room, dining room and kitchen in a single through space that organizes the rest of the rooms in the apartment.
The spaces are designed to be versatile so that the various occupants can adapt them for their own personalized use.
The residential brief consists of 120 homes, of which 106 homes are two-bedroom, 10 are three-bedroom and four one-bedroom, grouped around two entrance ways. The building, in the form of two bars, has a bioclimatic atrium in its central part. Most of the homes are located in the wide bar in the south façade to harness the sunlight, and the rest of the apartments and the communication shafts are housed in the narrow north-facing bar.

Urban context – Urban response
The layout of the building is determined by the desire to turn the maximum number of homes to face sunlighting and give them park views. The brief is arranged around a central bioclimatic atrium that organizes the entrances and connects visually and environmentally with the park. The main entrance is situated in the east façade, overlooking Carrer Josep Vicenç Foix, like a large plant-filled hallway open to the landscape.

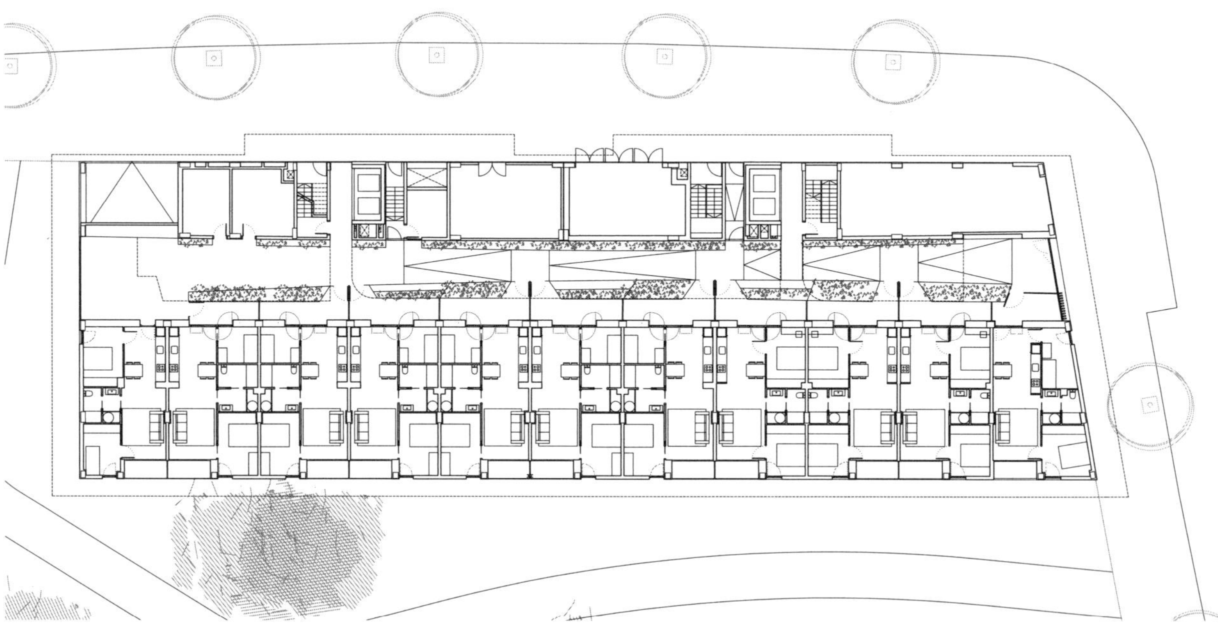

Ground floor plan

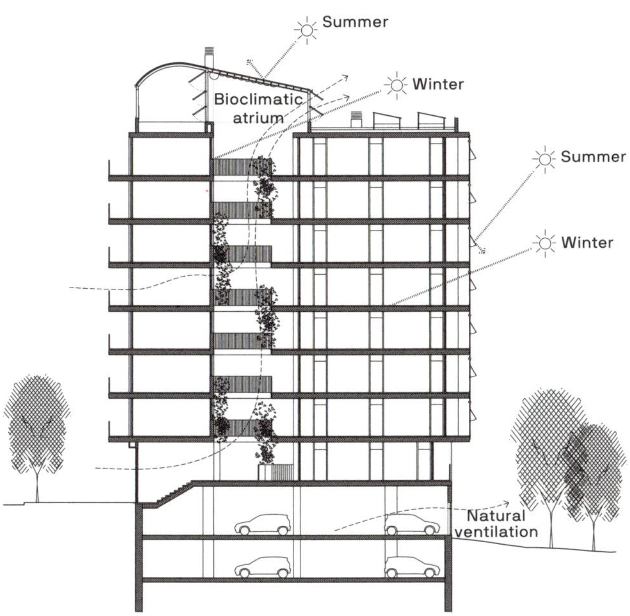

Bioclimatic section

0 5 10

Communal space
The brief is complemented by various communal spaces situated on the ground floor, in the end walls of the building on different floors, on two platforms overlooking the inner courtyard and on the roof. Their form and location allow the residents to carry out different activities according to their needs.

Energy strategy
- The central bioclimatic atrium serves to regulate the temperatures of the whole complex in both summer and winter.

Energy certification: A.
- Non-renewable primary energy consumption: A (19.1 kWh/m² year).
- Carbon dioxide emissions: A (3.5 kg CO_2/m² year).

Viladecans

120 homes

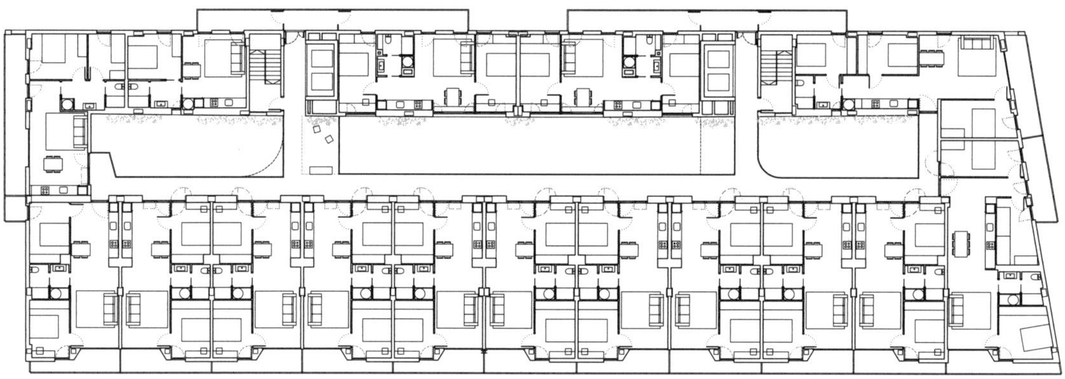

Typical floor plan

No. rooms	3	2	1
Total surface area (m^2)	79.53	57.91	42.51
Kitchen-living-dining room (m^2)	33.14	27.15	21.22
Terrace (m^2)	15.46	10.61	11.04
No. homes	**14**	**102**	**4**

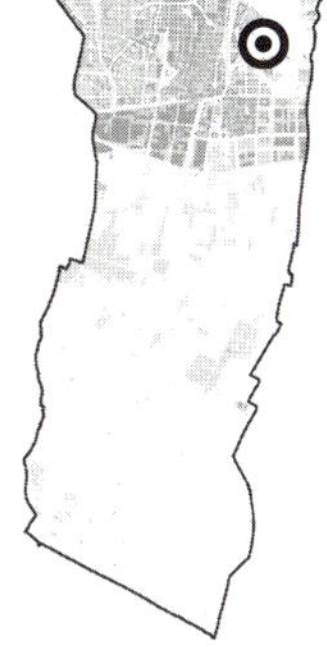

Site

Location

Architect: Isabel Rodon Bonet. Team: Enric Massip, Anna Suñe, Agustí Canadell, Laida Memba, Patrícia Gonzàlez, Nerea del Amo, João de Freitas. Works management: Francesc de Haro Macià, Francesc Xavier Aumedes Farré, Gemma Rius Macies (Arrevolt). Collaborators: Manuel Arguijo y Asociados (structures), AE-T Enginyeria (installations), Ivana Rossell (acoustics), Societat Orgànica (environmental consultancy), JPJ (BIM). Location: Avinguda de la Igualtat, 11. Floor area: 12,708.41 m^2. Construction budget: €11,110,793.65

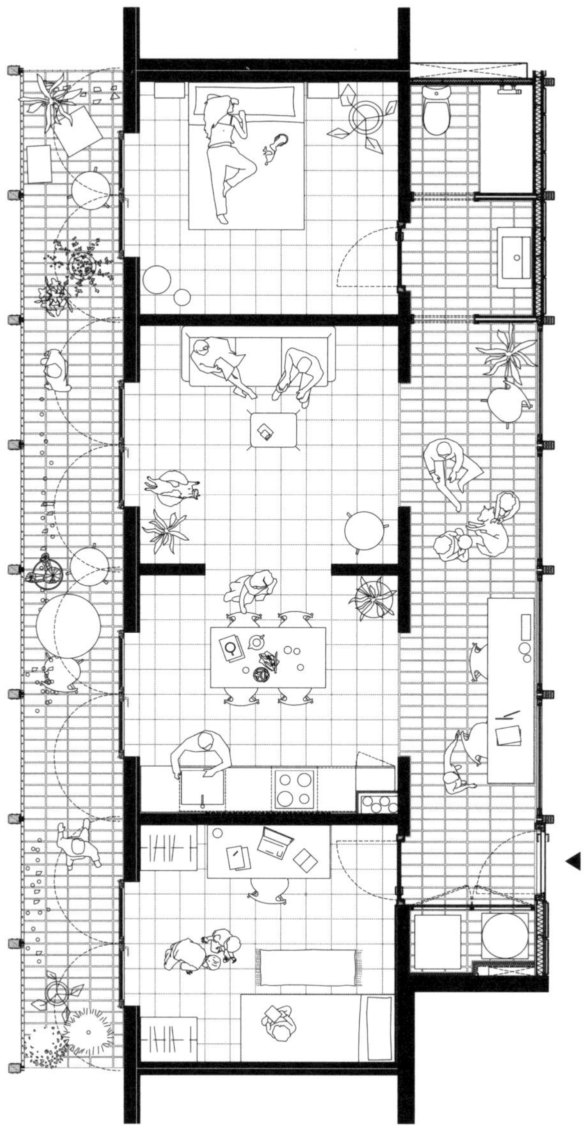

Housing unit type

Open-plan kitchen

Generic rooms

Interconnecting rooms

Intermediate climatic spaces

Intermediate social spaces

Housing unit type – Aggregation
The typological proposal, based on the continuous, linear aggregation of equal cells/modules (10.6 m^2) with no hierarchy, allows flexibility based on the characteristics of the space rather than the use. Each room is surrounded by transition spaces to the exterior: in the façade, a 1.5-m balcony; in the court, almost symmetrically, a gallery which, with its generous width of 1.70 m, enables circulation and offers the rooms complementary space; at the ends of the gallery are the toilet and bathroom, storage spaces and installations.
The homes are grouped in fours, two to either side of the stairs and lift shaft, situated in the inner court of the blocks; a total of eight cores that group together the 136 homes in the complex. The volume is built by means of a system of aggregation that maximizes the relations between living spaces and their surroundings. A continuous series of identical rooms follows the perimeter of each of the volumes, relating to the landscape via a generous terrace that also continues around the perimeter. Symmetrically to the terrace, the rooms are interrelated by a gallery that acts as a support and auxiliary space for conventional uses. The rings formed by terraces, rooms and galleries surround the inner courtyards, activating natural cross ventilation and providing all the homes with generous natural light.

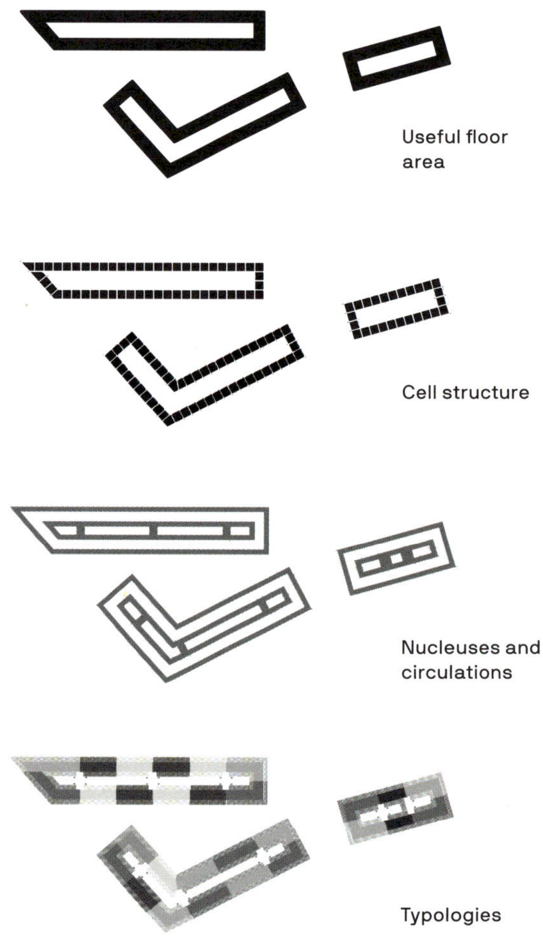

Diagrams

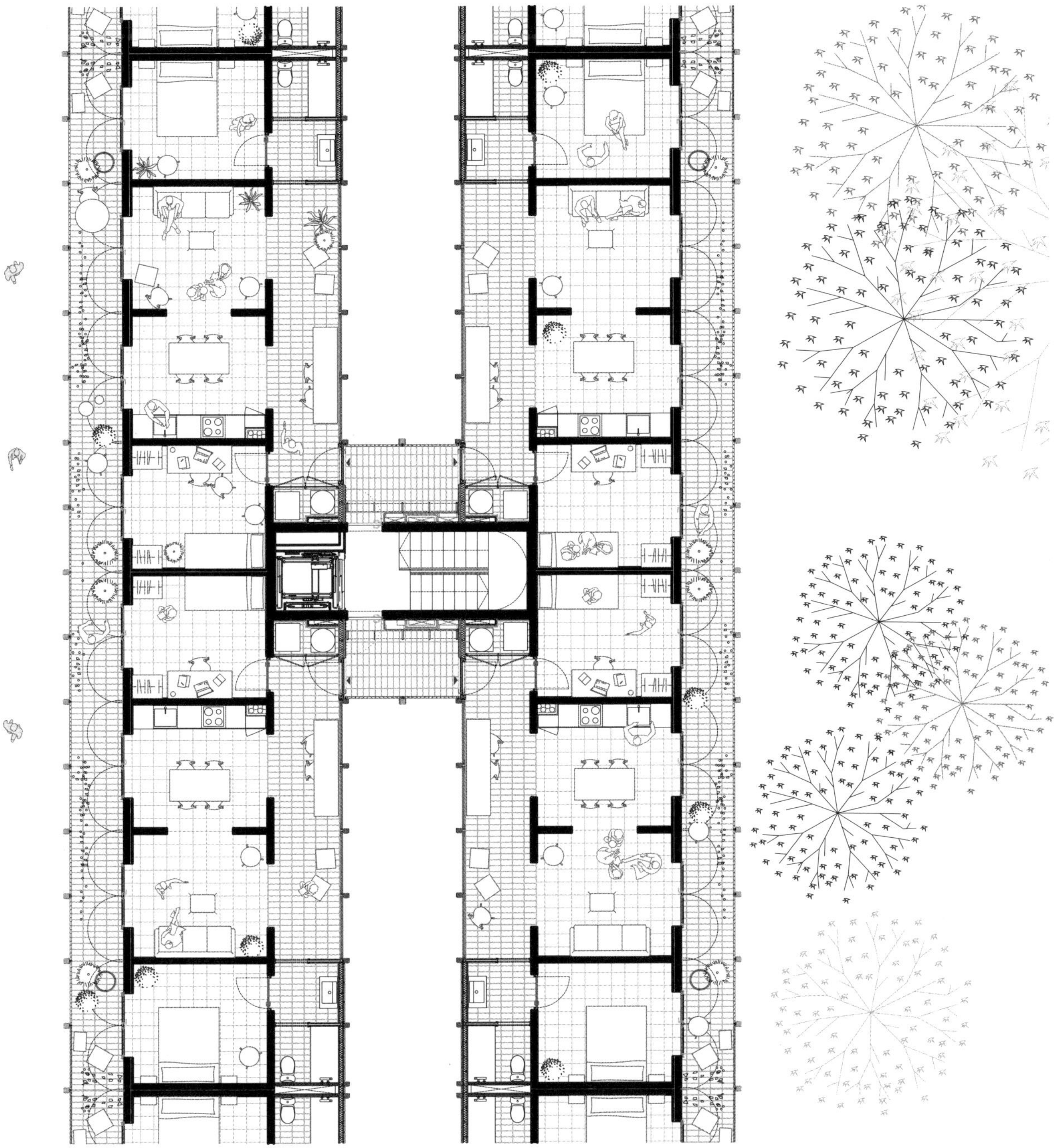

Aggregation floor plan

Urban context – Urban response
The arrangement of the volume according to planning encourages biological continuity between the Les Ferreres hill range and the Llobregat Agricultural Park; the building is completely surrounded by green spaces (Cim del Calamot, Masia de Can Ribes, Parc del Calamot and Plaça de les Tretze Roses). In this context of green continuity, the project aims to complement sea-mountain circulation with new routes that provide visual and biological continuity between the setting and the interior of the street block. The buildings, two linear blocks and one L-shaped comprising GF+4 and GF+5, are staggered to adapt to the plot's natural slope.
To promote the viability of a permeable garden with leafy trees, we house the car park in the projection of the building. The rest of the plot comprises draining surfaces that manage the natural water cycle and consolidate native vegetation.

Communal space
The big communal space is the garden at the centre of the street block, which is like a great foyer that provides access to the various stairways in the complex.
This strengthens the relationship between the residents and green space. There are two ways into the garden from the street. The main entrance, leading to two of the blocks, is a large double-height foyer with overhead daylighting that can be used to park bicycles and host community meetings. A path is built through the garden at the centre of the street block to get to the other, smaller building. The continuous terraces on the upper floors form a communal walkway to access the various stairways around the ground-floor garden.

Materiality
The project proposes a structure of screens and concrete slabs that directly participate in the spatial configuration, the materiality of the finishes and comfort based on inertia and cross ventilation. A repetitive series of screen walls shapes both the inside space of the rooms and the building's façade. The structural solution balances the projection, produces very short spans and optimizes the thickness of the walls and slabs. This materiality is complemented by laminated wooden door and window frames, and a series of uprights along the overhangs that form the terraces and inner courts with larch wood and climbing vegetation.

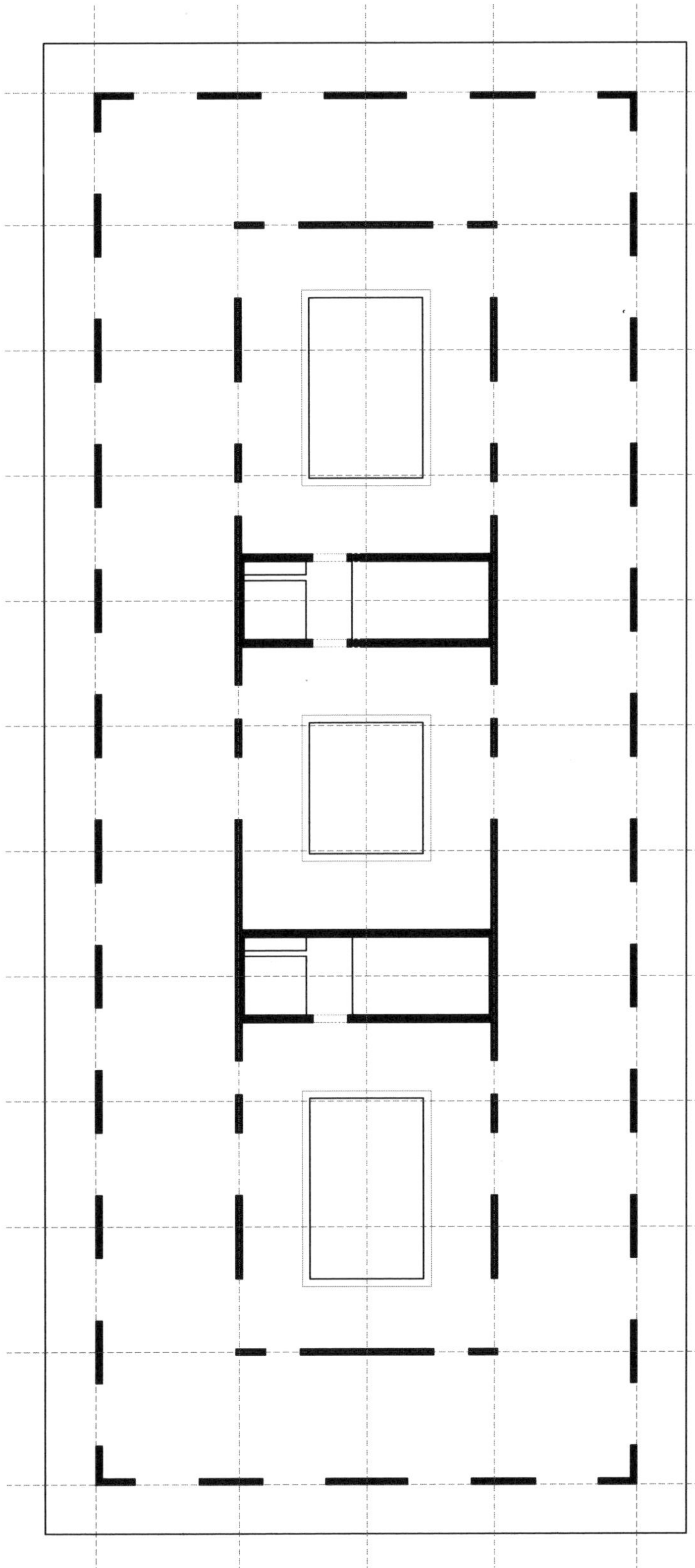

Structural floor plan

Energy strategy

- Cross ventilation in all the homes between the façade and the inner courtyards.
- High thermal inertia of the structure.
- The large openings guarantee a great deal of natural light, reducing electricity consumption.

The façades are protected from the sun's rays by the projections of the terraces and the wooden uprights that support climbing vegetation or roller blinds to complete sun control.

Energy certification: A.
Building A:
- Non-renewable primary energy consumption: A (24 kWh/m^2 year).
- Carbon dioxide emissions: A (4 kg CO_2/m^2 year).

Building B:
- Non-renewable primary energy consumption: A (26 kWh/m^2 year).
- Carbon dioxide emissions: A (4 kg CO_2/m^2 year).

Building C:
- Non-renewable primary energy consumption: B (28 kWh/m^2 year).
- Carbon dioxide emissions: A (4 kg CO_2/m^2 year)

Typical section

Section. Cross ventilation

0 1 2 3

136 homes

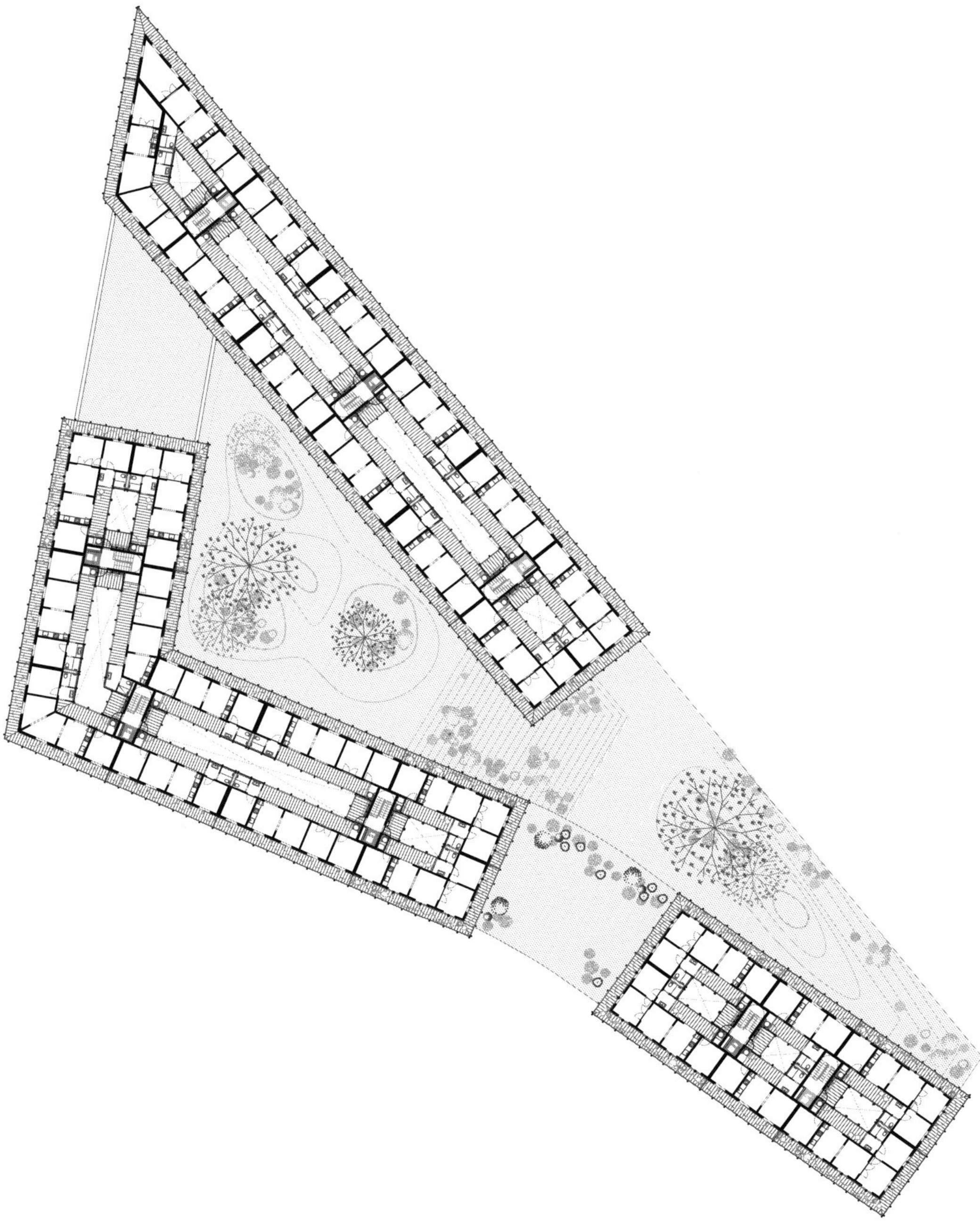

No. modules	5	4	3
Total surface area (m^2)	79,09	69,50	51,54
Module/cell (m^2)	10,60	10,60	10,60
Glazed balcony (m^2)	8,42	8,53	8,90
Intermediate space (m^2)	26,90	17,42	12,87
No. homes*	**58**	**52**	**8**

* Plus 18 homes on the ground floor

Complex plan

Architects: David Lorente, Josep Ricart, Xavier Ros, Roger Tudó. Team: Montse Fornés, Guillem Canudas, Néstor Morro, Nicolás Ortiz, María Espín, Meri Mensa, Eva Millán. Works management: Carles Bou. Collaborators: JFG Consultors (structures), Societat Orgànica (environmental consultancy), iA2 (acoustics), Oriol Vidal Ingeniería (installations), Barcelona Ingenieros (telecommunications), Bimetrical (BIM). Location: Passatge Marta Mata, 1-5 / Avinguda 8 de Març, 36 / Plaça de les Tretze Roses, 2-8. Floor area: 17,813 m². Construction budget: €13,137,507.39

Site

Location

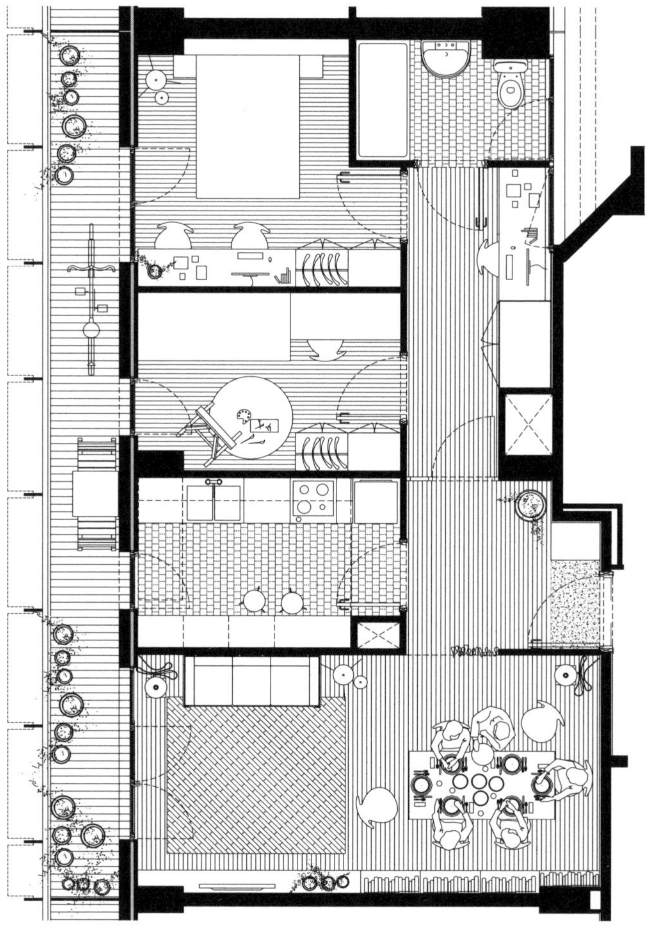

Housing unit type

Intermediate social spaces

Housing unit type – Aggregation
The organization of each home is linear, and the main spaces (living room, kitchen and bedrooms) are situated in the façade, giving onto a balcony. The service spaces (entrance hall, toilet and bathroom) are located on the inside, lit and ventilated via an inner court. The typologies vary: one bedroom (4); two bedrooms (53), three bedrooms (82) and four bedrooms (4).

The homes are grouped in fours, two facing east and two west in the linear blocks and, exceptionally, in twos, facing south, in the more organic volume. The stair and lift shafts and the light wells (seven in total) are located in the central strip of the volume in the linear blocks, and in the organic volume it has a compact, linear location in the centre.

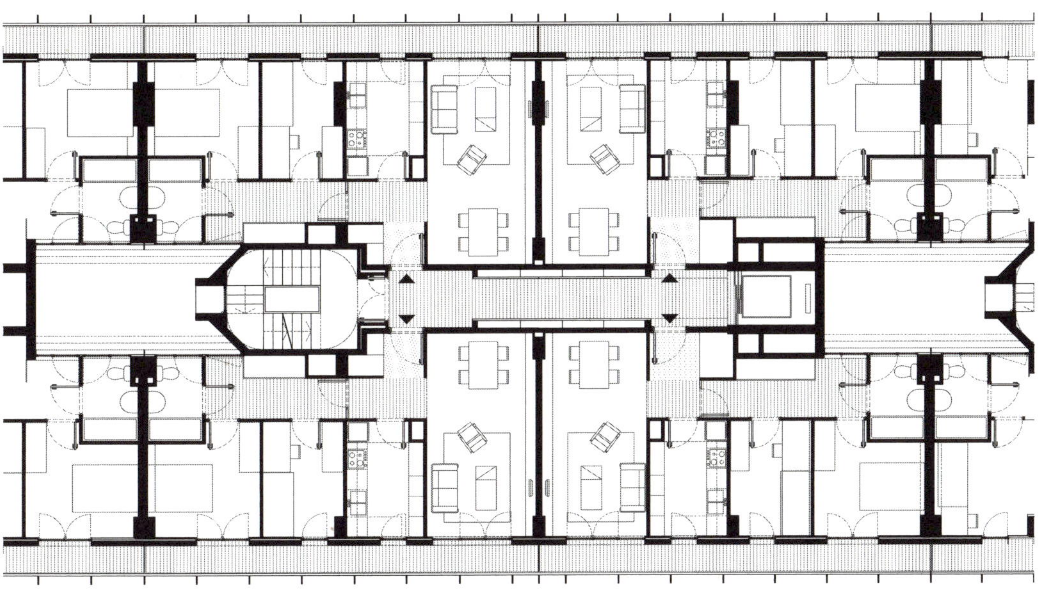

Aggregation floor plan

Urban context - Urban response

The proposal modifies the arrangement specified in the planning in order to improve lighting at the middle of the street block and the buildings, avoiding a dark north-facing façade and improving sunlighting for the homes at the corners. The proposed L-shaped volume is therefore broken down into a linear block and a smaller organic volume in the form of a ball joint. This new volume organizes the southern side of the free space, while giving the whole a more user-friendly image. The 143 homes are organized in four buildings: two linear volumes on the top edge of the plot, one on the lower edge, and a smaller one on the south side.

Communal space
The space at the centre of the street block is laid out as a large community garden with access to all the communication shafts of the buildings, maximizing sociability. The entrances to the buildings are customized and raised about 60 cm above the community space, creating an intermediate inside-outside space as a threshold.

Materiality
The linear buildings have a bare concrete plinth that levels out the unevenness of the site, and concrete end walls. The longitudinal façades comprise door and window frames in a basic module that responds to the different spaces and light-coloured, bare brick wall. These façades are lightened by long balconies that are defined by a metal substructure to support the protective sun awnings.
The organic volume has a large shadow at its base formed by the entrance and the porch to the garden, and a solid volume of bare brick in two alternating stripes of colour that accompany the change of scale. The balcony disappears to become an intermediate space within the volume.

Energy strategy
- There are no north-facing apartments.
- Shade elements are used to control sunlighting.
- The apartments have cross ventilation between the street façades and the inner courtyard, which acts as a thermal chimney.
- The central landscaped space allows water to seep into the soil.

Energy certification: B.
- Non-renewable primary energy consumption.
- Carbon dioxide emissions.

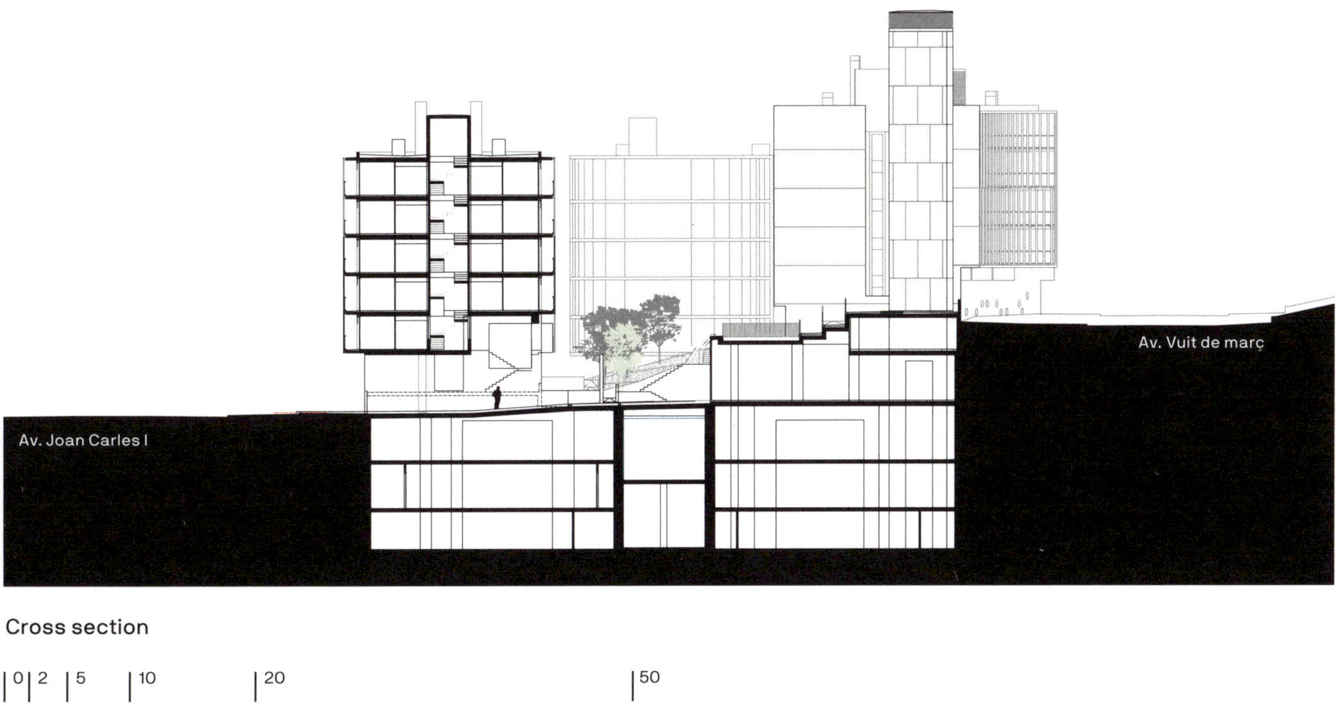

Cross section

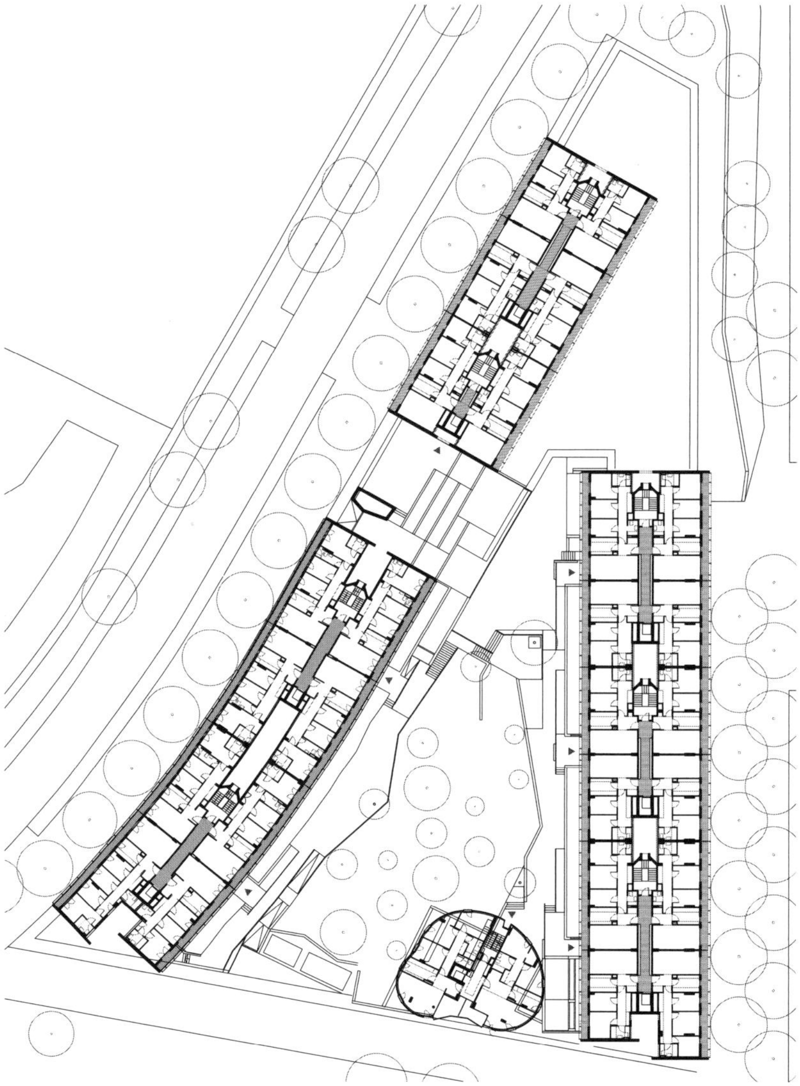

Typical floor plan

No. rooms	4	3	2	1
Total surface area (m^2)	99.86	88.90	66.05	55.30
Kitchen-living-dining room (m^2)	29.05	25.00	25.25	27.40
Balcony (m^2)	13.70	12.55	11.10	13.50
No. homes	**4**	**83**	**52**	**4**

Architects: Manuel Brullet, Alfonso de Luna, Jaume Piñol. Team: Mitra Modarressi, David Casadevall, Nil Brullet, Álvaro Valcarce, Volker Zimmermann, Roger Tremoleda, Laia Lara Sants, Bartolomé Olivares, Imma Domingo, Eva del Hoyo, Lali Daví, Wiliam Robison. Works management: Joan Ramón Soldevila, Lluís Llop (building engineers) Collaborators: Manuel Arguijo y Asociados (structures), Portell-Brunes Enginyers (installations).
Location: Avinguda Joan Carles I, 21-25. Floor area: 32,840.03 m^2.
Construction budget: €13,444,527.55

Site

Location

Competitions

2016—2021

Cornellà de Llobregat

Ideas competition to design a project for a social housing building, commercial premises and a facility in the PISA Cinema sector

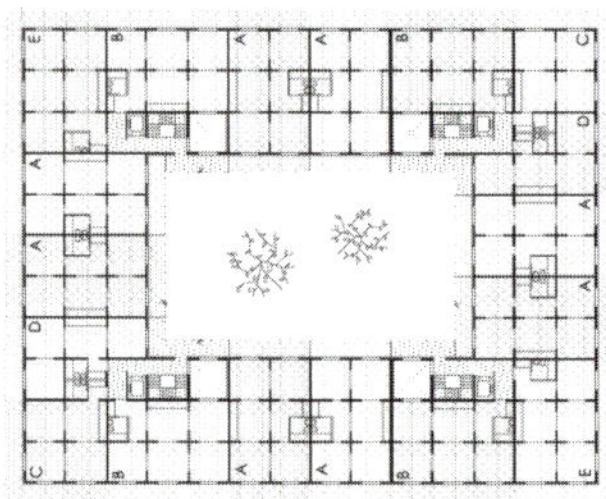

1

WINNING PROPOSAL (p. 210)
ENGAWA,
PERIS+TORAL ARQUITECTES

FIRST RUNNER-UP (1)
HYPNOTIC,
AV62 Arquitectos,
Pilar Calderón

SECOND RUNNER-UP (2)
LA DOBLE VIDA,
NUG Arquitectes

THIRD RUNNER-UP (3)
CIRCUMPISA,
Ibon Bilbao, Caterina Figuerola

FOURTH RUNNER-UP (4)
PISAMB PATI,
Conxita Balcells Associats

FIFTH RUNNER-UP (5)
KONIEC,
Bayona Valero Arquitectes,
Ensenyat-Tarrida Arquitectes,
Musquera Arquitectura

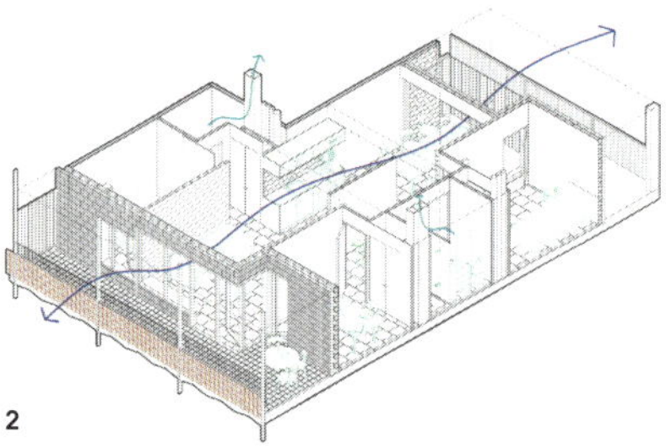

2

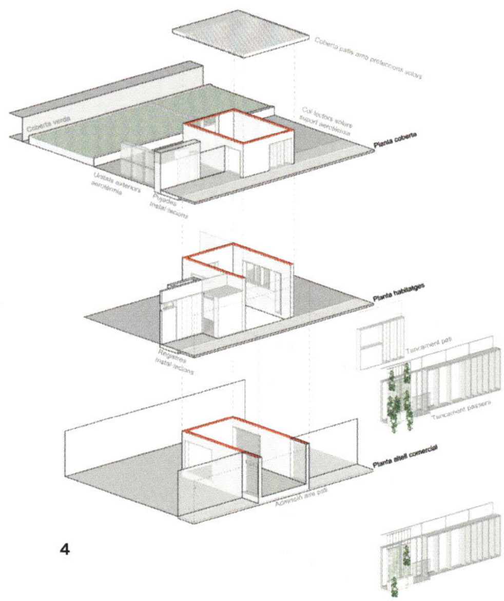

4

3

The winning proposal stands out both for its innovation in this housing type and for the extraordinary coherence between the structural, constructive, typological and energy efficiency systems. It skilfully distils the proposed formalisms and singularities, selecting what is strictly necessary for the project. This is an inspiring proposal.

5

Ideas competition for the planning proposal to define the specific modification of the Metropolitan Master Plan and the urbanization project in the Eix Bruc sector

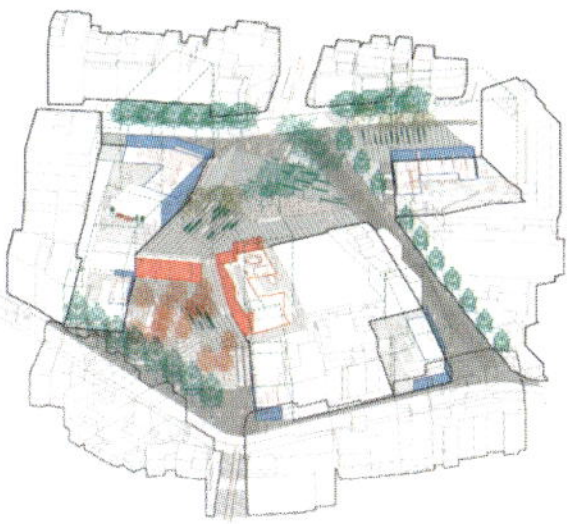

WINNING PROPOSAL PRINCIPAL (p. 36)
PINÇA URBANA,
Vora, Territori 24

Pinça Urbana successfully combines the necessary high density with the care required by the immediate setting, with a clear strategy for the integration of volumes that minimizes their effects on pre-existing construction.

UE1

WINNING PROPOSAL (p. 48)
ENTRAR PER PATIS,
narch

FIRST RUNNER-UP (1)
PUNTS DE SUTURA,
PERIS+TORAL ARQUITECTES

SECOND RUNNER-UP (2)
BRUC 123,
Jornet-Llop-Pastor Arquitectes

The apparent simplicity of both the volume and the aggregation was very positively rated. The jury highlighted the intermediate spaces proposed, which, due to their orientation, situation in the home and size, bring a very fitting degree of versatility to the homes.

UE2

WINNING PROPOSAL (p. 30)
JARDÍ D'HIVERN,
PERIS+TORAL ARQUITECTES

FIRST RUNNER-UP (3)
PLAÇA I JARDÍ,
AiB estudi d'arquitectes

The configuration of the building stands out, renouncing the chamfered corner and organizing three homes per landing with great qualities: optimal lighting and ventilation of the walkway and the homes, and a variable form factor depending on climatic conditions.

1

2

3

2016 Santa Coloma de Gramenet

UE 3

WINNING PROPOSAL (p. 36)
PINÇA URBANA,
Vora, Territori 24

FIRST RUNNER-UP (1)
PATI COBERT,
Pau Vidal Pont,
VIVAS ARQUITECTOS

SECOND RUNNER-UP (2)
TOT A LLOC,
Ibon Bilbao, Caterina
Figuerola, Marta Milà

The proposal resolves the difficulty of the plot and its orientation, and arranges the staircase landing in such a way that it becomes a flexible, potentially socializing space, while also optimizing the building's climatic functioning.

UE5

WINNING PROPOSAL (p. 66)
LES TRES TORRES,
Brullet de Luna

FIRST RUNNER-UP (3)
SALT,
Forgas Arquitectes

SECOND RUNNER-UP (4)
LORELEI,
Arriola & Fiol arquitectes

The jury highlights the efficiency of the aggregation system. Just two communication shafts organize the building and allow a simple distribution of up to four homes per landing, guaranteeing cross ventilation and a high degree of privacy for the homes from the entrance.

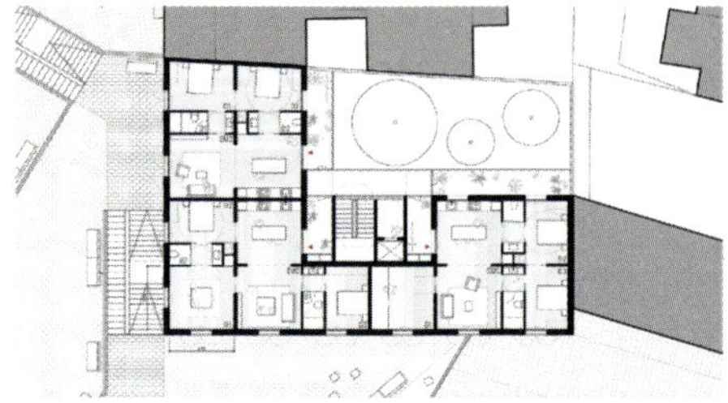

1

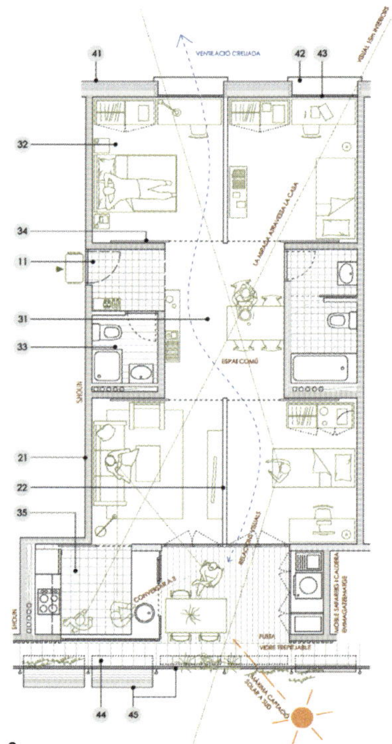

2

3

4

Ideas competition to draft a project for a social apartment building on plot B2.1 New neighbourhood of Can Ribes

1

2

3

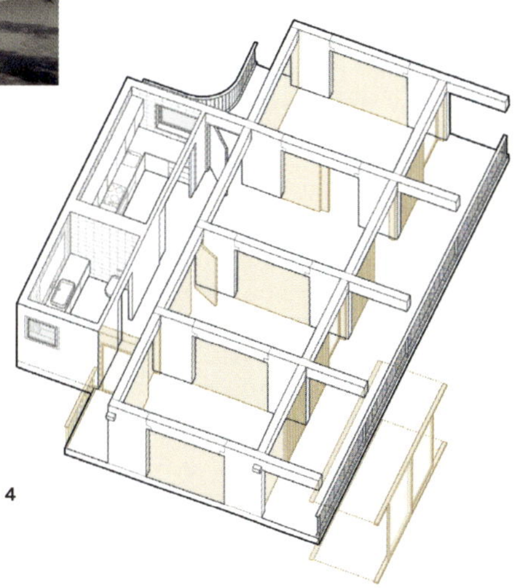

4

WINNING PROPOSAL (p. 238)
ENTRE,
HARQUITECTES

FIRST RUNNER-UP (1)
L'HABITACIÓ INTERMITJA,
FLEXOARQUITECTURA

SECOND RUNNER-UP (2)
FUSUMA,
Ileana Manea, Cristina Alsius Agustí, Joaquim Ortega Arévalo

THIRD RUNNER-UP (3)
SHÖJI,
Monica Escaño, Luis Lara

FOURTH RUNNER-UP (4)
A LA CARTA,
Estudi 08014

The winning proposal stands out both for the typological innovation of the proposed housing and for the extraordinary relationship of the parts with the immediate environment via intermediate spaces. The jury points out the quality of the aggregation and the functioning of the building, where all the rooms look out onto the landscape and all the typological variations are of the same quality in terms of size and position.

Sant Feliu de Llobregat

Ideas competition to draft a project for a social apartment building at 21-27 Carrer Anselm Clavé

WINNING PROPOSAL (p. 120)
GISCA,
MAIO

FIRST RUNNER-UP (1)
P4TI X CANTONADA,
Conxita Balcells Associats

SECOND RUNNER-UP (2)
ESPAIS INTERMEDIS,
FLEXOARQUITECTURA

THIRD RUNNER-UP (3)
ATRIUM,
Miquel Mas Arquitectes

FOURTH RUNNER-UP (4)
EMPATIA,
Ensenyat-Tarrida Arquitectes

The jury highlighted the winning proposal's capacity to neutralize openly hostile surroundings by means of a compact volume that is also user-friendly, lightweight and homogeneous. It values the democratic spirit, rationality, compactness and simplicity of the proposal that makes the most of the useful surface area and the interior layout to optimize the dimensions and connection of the parts, making for homes where the rooms are visually intertwined and create a feeling of space.

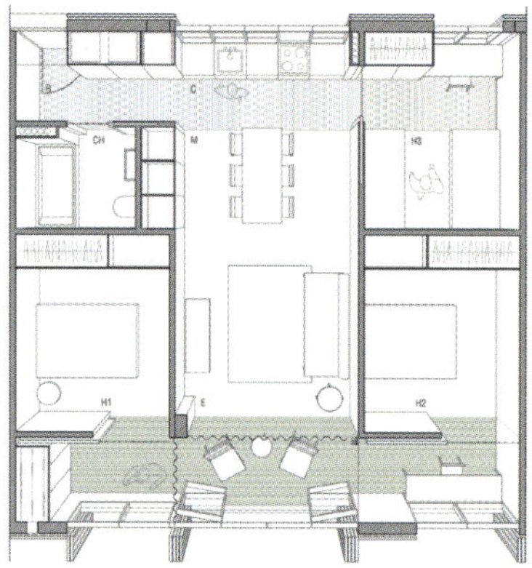

1

2

3

4

Ideas competition to draft a project for a social apartment building at 7 Carrer Carolina Catasus

1

WINNING PROPOSAL (p. 54)
VICENZA,
DATAAE — Xavier Vendrell

FIRST RUNNER-UP (1)
CUBO DE MENGER,
PERIS+TORAL ARQUITECTES

SECOND RUNNER-UP (2)
PINYOL,
HARQUITECTES

THIRD RUNNER-UP (3)
MARIA I CAROLINA,
Pablo Roel Herranz

FOURTH RUNNER-UP (4)
ESTANCES,
Pau Vidal Pont

The jury valued the proposal's search for the essential in these homes: housing and nature, with no added movements, accessories or personal traits. The open, extrovert image of the building and the strategic positioning of the rooms in contact with the outside spaces at the corners of the building, and the system of views and cross circulations maximize the value of the landscape context in which it is set.

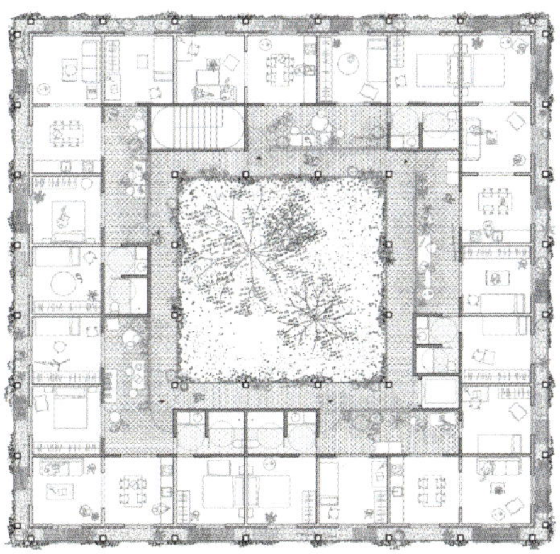

2

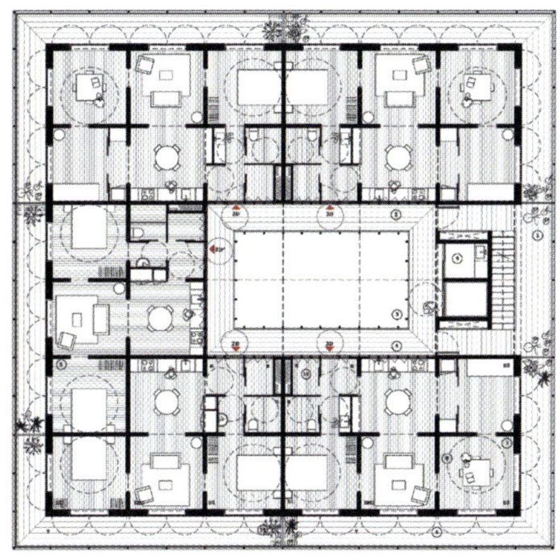

4

3

Sant Adrià de Besòs

Ideas competition to draft a project for a social apartment building on plot R19A of the La Catalana sector

1

WINNING PROPOSAL (p. 168)
VENTALL,
S.S.S.

FIRST RUNNER-UP (1)
DE QUATRE A NOU,
Ibon Bilbao, Caterina Figuerola

SECOND RUNNER-UP (2)
MEDITERRÀNIAMENT,
narch

THIRD RUNNER-UP (3)
REVERSIBLE,
Bayona Valero Arquitectes, Musquera Arquitectura

FOURTH RUNNER-UP (4)
TAMÍS,
Marmolbravo, Miel Arquitectos

The jury valued very positively the fact that the proposal is exceptionally generous and democratic but also addresses NZEB objectives in a simple, efficient way, returning to passive architecture. For its essence, on the site in question, the fact of transforming an available empty space into an emblematic terrace instead of a courtyard makes this proposal a winner.

2

3

4

Ideas competition to draft a project for a subsidized housing block on plot UE7 of the Bagaria-Alstom street blocks

WINNING PROPOSAL (p. 160)
DOS EN UN,
CASANOVAS, GRAUS, PÉREZ Arquitectes

FIRST RUNNER-UP (1)
ENROC,
Javier Hernani López, Carlos Albisu

SECOND RUNNER-UP (2)
CUADELLEÓ,
Jordi Truco Calbet, Sylvia Felipe Marzal

THIRD RUNNER-UP (3)
LA TARDOR,
Anna Codina

FOURTH RUNNER-UP (4)
ARTEMISA,
DDAP Arquitectes

The jury positively valued the delicacy and tenacity with which the building's response has been thought out, in terms of urban scale and in relation to the adjoining building, as well as its generosity towards the city. It also valued the appropriate degree of rationality, compactness and simplicity of this proposal, which seeks the best possible orientation on each level and for each home, and the best position for the living room to optimize sunlighting.

1

2

3

4

Montgat

Ideas competition to draft a project for a social apartment building in the Les Bateries-Turó del Sastre sector, plot 18A

WINNER
SEELE,
NITIDUS ARQUITECTES, Eduard Gutiérrez Colomé

FIRST RUNNER-UP (1)
MIRANT A MAR,
ESPINET/UBACH, Bajet Giramé

SECOND RUNNER-UP (2)
VIVET,
AV62 Arquitectos

THIRD RUNNER-UP (3)
LEBEN,
Carlos Valls Arquitectura, Álvaro Raventós Arquitectes

FOURTH RUNNER-UP (4)
VERD VERTEBRADOR,
Iván Egea Trujillo

The jury regarded this as a very functional, balanced proposal that optimizes the communal circulation spaces and atriums in such a way as to achieve the objectives of performance and efficiency. This favours the general criterion of economic viability, a fundamental aspect in rental developments.

1

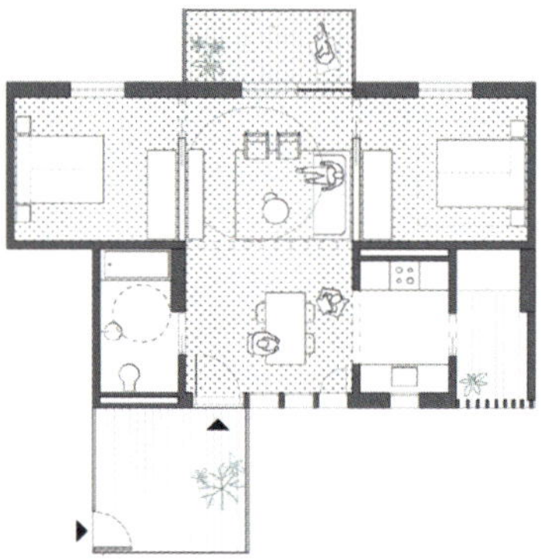

2

4

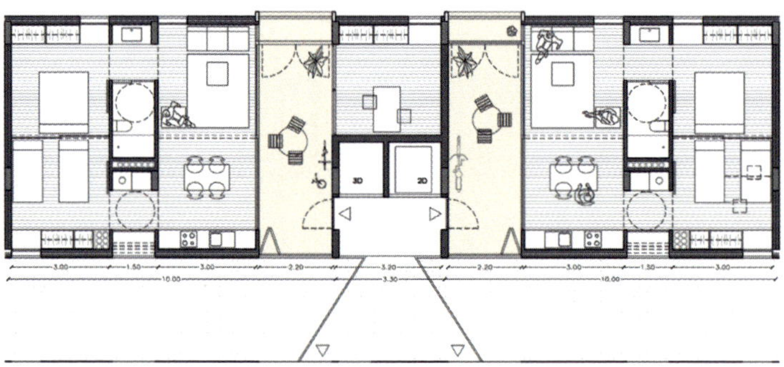

3

Ideas competition to draft a project for a social apartment building at the Les Bateries-Turó del Sastre sector, plot 18B

WINNER
ALEPH,
Pascual Ausió Fernández

FIRST RUNNER-UP (1)
MAR ENDINS,
VGV

SECOND RUNNER-UP (2)
KEKKAI,
Ileana Manea,
Cristina Alsius Agustí

THIRD RUNNER-UP (3)
HABITAR DES DEL CENTRE,
Cierto estudio, Franch Llonch

FOURTH RUNNER-UP (4)
XXXL,
Luis Lara Ambel,
Mónica Escaño Manso

The jury prioritized the rationality and professionalism of a proposal that perfectly synthesizes the site and proposes a building that is permeable to the park for citizens, but also sensible and intelligent in terms of the strategy of implementation, aggregation and typological resolution. The strategic positions of the kitchen and the bathroom clearly define the uses and enable the configuration of the home in a single space or in several undifferentiated, independent parts.

1

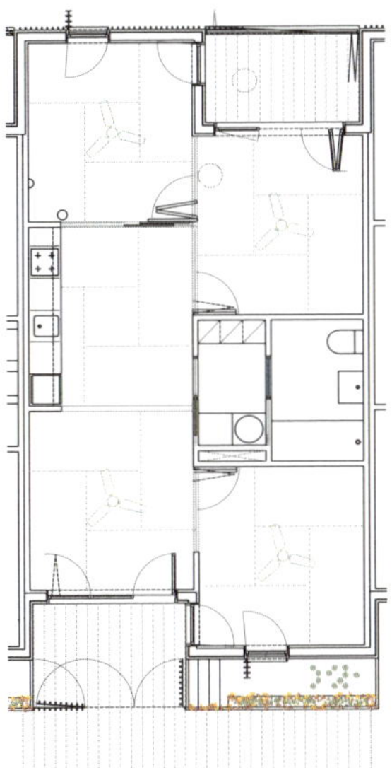

2

3

4

Sant Adrià de Besòs

Ideas competition to draft a project for a social apartment building on plot R16 of the La Catalana sector

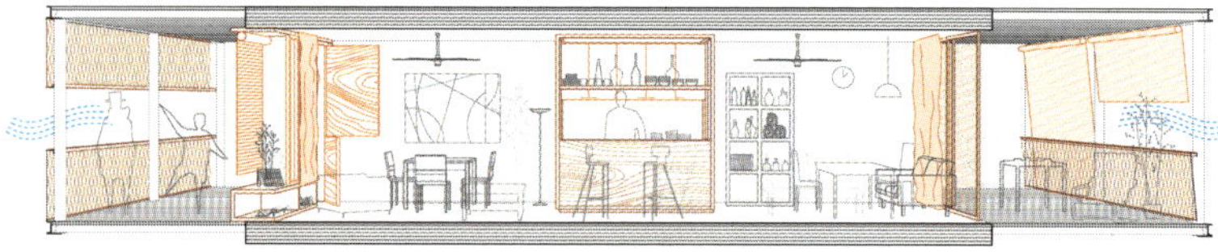

1

WINNER
56 DE BANDA A BANDA,
Ibon Bilbao, Caterina Figuerola

FIRST RUNNER-UP (1)
QUATRE,
Marmolbravo, Miel Arquitectos

SECOND RUNNER-UP (2)
PA(I)SSATGE,
Marta Milà, Erik Herrera

THIRD RUNNER-UP (3)
3 DE 3,
BOSCH.CAPDEFERRO

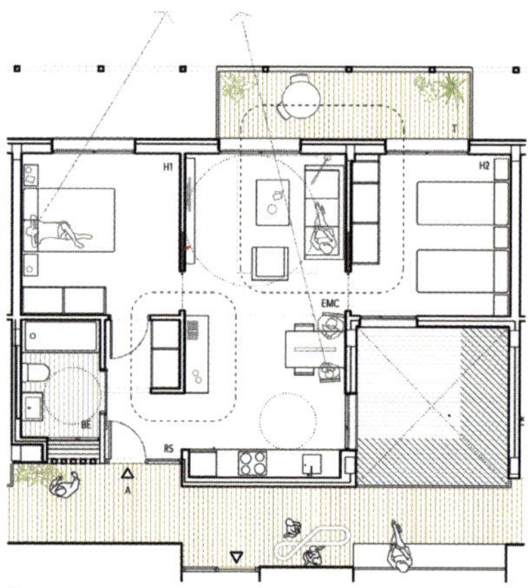

2

The jury positively evaluated the relationship between the metropolitan-scale façade and the domestic façade that fits into this complex environment, as well as the project's spatial generosity in giving the homes exceptional terraces that compensate for the decision of creating a through layout.

3

Ideas competition to draft a project for a social apartment building on plot R17 of the La Catalana sector

WINNER
CAPICUA,
FLEXOARQUITECTURA

FIRST RUNNER-UP (1)
HABITAT FLUVIAL,
Carles Enrich Studio

SECOND RUNNER-UP (2)
TRENCA LLUMS,
Ros-Sutries i Associats, Arquitectes, ikokora

THIRD RUNNER-UP (3)
ARCADIA,
Garcés-de Seta-Bonet Arquitectes

The jury valued the extroverted nature and spacious terraces of the proposal, which dialogues sympathetically with a complex environment and gives the homes their high quality. A very balanced proposal, in which the optimization of community circulation spaces and the versatility of the homes are some of the strong points that the jury unanimously valued in selecting it as a winning proposal.

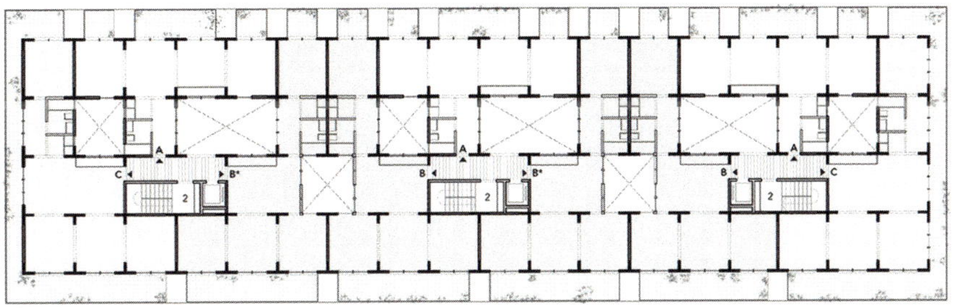

1

2

3

Ideas competition to draft a project for a social apartment building at 2, Plaça Duc Ahumada (Carsena-Mèxic planning intervention block)

WINNING PROPOSAL (p. 136)
KAUTTA,
PERIS+TORAL ARQUITECTES

FIRST RUNNER-UP (1)
CASES de CÓS,
Bajet Giramé

SECOND RUNNER-UP (2)
CUMBIERON,
Carlos Albisu Lledó, Frabic Office

THIRD RUNNER-UP (3)
MARIMONTANYA,
Feliu Llobet Arquitecte

FOURTH RUNNER-UP (4)
PLAÇA,
Un Parell d'Arquitectes

The jury highlighted how emptying out the corner of the building extends the street layout of Carrer Ciutat Reial and creates a new sea-mountain connection, which will become necessary. This cutout in the volume not only picks up the layout of its surroundings, it also improves the sunlighting of the homes situated at the corner.

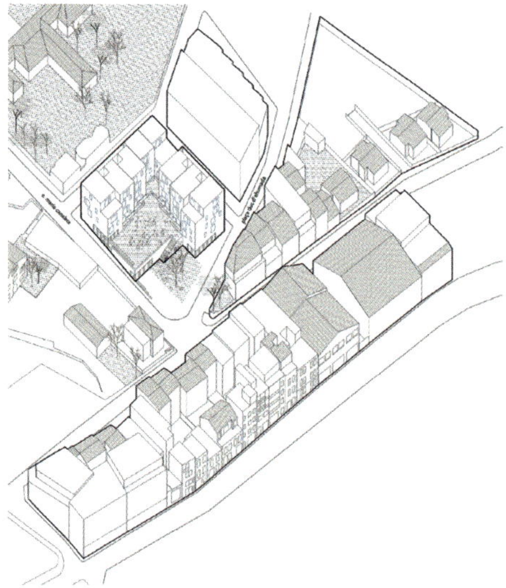

1

2

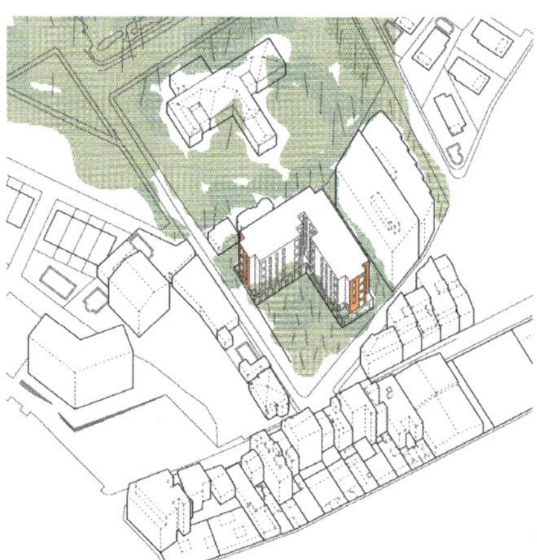

3

4

Ideas competition to draft a project for a social apartment building at 5, Carrer d'Itàlia (PAU IIIa Centre)

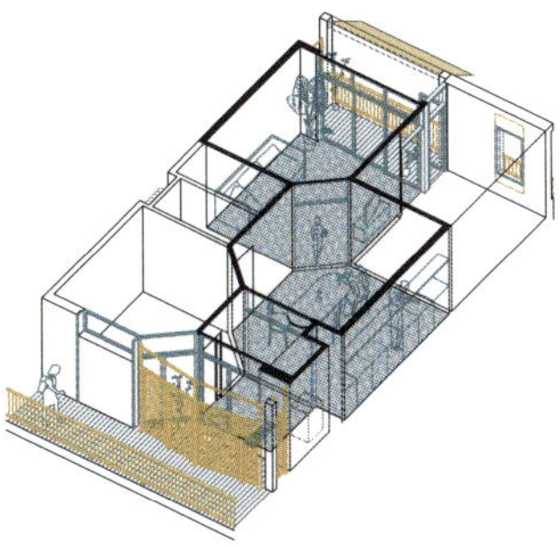

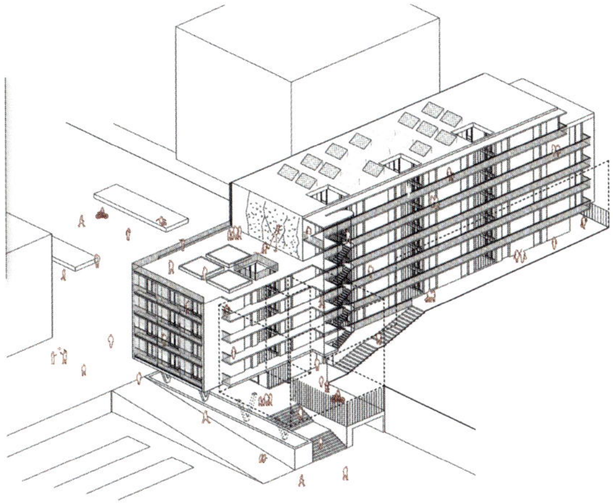

1

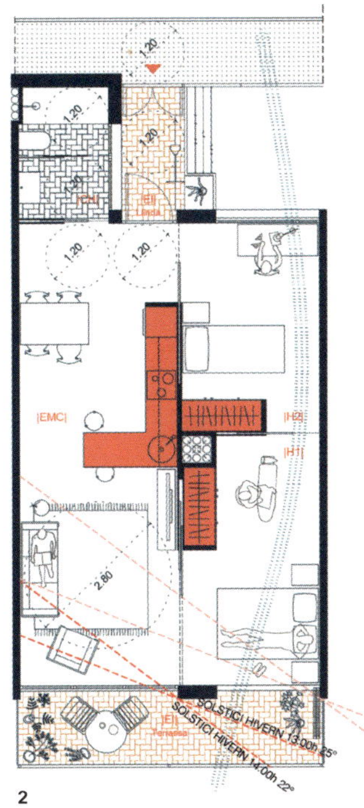

2

WINNING PROPOSAL (p. 184)
KITCH·ROOM,
Cierto Estudio, Franc Llonch

FIRST RUNNER-UP (1)
LIFE,
Pablo Roel Arquitectura

SECOND RUNNER-UP (2)
PLE DE +,
Franc Fernández Arquitectura, Estudi Mars

THIRD RUNNER-UP (3)
TRI CA PA,
Calderon Folch Studio

FOURTH RUNNER-UP (4)
GIRA-SOL,
Ros-Sutries i Associats, Arquitectes, ikokora

3

In its selection of the winning proposal, the jury prioritized its strategy of implantation. In this case, the aim is to occupy as much of the perimeter of the plot as possible to compact the building and promote the courtyard, giving it its own entity and personality. This is a singular project with great potential, based on democratic, rational values.

4

Castelldefels

Ideas competition to draft a project for a social apartment building in the discontinuous sector of Carrer Pietat, Avinguda Manel Girona and Avinguda Primer de Maig, plot H1

WINNING PROPOSAL (p. 190)
HALEPENSIS,
Carles Enrich Studio

FIRST RUNNER-UP (1)
6X8 & 7X7,
Calderon Folch Studio

SECOND RUNNER-UP (2)
DIVERSITAT,
narch

THIRD RUNNER-UP (3)
CASTELL de RELS,
Oriol Valls Guinovart, Izaskun González Barredo, Ramon Valls Ortiz

FOURTH RUNNER-UP (4)
LA GALERIA,
SUMO Arquitectes

The jury valued the proposal's perfect synthesis of the site for minimal impact and its integration into the surroundings of the castle. It aims to avoid excessive solidness and values the natural and the heritage environment by breaking down the volume of two compact buildings, making the project permeable to the park for citizens, but also practical and intelligent in terms of aggregation and typological resolution.

1

2

3

4

Ideas competition to draft a project for a social apartment building at 2, Carrer Jaume Balmes, plot UA2a

WINNING PROPOSAL (p. 42)
ADARVE,
AV62 Arquitectos, Calderon Folch Studio

FIRST RUNNER-UP (1)
XARRANCA,
Pablo Joel Herranz

SECOND RUNNER-UP (2)
QUE PASSI L'AIRE,
Oikosvia Arquitectura

THIRD RUNNER-UP (3)
CARXOFA,
Arantxa Manrique Arquitectes

FOURTH RUNNER-UP (4)
VILAHAUS,
Argepro

The jury rated very positively the skilful resolution of the difficult transition between the arrangement permitted on Passeig Marina and Carrer Jaume Balmes, clearly intertwining the two volumes. The building maximizes the possibilities of the site and generates two different universes, the domestic and communal in the inner garden, and, outside, a more urban character, with specific openings.

1

2

3

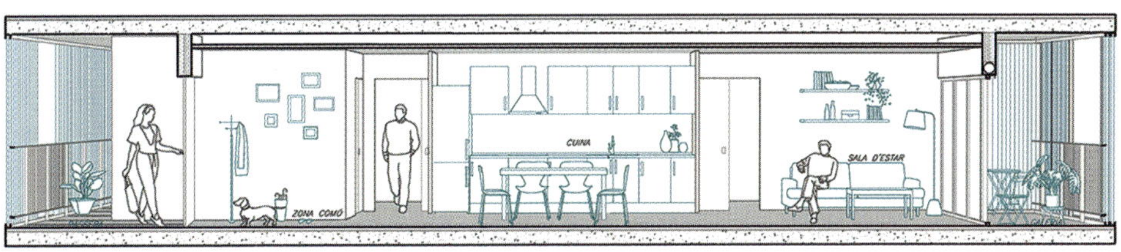

4

2021 Molins de Rei

Ideas competition to draft a project for a social apartment building on plot R10 in the Les Guardioles sector

WINNING PROPOSAL (p. 154)
BLOK50x15,
Carlos Valls Arquitectura,
AAAR Arquitectes

FIRST RUNNER-UP (1)
INDIVIDUAL + COMPLEX,
MIR & Ituarte

SECOND RUNNER-UP (2)
OHOHOHOHOH,
PLYSTD

THIRD RUNNER-UP (3)
51 A LA RIERA,
ikokora

FOURTH RUNNER-UP (4)
153HABITACIONS,
ABAA Arquitectura,
Albert Brito Ferraz

The winning proposal stands out for the formalization of a neutral block, with a single communications shaft and access via a walkway in the northeast façade, giving the living areas of all the homes the best orientation. The resulting typology is noteworthy for the versatility of the undifferentiated rooms. The jury highlighted the generous space of the exterior room, almost three metres deep.

1

2

3

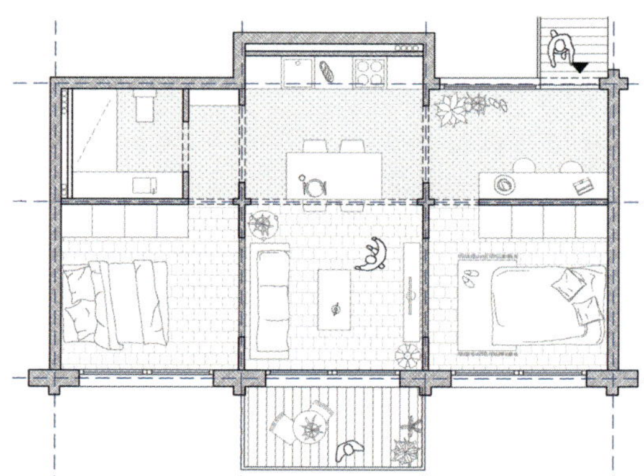

4

Ideas competition to draft a project for a social apartment building on plot R13 in the Les Guardioles sector

WINNING PROPOSAL (p. 86)
SUASTI,
METRONOM

FIRST RUNNER-UP (1)
96HABITACIONS,
Pablo Roel Herranz

SECOND RUNNER-UP (2)
QUATREEMESUNAMOLINS,
CASANOVAS, GRAUS, PÉREZ Arquitectes

THIRD RUNNER-UP (3)
MOLINS.01OCT,
GMG Plans I Projectes

The jury highlighted the proposal's skilful central arrangement of communal spaces, and the resulting clarity and compactness of the corner homes, with clear layouts and no corridors. This allows maximum use of the available surface area and a large multifunctional terrace-glazed balcony that gives the design character and identity in every sense.

1

2

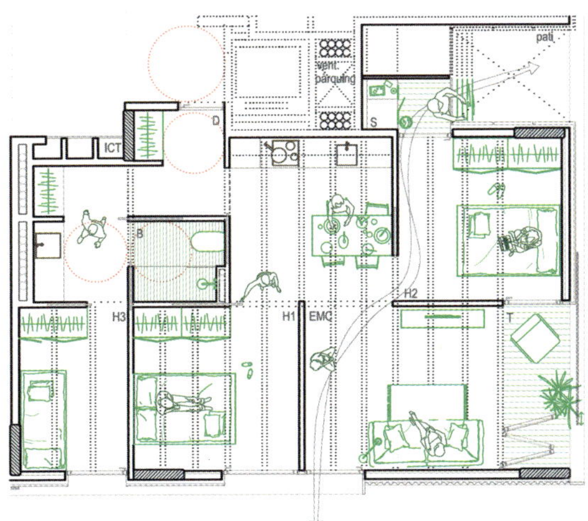

3

Ideas competition to draft a project for a social apartment building on plot 25+26 in the Llevant sector

WINNING PROPOSAL (p. 232)
VILADEMETER,
Rodon Arquitectes

FIRST RUNNER-UP (1)
WABI SABI,
PERIS+TORAL ARQUITECTES

SECOND RUNNER-UP (2)
DOS PER TRES 5,
Alex Gallego Urbano, Jordi Adell Roig, David Tapias Monné, Gerard Puig Freixas

THIRD RUNNER-UP (3)
SOL D'HIVERN,
Yaiza Terré, Pau Vidal

FOURTH RUNNER-UP (4)
MINAMICANS,
Joaquim Ortega Arévalo

The jury highlighted the fact that the layout of the project ensures good sunlighting for more than 85% of the homes. It highlighted the proposal as the most balanced and the one that makes the most of the plot conditions. It positively valued the incorporation of an alternative layout proposal, with an increase in homes in the end walls without altering their volume or built surface.

1

2

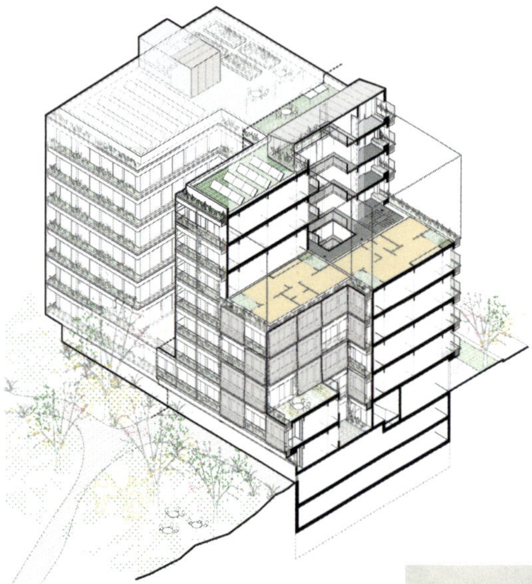

3

4

Ideas competition to draft a project for a social apartment building on plot HD2 in the Saló Central sector

WINNING PROPOSAL (p. 148)
XARRANCASANTBOI,
FLEXOARQUITECTURA

FIRST RUNNER-UP (1)
IT.ISNICE.TODAY.SANT.BOI,
narch

SECOND RUNNER-UP (2)
RETI,
Nogué Onzain López Arquitectes

THIRD RUNNER-UP (3)
PAREILLE,
Roger Such Sanmartín

FOURTH RUNNER-UP (4)
06CAPES,
SUMO Arquitectes

The jury valued this compact building design that is sensitive to the environment and oriented southeast, where the top three floors are emptied out to promote sunlighting and ventilation of the homes, also creating a large communal terrace. The jury positively valued the position of the living rooms at the corner, giving them a dual orientation.

1

2

3

4

Awards

Cornellà | 85 homes | 2017–2021 | PERIS+TORAL ARQUITECTES

Construmat Award, 2024
Special Prize, Asturiana de Zinc. Premios ATEG, 2023
Silver Medal. Premio Italiano Architettura Sostenible Fassa Bartolo, 2023
Outstanding work. IV Mostra d'Arquitectura Catalana, 2023
Finalist. EUmies Awards, 2022
Spanish Architecture Prize. Premios Arquitectura CSCAE, 2022
Prizewinner. Eduwik Architecture Excellence Awards, 2022
Construction Prize. Egurtek, 2022
Gold Medal. Best Architects Award, 2022
Collective Housing Prize. Best Architects Award, 2022
Best Collective Housing of the Year. Future House Awards, 2022
Honour Prize. Wood Design & Building Award, 2021-22
Premio Europeo di Architecttura Matilde Baffa Ugo Rivolta, 2021
First Prize. Premio MAPEI a la Arquitectura Sostenible, 2021
Collective Housing Prize. The Plan Award, 2021
Jury's Favourite in Architectural Design - Social Housing. BLT Built Design Awards, 2021
Best of Best, collective housing. Architecture MasterPrize AMP, 2021
Ex aequo award for innovation in construction. Premis Catalunya Construcció 2021
Best multi-family housing architecture project. Premios Arquitectura Plus by Daikin, 2021 - Habitatge plurifamiliar 2021
Opinion Prize. FAD Arquitectura, 2021
Prizewinner. XV Bienal Española de Arquitectura y Urbanismo, 2021
Best Residential Construction Project. Premios NAN, 2021
Finalist. BIGMAT Awards, 2021

Gavà | 136 homes | 2017–2022 | HARQUITECTES

Shortlisted. EUmies Awards, 2024
Premio Europeo di Architecttura Matilde Baffa Ugo Rivolta, 2023
Best Sustainable New Build. Premis AVS, 2023
Prizewinner. XVI Bienal Española de Arquitectura y Urbanismo, 2023
Ex aequo Prize, IX Premios de Arquitectura Ascensores ENOR, 2023
Opinion Prize. FAD Arquitectura, 2023
Finalist. FAD Arquitectura, 2023
1st Runner-up. Premis El Temps de les Arts, 2023
Outstanding work. IV Mostra d'Arquitectura Catalana, 2023

Montgat | 39 homes | 2009–2022 | DATAAE — Xavier Vendrell

Finalist. Premios Arquitectura CSCAE, 2022

Montgat | 40 homes | 2009–2017 | Isabel Bennasar

Outstanding work. Mostra d'Arquitectura Catalana, 2017

Sant Boi de Llobregat | 79 homes | 2009–2020 | Estudio Herreros — MIM-A

Shortlisted work. EUmies Awards, 2022
Prizewinner. FAD Arquitectura, 2020
Opinion Prize. FAD Arquitectura, 2020
Finalist. XV Bienal Española de Arquitectura y Urbanismo, 2021

Sant Feliu de Llobregat | 34 homes | 2018–2022 | MIM-A

Special mention, Millor Rehabilitació Funcional. Premis Catalunya Construcció, 2023
Special mention, New European Bauhaus. European Award AHI (Architectural Heritage Intervention), 2023
Outstanding work. IV Mostra d'Arquitectura Catalana, 2023
Shortlisted work. Premios Arquitectura CSCAE, 2022

Sant Feliu de Llobregat | 40 homes | 2018–2023 | MAIO

Shortlisted. EUmies Awards, 2024
Best Sustainable New Build. Premis AVS, 2024

IMPSOL Team

List of employees of the Metropolitan Institute of Land Development and Property Management (IMPSOL)

CHIEF EXECUTIVE OFFICER
Ramon M. Torra i Xicoy

MANAGING DIRECTOR
Amadeu Iglesias i Unzué

TECHNICAL COORDINATOR
Josep M. Borrell Bru

HEAD OF CONSTRUCTION SERVICE
José Antonio Sánchez Rincón

HEAD OF ECONOMIC AND FINANCIAL SERVICE
Isabel Calles Martín

HEAD OF ADMINISTRATIVE LEGAL SERVICE
Àlex de la Torre Sánchez

HEAD OF PROCESS CONTROL AND MANAGEMENT SERVICE
Josep Ramon Murillo Anzano

HEAD OF MANAGEMENT OFFICE
Marta Alarcón Puerto

HEAD OF WORKS SECTION I
Daniel Rangel Navarro

HEAD OF WORKS SECTION II
Montse Jané Franch

HEAD OF AFTERSALES SECTION
Remei Granados Pérez

HEAD OF BIM OFFICE
Rosa M. Cano Santander

HEAD OF ADMINISTRATIVE OFFICE
Rafael Ríos Fernández

HEAD OF COMMERCIAL OFFICES
Dolors Martínez Herrera

MANAGEMENT SECRETARY
Mónica Hidalgo Angulo

ARCHITECTS
Yolanda Larrubia Garcia
Xavier Gracia Marcos

BUILDING TECHNICIANS
Elisabeth Torilo Moyano
Macià Parés Grau

DRAFTING SPECIALISTS
Marta Lázaro Sanjuan
Jordi Sánchez Monteagudo

SENIOR ECONOMIC MANAGEMENT TECHNICIANS
Laie Estasio Solé
Carlos Morales Hernández
Aleix Caminal Bobet

SENIOR LEGAL TECHNICIANS
Anna Zhukova Guz
Raquel Amor Llurba

SENIOR ADMINISTRATIVE MANAGEMENT TECHNICIAN
Anna Piqué Puchercós

ADMINISTRATIVE ASSISTANTS
Dulce M. Peña Mateo
Judith Sansó Antoli
Anabel Sánchez Acosta
Patricia Ezquerro Ortiz
Yolanda Corpa Herrero
Jenifer Blanco Patiño
Cristina Jiménez Santos
Elisenda Huguet Romero
Vanesa Contreras Ortiz
Marta Cabezudo Martínez
M. Rosa Calduch Dordal
Susana Alcaraz Gutiérrez
Andrea Alarcón Sabadell
Jesús Galván Romero
Miquel Àngel Caelles Garcia
Esteban Ceacero Romero
Jordi Sanahuja Soler

List of employees who formed part of the IMPSOL | 2015–2023

HEAD OF ECONOMIC AND FINANCIAL SERVICE
Begoña Antonell Massuet

HEAD OF ADMINISTRATIVE LEGAL SERVICE
Joan Serra Barceló

MANAGEMENT SECRETARY
Maria Àngels Herrera Pérez

BUILDING TECHNICIANS
Montserrat Cabo Mañogil
Noelia Miranda Tomás

DRAFTING SPECIALIST
Dídac Martí Martínez

SENIOR LEGAL TECHNICIANS
Marina González Moro
Imma Serrano Lorenzo

ADMINISTRATIVE ASSISTANTS
Montserrat Aguilar López
Verónica Fernández Antón
Mercedes Mayoralgo Serrano

Members of the Board of Directors of IMPSOL

PRESIDENT
Antoni Balmón Arévalo
Mayor of Cornellà de Llobregat | Executive Vice President of AMB

VICE PRESIDENTS
Jordi San José Buenaventura
Mayor of Sant Feliu de Llobregat | 2015-2019

Lídia Muñoz Cáceres
Mayor of Sant Feliu de Llobregat | 2019-2023

Miguel Comino Haro
Mayor of Sant Vicenç dels Horts | 2023-present day

CHIEF EXECUTIVE OFFICER
Ramon M. Torra i Xicoy

SECRETARIES
Sebastià Grau Àvila
2015-2019

Marcel·lí Pons Duat
2019-2021

Glòria Vendrell Garrido
2021-present day

BOARD MEMBERS
Manuel Ceballos Morillo
Deputy mayor and councillor for Territory and Sustainability of Cornellà de Llobregat | 2015-2019

Lídia Montero Cos
Second deputy mayor of the Urban Planning, Housing, Environment and Urban Ecology Department of Santa Coloma de Gramenet | 2015-2019

José Ángel Carcelén Luján
First deputy mayor, Territory and Economic Development, of Sant Boi de Llobregat | 2015-present day

Laura Campos Ferrer
Mayor of Montcada i Reixac | 2015-2019

Francisco Javier Burón Cuadrado
Housing manager of Barcelona City Council | 2015-2019

Vanesa Vilaño Esparducer
Head of the Housing Department of Barcelona City Council | 2015-2019

Ramon Sánchez Gil
Deputy mayor, President of Sustainability, Territory, Construction Work and Economics of Molins de Rei Council | 2017-2019

Miguel Rodríguez Rosillo
Alternativa d'Esquerres per Badia | 2015-2017

Alba Sanjurjo Castro
CUP-PA | 2017-2019

Jaume Campreciós Colet
ERC | 2015-2016

Jordi Albert Caballero
ERC | 2016-2018

Íñigo García de Enterría Adan
ERC | 2018-2019

Raquel Albiol Gilabert
ERC | 2015-2023

Eduardo Bolaños Rodríguez
PP | 2015-2019

Miguel Raposo Riesco
PP | 2019-2021

Esteban Gesa Para
PP | 2021-2023

Luis Ignacio Ruiz Gandullo
Ciutadans | 2015-2017

Koldo Blanco Uzquiano
Ciutadans | 2017-2023

Antonio Martínez Flor
Deputy mayor of Cornellà de Llobregat | 2019-present day

Francesc Josep Belver Vallès
Deputy mayor of L'Hospitalet | 2019-present day

Antonio Suárez Pizarro
Deputy mayor of Santa Coloma de Gramenet | 2019-present day

Carles Cordón Núñez
Mayor of Cerdanyola del Vallès | 2019-present day

Candela López Tagliafico
Deputy mayor of Castelldefels | 2019-2023

Cristina Paraira Beser
Junts | 2019-2023

Pedro Maqueda de Anta
Barcelona pel Canvi | 2019-2020

Oscar Benítez Bernal
Valents | 2020-2023

Mireia Ingla Mas
Mayor of Sant Cugat del Vallès | 2019-2023

Joan Basagañas Camps
Mayor of Sant Just Desvern | 2023-present day

Damià Calvet Valera
Vice president of Urban Planning Policies, AMB | 2015-2017 / 2023-present day

Angel Pedrós Bochaca
Councillor for Urban Planning and the Natural Environment of Sant Cugat del Vallès | 2023-present day

Lluís Mijoler Martínez
Mayor of El Prat de Llobregat | 2023-present day

Jordi Gil Dorado
Councillor for People Services of Sant Vicenç dels Horts | 2023-present day

Guillem Esteve Higuera
First deputy mayor of Sant Climent de Llobregat | 2023-present day

Joana Crespo García
Coordinator of the Urban Planning and City Transformation Department of Barcelona City Council | 2023-present day

Housing in the Metropolitan Area of Barcelona
IMPSOL 2015—2024

PUBLISHED BY
Barcelona Metropolitan Area (AMB)
Metropolitan Institute of Land Development and Property Management (IMPSOL)

DIRECTION
Ramon M. Torra i Xicoy,
General Manager, AMB
Amadeu Iglesias Unzué,
Director Manager of IMPSOL

EDITOR
Marta Poch
POCH·CAPDEVILA

IMPSOL COORDINATION
Josep Maria Borrell Bru
Xavier Gracia Marcos

GRAPHIC DESIGN
spread. Tomoko Sakamoto - David Lorente

CONTRIBUTIONS
Maria Amat
Mariona Benedito
Josep Maria Borrell Bru
Rafael Gómez-Moriana
Marta Peris

PROOFREADING AND TRANSLATION
Elaine Fradley

PAPERS
Arena Natural Smooth 140g
and Woodstock 110g by Fredigoni

DIGITAL IMAGE CORRECTION, COLOUR PROOFS, PRINTING AND BINDING
Gràfiques Ortells SL

SAMPLERS
500

INDEXATION
DL: B 8849-2024
ISBN: 978-84-87881-56-5
Printed in Spain
Barcelona, June 2024

Also available:

Catalan edition: *Habitatge a l'àrea metropolitana de Barcelona. IMPSOL 2015—2024*
ISBN (Catalan): 978-84-87881-54-1

Spanish edition: *Vivienda en el área metropolitana de Barcelona. IMPSOL 2015—2024*
ISBN (Spanish): 978-84-87881-55-8

PHOTOGRAPHIC CREDITS
© Íñigo Bujedo: 24 (bottom), 25 (centre), 56, 57, 59, 74, 99, 100 (right), 101 (top), 102 (top left, bottom left), 113, 115, 122, 125, 128, 131, 178, 179 (top left), 180, 200 (bottom, centre right, bottom right), 201, 213, 218 (bottom), 220, 223, 226 (top right, centre right, bottom right), 240, 242, 243, 253, 254. 258 (bottom left, top right), 259, 261
© Andrés Flajszer: 177, 179 (top right, bottom), 181, 183, 200 (top right)
© Adrià Goula: 22 (top), 25 (top, bottom), 26 (centre), 55, 58, 60, 61, 62, 65, 100 (left), 101 (bottom), 102 (top right), 103, 104, 105, 106, 107, 108, 111, 116, 117, 119, 161, 162, 163, 164, 165, 167, 239, 244, 246, 249, 251, 255, 256, 257, 258 (bottom right)
© José Hevia: 22 (bottom), 24 (top, centre), 26 (top, bottom), 73, 75, 76, 78, 79, 80, 81, 83, 121, 123, 124, 126, 129, 137, 138, 140, 141, 142, 144, 147, 199, 203, 204, 206, 207, 209, 211, 212, 216, 218 (top), 219, 221, 225, 226 (bottom left), 227, 228, 229, 231
© Pol Viladoms: 169, 170, 171, 172, 173, 175

IMPSOL
Institut Metropolità de Promoció de Sòl i Gestió Patrimonial
Carrer 62, núm. 16-18, edifici A
08040 Barcelona (Zona Franca)

www.amb.cat/en/web/habitatge/impsol